Out of the Stockpot

Out of the Stockpot

WILLIAM J. DUNN

CHARLES SCRIBNER'S SONS   NEW YORK

Printed in the United States of America
Library of Congress Catalog Card Number 76-162741
SBN684–12483–1

à mes trois petits-fils,
who prefer burghammers *to* hamburgers

Contents

Introduction

Why a "stockpot" cookbook?

Webster's Collegiate *defines a stockpot as a "pot in which soup stock is prepared," which is, roughly, something like defining Massachusetts Institute of Technology as a school where arithmetic is taught.*

Webster's New International *is somewhat more specific. It terms the stockpot "a pot in which stock (sense 12) is prepared." And when you check back to "sense 12," you find stock defined as ". . . a rich extract of the soluble parts of meat, fish, poultry and, sometimes, of vegetables, used as a basis for soups, gravies, etc." This is correct, but still far from complete.*

Not too surprising, perhaps, the French have the best definition of all in their everyday name for stock, fonds de cuisine—*literally,* base of cooking,—*because stock is truly the base of most really good European cooking, particularly that of France. There are so many things you can do with stock to improve the taste and heighten the nutrition of everyday cooking—and at a cost far less than almost any other adjunct to good cooking—that it really is surprising that more hasn't been written on the subject.*

As a matter of fact, even the French themselves haven't written too much on the subject, probably because they take it for granted that everyone old enough to read a cookbook knows what stock is and how to prepare it. It is one of the first things a French child is taught in his mother's kitchen and the thought that anyone wouldn't at least understand the uses and advantages of stock is beyond Gallic comprehension.

Unfortunately, however, this is not true in the United States. Here we have many good cooks who know stock and depend on it in their daily routines, but they are in the vast minority. Certainly there are few children learning to know and use stock in their mother's American kitchen. And the loss is ours.

I first became conscious of stock and its value some ten years ago shortly after we established a home in Saint-Laurent-du-Var, Provence, just outside Nice. My favorite butcher insisted on saluting my purchase with the gift of un bon os—*a good bone—which usually took the form of a large veal knuckle cracked into several pieces and folded into my package with all the air of conferring the Croix de Guerre (happily, without the customary kiss on both cheeks!).*

When I brought le bon os *home the first time, I really didn't know what to do with it. All I knew was that it should be used in cooking and, moreover, that no gift as ceremoniously bestowed as that veal knuckle was to be lightly discarded.*

Fortunately, we had a Belgian neighbor whose gentleman friend was a cook in one of Nice's better restaurants. When I turned to her for advice, she put me in the hands of a top professional and I quickly learned the value and uses of le bon os.

As an old pro in the French tradition, Lou-Lou (I never learned another name) was all for le fonds brun *(chapter one) because that stock is, of course, the premier stock of the real French* cuisinier. *(Lou-Lou also taught me the invaluable uses of* beurre manié *[chapter nine] among many other things.) It soon became apparent, however, that the preparation of brown stock was too time-consuming for the average nonprofessional cook. So once I had mastered the fundamentals of stock, particularly its preparation, I set about the development of a simpler multi-purpose stock that even Lou-Lou admitted was a good stock for the home kitchen.*

From that time forward my wife and I became devotees of the stockpot and not only welcomed the gift of un bon os *when it was bestowed but solicited it if the butcher was remiss. We kept a supply of both chicken and multi-purpose stocks on hand all the time and brewed up a special stock any time our culinary program suggested one.*

This has never changed for us, although the idea of a good bone as a gift vanished with our return from Europe. Today we buy our bones, just as we buy the other components of our stockpot, but nevertheless the price is reasonable and considerably lower than the cost of canned substitutes in equal quantity. And the quality is superior.

Most of the recipes in this book concern themselves with meat or poultry, but fish too is at its best in many recipes when cooked with stock—in this case, usually fish stock—and a modest section of this book addresses itself to that subject. There are also quite a few recipes devoted to the use of stock in the preparation of certain vegetables, something else not too familiar in the United States.

In truth, stock can be used in almost every branch of cooking, possibly excepting the preparation of breads, pastries, and most types of desserts. And, to repeat by way of emphasis, the proper use of stock in the preparation of almost any dish will enhance both its flavor and its nutritive value.

This, then, is the fundamental purpose of this volume—to show you how to use simple, nutritious stocks to improve your everyday cooking and to place at your command a battery of pretested, outstanding dishes which you can call on when the daily routine palls or when you feel yourself in the venturesome mood for something different.

Finally, this is a kitchen manual by a nonprofessional cook primarily for other nonprofessional cooks. All these dishes have been tested in an ordinary kitchen, using only the utensils and equipment found in your own kitchen. You don't need to possess a cordon bleu *diploma—just the ordinary amount of common sense and judgment.*

Approach the subject with an open mind and you'll be thrilled with what you can accomplish. This is, above all, a cookbook for people who like flavor in their food and want to savor it to the utmost!

Bon appétit!

CHAPTER I

The Stockpot

Cookery is become an art, a noble science;
cooks are gentlemen.

ROBERT BURTON, *1621*

The preparation of a good stock takes time and good basic ingredients, *but* the personal time required of you is relatively small (the back burner does the rest) and the ingredients are cheap and normally easy to obtain. Moreover, *the rewards are great!*

There are, of course, many types of stock, each concocted originally for some particular dish. In this book we are going to examine several of the most important ones, their preparation and use. But first of all, we are going to show you how to produce one basic all-purpose stock that is simple to make and can be used in over 90 percent of the recipes in this book. If you are not too familiar with stocks, I suggest that you master this one first; then, when you feel the confidence that comes with familiarity, you can try the others.

The obvious strategy at this point, of course, would be to set down a recipe detailing every move, every component you need, and the exact amounts. The truth of the matter is, however, that in a dozen years of making stock once or twice a week while living in the Far East, France, Italy, and the United States, I doubt that I have ever used the same formula twice. It just isn't possible to obtain identical ingredients every time you set out to build a stock. And bones are not easy to measure. Fresh veal knuckles, properly cracked, are plentiful and free in both France and Italy, provided you trade with the same butcher regularly. The average butcher I've met in this country wouldn't understand why you wanted the knuckles cracked, if he had any, and they certainly would not be free—unless you have a butcher more liberal than mine. Leeks are so common in France that the French call them *l'asperge du pauvre*, literally the poor man's asparagus. In those parts of the United States I know best, however, leeks are neither common nor cheap. And the same is true of many meats, bones, and vegetables; they may be easily and cheaply available in one place at one time and considerably less so elsewhere at another time.

MEAT AND BONES FOR PROTEINS

For this reason it would seem best to examine the various ingredients that might be used in a stock, their characteristics, and the way they react in combination. We'll start with the meats and various types of bones that make your stock rich in protein.

BEEF: I prefer the shank to all other cuts of beef for making stock, because it has a fine flavor of its own and the meat (unless very old) is seamed with natural gelatin that contributes both flavor and texture. Oxtails, to my taste, have too pronounced a flavor and are often quite oily. Brisket, flank, or chuck may be used successfully, but shank is best. The beef bones should be marrow bones, like that in the shank. These are not hard to come by, and your butcher will probably supply them at very little cost. Remember, however, that neither beef nor beef bones should ever be used in a white stock.

VEAL: Veal bones are the most popular component of both the French *fonds de cuisine* and the Italian *brodo*. And the fact that veal is the most popular meat in both countries is only part of the reason. Veal bones actually usually have more flavor potential than the veal itself, and the joints are rich in gelatin. The veal shank, like the beef shank, is the preferred cut for stock because few of the other cuts, possibly excepting the breast, will add any flavor to the finished product. Veal and veal bones can be used to augment almost any stock. They often go into chicken stock, and oven browned, are always the base of *fonds brun,* the classic French brown stock.

LAMB: As a general rule, lamb has too pronounced a flavor to blend with any other meat. For this reason lamb stock should be used only in the preparation of lamb dishes. This is true of both the bones and the meat. It helps to know, however, that most lamb dishes requiring stock will respond just as satisfactorily to the all-purpose stock described in this chapter.

PORK: This is another meat that does not lend itself well to the preparation of stock, although many people are fond of soup made from pork bones. Pork is usually too fatty, and the flavor of both the meat and the bones is likely to be sweet. Certainly, no stock should ever be sweet. However, pork can be cooked, as lamb can, with the multi-purpose stock with outstanding results.

CHICKEN: Chicken, like veal, is ideally suited to the production of stock. It has both flavor and, when enough bones are used, the gelatin that is the hallmark of a rich stock. As far as the meat is concerned, there is no point in using anything but the flesh of sturdy old fowls. The flavor to be simmered out of a young fryer or broiler is not sufficient to warrant its use. The bones, however, are a different matter. The cooked or uncooked carcass, the neck, the back, and, above all, the feet—if you can get them—are valuable no matter how young the bird. For chicken stock I seldom use more meat than can be found on the necks, backs, wingtips, and giblets. When I plan to make a chicken stock in the immediate future, I never discard a single chicken bone, storing even leftovers in the freezer until needed.

OTHER POULTRY: The carcass of a roast duck can be boiled to make a really excellent duck soup (maybe that's where "easy as duck soup" originated!), and there is no reason why duck bones should not be added to the stockpot. The same is true of turkey. Frankly, I have never tried to make stock of either guinea hen or rock cornish fowl, but either should produce a good soup.

One thing to remember is that the term *poultry* should never be interpreted to include eggs. There is no place for eggs or dairy products in any stock, although you can use eggshells to clarify a stock.

FROM THE GARDEN

In selecting vegetables for the stockpot you will find there are several not acceptable, including some of the more familiar. Many everyday vegetables have too distinctive flavors or unsuitable color. Examples include such favorites as turnips, cabbages, parsnips, and beets, the first three taboo because of their heavy flavor and aroma and the fourth because of its dominating color. Some of the favored vegetables are:

ONIONS: Onions are a *must* in every stock, whether white, brown, chicken, all-purpose, or whatever. The familiar yellow onion is the most popular in both this country and most of Europe except Italy, where the big purple onion predominates. Although it contributes an excellent flavor, the purple onion does tend to turn the *brodo* or stock dark. I do not consider this a handicap unless I happen to be using the stock to make a very light sauce. There is no reason why the small white onions cannot be used, but they are relatively expensive and their flavoring talent is not that much superior for making stock. Green onions are always acceptable, of course.

SHALLOTS: Shallots have such delicate flavor and, in most of the United States, such robust cost that it seems doubtful that their use can be justified in the stockpot. Even in France where they are not quite so expensive, shallots are generally regarded as too dear in proportion to the contribution they make.

LEEKS: Because it definitely contributes to the finished stock and is easy to come by, the leek is a standard component of the average French stockpot. In the United States, where leeks are not so plentiful and rather expensive, I would recommend using only the green tops. The white stalks make fine soups and, when lightly parboiled and fried in butter, a magnificent vegetable dish. Some cooks believe the leek tops, like the purple onion, darken a stock too much, but this shouldn't matter except, perhaps, in the brewing of a white chicken stock.

CARROTS: Like onions, carrots, usually in large chunks, are a must in any stockpot. In most urban markets today it is difficult to buy carrots with the lacy green tops still fresh and intact; if these tops are available, however, by all means include them.

CELERY: Celery, onions, and carrots are the big three of the vegetable kingdom in the stockpot. Here again you are likely to be hampered, if you live in a large city, by the tendency of the merchants to strip celery of most of its foliage in the interest of easier handling and packaging. This is unfortunate because the leaves can contribute more flavor to the stock than the stalks. Always prefer the leaves first and the coarse outside ribs next. The closer you get to the heart the more delicate the flavor, and your stockpot needs a boost from the celery department.

GARLIC: You can use garlic freely *if you don't peel it.* It will impart a nuance all its own to the stock, but it won't be what you ordinarily regard as a garlic smell or flavor.

PARSLEY: Parsley is an excellent addition to any stockpot.

HERBS AND SPICES

The seasoning of a stock is just as important as the right basic ingredients. Meat, bones, and vegetables will determine the fundamental flavor and richness of a stock, but the proper seasonings are absolutely necessary to accentuate that flavor and, of course, the aroma that is a vital part of the flavor.

SALT: Care should be taken not to salt the stock too heavily during the cooking process. Almost any dish in which stock is used will require salt on its own account. A stock that is too salty can ruin a delicate sauce, even a robust ragout. A couple of teaspoons in four to six quarts of water are usually enough for a beginning. More salt can be added as needed, but too much is really tough to remove! I prefer the coarse (usually kosher in this country) salt, mainly because it seems to be easier to control. Fine salt can pour too easily, sometimes with troublesome results.

PEPPER OR PEPPERCORNS: Prefer the latter because these fiery buckshot are ideal for making stock. They make their contribution and then surrender their person when the stock is strained. The amount used will vary with the amount of liquid, but I stick to the ratio of one generous teaspoonful to each four quarts of water.

HERBS: First of all comes the ubiquitous bay leaf, a herb that must have graced more stockpots than any two or three others combined.

The classic French recipes always call for a *bouquet garni,* which is nothing more than a simple bouquet of herbs, based on the bay leaf, tied together or stitched into a fold of cloth so that it can be removed after use. Inasmuch as stock is always doubly strained, however, there is no need to secure the herbs, fresh or dried, in order to keep them out of the finished stock. The second straining, through a cheesecloth or a fine sieve, will remove even the finest flecks of crushed or ground herbs.

Most of the herbs on your shelf—even mint leaves—can be used in stock, excepting such pronounced flavors as dill seed and tarragon. I use the bay leaf without exception and other herbs as the whim strikes me, generally choosing among thyme, oregano, rosemary, marjoram, basil, chervil, sage, and savory or a combination of two or three. Thyme and oregano are first on my list by personal preference.

Actually, parsley should properly be considered a herb because it *is* a herb, but, since it is usually available fresh, I automatically think of it as a vegetable, If fresh parsley is not available at stockpot time, the dried leaves can—and should—be used, just as other dried herbs.

There are two reasons for including the herbs: primarily, because they are essential to the final flavor and, secondarily, because they aromatize your kitchen while the stock is simmering on the back burner. A simmering stock without herbs would hardly please the nostrils.

SPICES: The only spice that might contribute to an ordinary stock, aside from peppercorns, of course, is the clove, although some cooks do use a trace of nutmeg or mace. I usually spike the onions with cloves before dropping them into the pot, but such spices as ginger, juniper, cinnamon, cumin, and others of really pronounced and distinctive flavor should not be considered. Your stock is going to serve as a base for finished dishes with their own flavors. The flavor of the stock should always enhance, but never dominate, those flavors.

To sum up, beef, veal, and fowl provide the best meat and bones for stock. In the vegetable realm carrots, onions, and celery are a must, while leeks and parsley are a welcome addition. Salt in moderation, peppercorns, bay leaf, and a couple of other herbs of choice are vital. With these basic components, a stockpot, and a good supply of pure water, you are ready to begin.

We are going to start with the multi-purpose stock indicated wherever the word *stock* appears in this book, unless, of course, another is specified. You will need a metal pot that will hold at least eight quarts, probably heavy aluminum, with a smooth-fitting lid that is not too tight. Stock can be made in smaller amounts, using smaller pots, but the work will be as great and will just have to be repeated more often.

MULTI-PURPOSE STOCK

This sample recipe yields about three quarts of stock which can be stored for future use, as will be explained later.

In the bottom of the pot place:

1-1/2   *lb beef shin with the bone, cut coarsely*
2   *lb beef marrow bones*
2   *lb chicken necks with backs (if included)*
1   *lb veal bones (cracked knuckles, if available)*

Cover with sufficient water to immerse completely, the colder the water the better. Place on a high flame and bring to a boil. Turn the flame down somewhat, but maintain enough heat to keep the water boiling briskly. A gray froth will start to form on the surface of the water in a very short time, and this must be skimmed off. Continue skimming until no more froth forms.

In the meantime, prepare:

> 3   *medium onions, quartered*
> 6   *cloves, speared in the onions*
> 2   *large carrots, cut in 1-inch chunks*
> 4   *ribs celery (outside ribs), cut in 1/2-inch lengths*
>   *leaves from 1 full stalk celery (if available)*
> 8   *sprigs parsley*
> 2   *cloves garlic, unpeeled*

When the broth no longer needs skimming, add the vegetables and bring the stock to a boil. Then lower the flame to the merest simmer. While the liquid is coming to a boil, add the seasoning:

> 1   *tsp peppercorns for each 4 quarts water*
> 2   *bay leaves*
> 2   *heaping tsp coarse salt*
> 1/4 *tsp each of any 2: thyme, oregano, marjoram, sage,*
>   *chervil, basil, or rosemary*

Cover the pot and let simmer as slowly as possible for 6 to 12 hours. Some cooks remove the meat after 2 or 3 hours for use in another dish. Actually, there is little, if any, food value left in the meat after that much simmering and absolutely no flavor. My advice is to leave it in the pot until you are ready to strain the stock, then discard it. If you do rescue it earlier, you may be able to make the meat edible with the aid of horseradish and ketchup. Or you may grind it into a salad with onions, pimientos, and mayonnaise, but, frankly, it isn't worth the effort and there's always the chance it might add one final something to the stock.

The reason for the long simmering (I almost always simmer a stock overnight) is to extract every bit of nutrition and flavor from the ingredients and to turn out a stock that will jell in the refrigerator. It is not necessary for the stock to jell, of course, but it is easier to store.

Once the stock is ready (be sure to taste it for salt), strain it through a coarse sieve or collander into a second pot, so that you can get some idea of how much you have to store. By adding a bit of water from time to time during the simmering process to keep the liquid level just above the ingredients, you should wind up with about 3 quarts of coarsely strained stock.

SIMPLE STORAGE

Wash three one-quart jars with tight-fitting lids (mayonnaise jars are excellent) in boiling water. Dry, but don't cool the jars if the stock is still warm, as it should be when strained. Fill these jars, a little at a time, straining the stock through a bit of cheesecloth or a sieve no coarser than a tea strainer.

It is essential that you fill the jars at the same time, alternating a ladleful in each, in order to keep the fat from concentrating in one jar. This fat, which solidifies at the top of each jar to form a natural seal, is essential to successful storage of the stock, and each jar should have about the same amount.

The fat will come to the top immediately to form a cap from one-half to one-inch deep according to the fat content of the meat and bones, another factor that is never constant. Cover the jars loosely and let them stand until cool enough to store in the refrigerator.

Once the fat has solidified, as it will do very rapidly in the refrigerator, it will seal the stock as effectively as wax. This is the same method the French use to store homemade pâtés and terrines. As long as this seal is not disturbed, the stock will stay sweet in the refrigerator for two to three weeks. It is not necessary to freeze or use the stock immediately *if this seal remains intact.*

When you use the stock, take one of the sealed jars out of the refrigerator and cut the congealed fat into quarters, like a pie. The fat will lift out easily and can be discarded. (There may be a use for this fat but, if so, I have never discovered it.) If there is a layer of brown sediment directly under the fat, skim it off and discard it also. What is left is excellent neutral stock, slightly brown, opaque, and at least slightly jelled, that will be a genuine asset to your culinary aspirations.

After the fat is removed, the stock will stay good, refrigerated, for about four days. When it starts to deteriorate, it will signal the event by forming a watery layer on the surface. If this happens, pour the stock into a pan on a hot flame and bring to a boil. After it boils one minute, you can return the stock to its container and it will be good refrigerated for another four to five days.

Actually, you should never need to keep an opened quart of stock that long once you learn more about its many uses. Three or four quarts of stock rarely last more than a couple of weeks in my household and not that long if soups are on the agenda.

It is possible to freeze stock in ice trays, remove the cubes to plastic bags, and keep them in the freezer indefinitely, using the cubes (four of them are roughly the equivalent of a cup) as needed, but I have never found this necessary. By packing the stock in fat-sealed jars (the lids are left on, but not hermetically sealed) I find we seldom have any surplus.

Although it can be further seasoned for use as bouillon, this stock cannot be used as consommé until it has been clarified, a simple but somewhat tedious process that will be explained in the next chapter.

As I have emphasized, this is an all-purpose stock that will serve for the vast majority of recipes in this book and for any recipes calling for the use of stock. Now we'll turn to some of the standard stocks in general use, particularly among the proponents of French cuisine.

BROWN STOCK [Fonds Brun]

Brown stock is the classic stock of the French kitchen, differing from the all-purpose stock in two important features. First, it is entirely a meat stock—no chicken or chicken bones are used in its preparation—and is only used in meat dishes, soups, and sauces. Second, the bones, meat, and vegetables are browned in the oven before being simmered in water, giving the stock the characteristically dark brown color from which it takes it name.

There is no doubt that this is an excellent stock, but there is definitely doubt that the work required in its preparation is justified by its probable use in the non-French kitchen. But this is a practical formula that is not too complicated.

First, take a fairly large baking pan and oil the bottom liberally. Place in the pan:

> 1-1/2   *lb beef shin, cut into 1-inch cubes*
> 1-1/2   *lb beef marrow bones*
> 3   *lb veal knuckles, cracked*
> 1/2   *lb raw ham, chopped (optional)*

Preheat the oven to 450° and roast the meat and bones for 45 minutes, stirring occasionally. Then add to the pan:

> 3   *carrots, cut into 1/2-inch chunks*
> 2   *medium onions, quartered*
> 4   *ribs celery, chopped*
> 2   *cloves garlic, unpeeled*

Continue roasting for another 15 minutes, again stirring every few minutes.

You will now need a large (at least 8-quart) stockpot, into which you transfer the roasted bones, meat, and vegetables. Rinse the baking pan well with boiling water to cover the components by at least 1 inch. Bring to a boil over a hot fire and skim carefully until all froth is removed from the surface. Then add:

> 2   *tbsp coarse salt*
> 1   *tbsp peppercorns*
> 2   *bay leaves*
> 1/2   *tsp thyme or herb of preference*
> 6   *sprigs fresh parsley*

Bring the stock to a boil again, then reduce the fire to a minimum and simmer 8 hours, adding more water occasionally to maintain a fairly even level. After the simmering period is ended, process the stock just as you would the multi-purpose stock.

Once the *fonds brun* has been strained, it can be returned to the fire and boiled down to a very small fraction of its volume and to a very thick consistency for use as a glaze—a perfect substitute for commercial glazes, which are quite expensive.

WHITE SAUCE [Fonds Blanc]

Another classic of the French kitchen is the white stock (*fonds blanc*) which is prepared just as the multi-purpose stock, but without beef or beef bones and, of course, without browning. *Fonds blanc* is used in making a *velouté* sauce that is nearly as white as its first cousin, *béchamel* (see chapter four). *Fonds blanc* can be used in cream soups and in any chicken dish requiring stock. Here is a sample formula.

Follow the recipe for the multi-purpose stock, except to substitute a stewing chicken for the beef and beef bones and to increase the amount of veal and veal bones by 50 percent. The vegetables, seasonings, and aromatics can remain the same, except that the garlic should be omitted. The entire stock can be simmered to completion in about 6 hours, but, if you are using a whole stewing fowl, you can remove it from the pot after 2 or 3 hours, take the meat off the bones, and return the bones to the pot. The meat can then be used in chicken salad or other dishes in which sufficient condiments are added to disguise the fact that there is very little, if any, flavor left in the meat.

This stock will probably not have the same proportion of fat as the multi-purpose stock, unless you select an unusually fat hen for the pot. If it has sufficient fat to form a protective seal in its storage containers, the stock can be kept refrigerated for a considerable length of time without worry. Without this seal, however—and it should be at least 1/2-inch thick—the stock must be frozen for long storage or boiled again every 4 to 5 days.

There really is no difference between white stock and chicken stock, although some chefs do indicate such a difference. Veal is widely used in France to augment the meat in an otherwise bona fide chicken stock, in spite of the fact that it should, by definition, contain no other meat or bones than those of the *poule.*

During my years in France I always kept a supply of pure chicken stock in the refrigerator, chiefly because I used lots of chicken in my daily cooking and it was easy to use the bones, giblets (sometimes), necks, backs, and feet to prepare small quantities of stock once or twice a week. In this stock I rarely used veal unless I had veal trimmings or bones on hand. In other words, I sometimes added veal to use up the trimmings, but seldom merely to augment the chicken.

There is one important point I wish to make before we conclude the consideration of chicken stock. *There is no part of a chicken that can contribute more to the quality of a good stockpot than the feet.* In both France and Italy, where chickens are sold plucked and drawn but with head and feet intact, I always compromised by having the feet included with my purchase while the head was left for others. And you can be sure it was always claimed!

By chopping off the claws and soaking the feet in boiling water for 60 seconds, the hard, scaly outer skin can be peeled away. What remains provides a rich source of flavor and gelatin for the pot. The French housewife invariably uses the head as well as the feet in her stock, but not having been brought up with a taste for chicken heads in my native Indiana, I skipped that useful part of the *poulet* and concentrated on the remainder.

OTHER STOCKS

Another basic stock is lamb stock, prepared as the name implies principally from lamb and lamb bones. This stock is always made in small quantities, because its flavor is too pronounced to be used except in lamb dishes. It is prepared basically like the multi-purpose stock, except that lamb bones and some meat, preferably the shank, are substituted for the veal, beef, and chicken. If some veal and chicken trimmings are on hand, they can be added, but beef should be omitted. It is not necessary to simmer lamb stock for more than 2 or 3 hours to gain its full flavor.

Other stocks can be made from almost any type of meat or game you have on hand, using the same formula for other ingredients. For instance, if you have a cut of venison by virtue of your own skill or that of some sportsman friend, you might want to take the trimmings and any spare bones to brew up a quick stock for use in later preparation. It is unnecessary to simmer the components for more than a couple of hours to achieve a satisfactory stock from any type of game.

WHEN THE STOCKPOT IS EMPTY

There will be times, of course, when the stockpot is empty, and you don't have time to simmer another before preparing that special dinner. Over the years I have tried almost every possible substitute and, fortunately, the best ones are easily available in this country. Canned chicken broth, canned chicken and rice soup (with the rice removed), and canned beef bouillon are all quite acceptable because they have food value to contribute as well as flavor.

I have on occasion used bouillon cubes dissolved in hot water. These certainly have flavor, but no body or richness to impart. Nevertheless, I prefer them to the plain water that would probably be the alternate. Consommé, as sold in American stores, is usually delicious, but it often tends to be sweet and is not recommended for that reason.

None of these substitutes are expensive really, but they do cost much more than the stock you can make so easily in your own kitchen. And in my personal opinion, they are never quite as effective. The preparation of the all-purpose (or any standard) stock does, admittedly, take time, but *very little of your own time*. Most of the hours of simmering require no effort on your part aside from an occasional peek into the pot to make sure the liquid level isn't too low.

In conclusion let me repeat: *there is no rigid recipe or formula* for making any type of stock. In only one or two sessions you can develop a sort of second sense that enables you to ad-lib a stock from whatever ingredients are available and for any specific purpose. You will quickly learn how to balance the various components against each other—meat versus vegetables, aromatics versus seasonings—and how long to cook the whole. When you do, you will have made a long stride toward mastering "cooking by ear"—the art of preparing something memorable for your table from whatever ingredients you have at hand, and without detailed recipes or formulas.

And on that day you have won your own private *cordon bleu* as a cook of more than ordinary ability!

CHAPTER II

Soups from the Stockpot

Je vis de bonne soupe et non de beau langage.

MOLIERE, 1622-1673

Returning to the United States after a quarter-century overseas, one is tempted to believe that the can opener has completely replaced domestic skill and ingenuity in the preparation and serving of soup. Even the better restaurants too often settle for stereotyped broths that could only come out of a can. And this despite the fact that there are no divisions of the culinary art that the neophyte—the inexperienced beginner—can master with less effort and better results than the preparation of good soup.

It is not my intention to disparage canned soup. Most of them are excellent and many are outstanding. But the real importance of mastering the art of making your own soups, at least part of the time, lies in the fact that there is no type of canned, frozen, or dehydrated soup on the market that your neighbor can't prepare and serve just as expertly as yourself. And there's no sense of accomplishment to glorify the simple act of opening a can. When Molière remarked the superiority of soup over beautiful language as a means of sustaining life, one can be sure he was not referring to the canned variety.

So . . . with a supply of stock in your refrigerator, the joys of dreaming up your own soups can be as infinite as the far reaches of your imagination—certainly as easy to achieve as the business of opening a can and heating the contents.

Let's assume you have informal guests drop in for what develops into a Saturday night supper. You would like to serve a hot soup with the cold cuts and potato salad that will highlight the impromptu two-bit-limit card session. You have a jar of stock in the refrigerator just waiting for a moment like this, and you have a cupboard that isn't entirely empty. For instance, there's a can of tomatoes, an onion and some elbow macaroni on the shelf. Almost between deals you sauté the onion, chopped, in a bit of butter or oil, add two cups of stock, the can of tomatoes, and a handful of the macaroni. Next put in a bit of salt, freshly ground pepper, and a pinch of oregano or some other handy herb, and let the whole thing simmer for just long enough to blend the ingredients and cook the pasta—but not too much.

The result will be a soup your guests can never duplicate from a can, and their appreciation will let your ego enjoy several minutes of unashamed preening.

Actually, you may not even look to the pantry. Your refrigerator usually has quite a complement of leftovers waiting for a good idea—and soup is usually a very good idea. There are two stalks of broccoli shivering in their icy bed of congealed butter. If you reheat them, they'll be mush; if you throw them away, you're a poor economist. And who ever heard of cold broccoli being incorporated into a stew?

Into the blender go a couple of cups of stock, the broccoli, a stalk of celery, coarsely chopped, and a heaping tablespoon of minced onion. In thirty seconds you have the foundation for a potage that needs only heat, a bit of salt, pepper, and a pinch of powdered thyme to achieve perfection. If you were a French housewife or chef, you probably would bind the soup with a couple of tablespoons of heavy cream, just before you serve it. But you don't need to use cream in order to produce an excellent soup in just about the same time it would take you to open and warm a can of cream of alfalfa.

The combination of stockpot, blender, pantry, and refrigerator, plus a generous helping of imagination, can provide you with an unlimited supply of delicious soups—all of them different and all original, at least as far as you are concerned. What difference does it make if someone else first thought of pouring a can of black beans, a pint of stock, some herbs, salt, and pepper into a blender and serving the result, piping hot, with a sprinkle of crumbled egg yolks or sour cream on top? When you make it, black bean soup becomes your own creation and the plaudits it prompts will belong to you personally and not to the head cook in some canning factory.

Nor is it necessary to ad-lib your own creations all the time. Included in this tome are some of the finest stock soup recipes to be found anywhere, collected during my years of roaming around the globe. Most of them are quite simple and all of them are delicious. And when you have mastered your favorites among them, you doubtless will come up with some innovations to make them your private property.

In the meantime, keep experimenting. There's a lot to be learned about cooking in general just from studying the art of making good soup.

TEN-MINUTE-STRONE

Ten-minute-strone is one of my favorite quick soups, named with more or less whimsy because it is faintly reminiscent of minestrone and can be prepared in about ten minutes if you like your pasta *al dente*—tender, but not too soft. Actually, fifteen minutes might be a more accurate estimate, but who's timing it? This recipe should be sufficient for four servings.

1	large onion, minced
1	tbsp oil
1	1-lb can tomatoes
1	cup stock
1	cup water
1/3	cup tiny elbow macaroni or other small pasta
1/4	tsp celery salt
1/4	tsp garlic salt
	thyme
	oregano
	freshly ground pepper
	Parmesan cheese, grated

Sauté the onion in the oil until golden, but not browned. Add all the other ingredients except the cheese, cutting the tomatoes a bit and using a pinch only of the herbs. Bring to a boil, then turn the fire low, and let the soup simmer until the pasta is to your liking. Taste for seasoning, then serve with the grated Parmesan.

GULYASUPPE [Goulasch Soup]

I first tasted goulasch soup in an Innsbruck *bierhaus* one wintry night several years ago and immediately fell in love with it. After consuming a steaming bowl, accompanied by a huge stein of beer, I walked directly into a neighboring *bierhaus* and did it all over again. The thing that intrigued me most was the faint hint of chili—a savor I didn't even know existed in Austria—and when I finally tracked down this recipe I realized that the elusive flavor was actually cumin, the same spice that distinguishes real Texas chili powder. In our family parlance this dish is known as "droolin' soup" because the very thought of it makes us drool! This recipe should be sufficient for four servings.

3/4	lb beef, diced in 1/4-inch cubes
1	tbsp olive oil
1	tbsp butter
1/2	cup onions, chopped
1	tbsp flour
1	tsp ground cumin
2	tbsp paprika
	salt
	freshly ground pepper
	dash of cayenne pepper
2	cups water, boiling
3	cups stock
1	medium boiled potato, diced in 1/4-inch cubes

Sauté the beef in the oil and butter, mixed, until lightly brown. Add the onions and cook until just golden. Mix the flour, cumin, paprika, salt, pepper, and cayenne together and, off the fire, mix thoroughly with the meat and onions. Return the pan to the fire and slowly add the 2 cups of boiling water, stirring constantly until smooth. Cover the pan and let simmer for 45 minutes or until the meat is tender. Now add the stock, preferably heated, and the potatoes. Simmer another 15 minutes and serve when the potato is thoroughly heated.

SOUPE PROVENÇALE

Soupe provençale is a thick potage of the type often found in rural France, particularly along the Mediterranean. It is also often served with a little grated Gruyère or Parmesan cheese on the side in that section of Provence near the Italian border. To make this soup properly you should have a food mill—standard equipment in every French kitchen—but the vegetables can be forced through a coarse sieve or run through a blender a little at a time. When served, it should be about the consistency of heavy pea soup.

3   *large potatoes*
4   *medium tomatoes, peeled and seeded*
2   *large onions*
1   *clove garlic, chopped*
    pinch of thyme
1   *tsp salt*
    freshly ground pepper
1   *quart stock*
1   *quart water*
1   *tbsp butter*
    parsley, chopped

Chop all the vegetables in small pieces and put them in the combined stock and water, together with the garlic, a generous pinch of thyme, the salt, and several grinds of fresh pepper. Bring to a boil, then reduce the fire and cook, covered, for 1 hour at moderate heat. Strain the vegetables, reserving the liquid, and puree them through a food mill or sieve or in a blender. Add enough of the cooking liquid to the vegetables to achieve the proper consistency and discard any left over. On the other hand, if the liquid is insufficient, add boiling water. Return the soup to the fire and bring just to the boiling point. Shut off the fire and stir in the butter. Sprinkle with chopped parsley. This soup is superb served over very dry toast spread with garlic butter (page 282).

BOHNENSUPPE [Bean Soup]

Several years ago I was traveling through Europe doing research for a book on train travel. One evening, heading south out of Salzburg, the train pulled into an attractive village, *Bischofshofen,* and on a whim I picked up my bags and got off. (You can do that with a Eurailpass.) The village was well worth the evening I devoted to it, but the thing that I remember above all is the *bohnensuppe* served in the little inn where I spent the night. Language limitations forbade my asking for a recipe, but I did start a study of German bean formulas and this is the one that meshes with my memory of that Austrian interlude.

2	*cups white beans*
	water
6	*cups stock*
1	*tbsp butter*
1/4	*lb salt pork or 4 slices bacon, chopped finely*
1	*medium onion, chopped*
1	*medium tomato, peeled, seeded, and chopped finely*
1	*clove garlic, crushed*
	marjoram
	salt (perhaps)
	freshly ground pepper

Wash the beans, discarding the broken or bad ones, and bring them to a preliminary boil in plenty of water as for *cassoulet à l'agneau* (page 182). When they have soaked for 1 hour, drain the water off and put the beans into the stock. Bring them to a slow boil and let simmer until tender. Put both the stock and the beans through a food mill, a heavy sieve, or a blender until smooth, then return to a low flame. Melt the butter in a skillet and sauté the salt pork or bacon. Before the meat is brown, add the onion. When the onion is golden, add the tomato and the garlic. Put in the marjoram, several twists of fresh pepper, but hold the salt for later. Sauté the meat, onion, and tomato for about 3 minutes, then pour the entire contents of the skillet into the pureed beans. Put a small amount of stock into the skillet, heat to the boiling point, and scrape bits and pieces from the sides and bottom, adding them to the soup. Simmer another 30 minutes, taste for salt, and serve very hot.

CREAM OF TOMATO BRESSE

Cream of tomato Bresse is a simple but delicious soup that can be made in minutes. The recipe comes from Bresse, an ancient name for the region north of Lyons, France, that produces what may be the world's finest chickens. It calls for chicken stock, as would any recipe originating in Bresse, but I have made this soup with the all-purpose stock with excellent results. Care must be given to the seasoning.

> 3   *cups chicken stock*
> 1   *cup water*
> 3   *tbsp tomato paste*
> 1   *cup fresh heavy cream*
> 2   *egg yolks*
>   *salt*
>   *freshly ground pepper*

Heat the combined stock and water and stir in the tomato paste. Let simmer for 10 minutes and season to taste. While the soup is simmering, stir the egg yolks into the heavy cream and mix thoroughly. *Off the fire,* stir the cream into the soup and, when well blended, return to the fire and heat to *just below the boiling point.* At the appearance of the first bubble, turn off the fire and serve the soup at once, steaming hot.

SOUPE À L'OIGNON [French Onion Soup]

Of all the countless *soupes* and potages of France, onion soup is undoubtedly the best known in the United States and understandably so. It is delicious and easy to prepare. It goes well with any meal and is a wonderful snack all by itself. Here is my favorite recipe—one that has withstood the test of time. You can prepare this for four people in about twenty minutes.

4   large white onions, thinly sliced
1   tbsp oil
1   tbsp butter
1/2   clove garlic, minced
2   tbsp flour
3   cups stock
1   cup water
    salt
    freshly ground pepper

toast (French bread preferred)
Parmesan cheese, grated

Brown the sliced onions in the combined oil and butter, add the garlic, and immediately stir in the flour. Continue to stir until the flour is browned—how much is up to you. Meanwhile, heat the stock in a separate pan and, just before it starts to boil, add the browned onions. Pour the water into the pan in which the onions were browned and bring to a boil, stirring constantly with a wooden spoon so that nothing is left behind when you add this water to the soup. Taste for seasoning with salt and pepper.

Now you have two options:

1. Let the soup simmer for 15 minutes, then pour over toasted rounds of bread (French type preferred), and sprinkle generously with grated Parmesan cheese. And *always* prefer the freshly grated cheese.

2. As soon as it starts to bubble, divide the soup into 4 ovenproof dishes, pottery or glass, place a round of bread in the center of each, moisten, and top with grated Parmesan. Slide the dishes under the grill

and let them remain for 15 minutes until the soup is blended and the cheese is melted and browned. Serve with *extreme care* because everything concerned will be blistering hot—and delicious!

IRISH ONION SOUP

Irish onion soup is as great a contrast to French onion soup as Galway is to Normandy, but it is just as good in a completely different way. This soup is often prepared in Ireland after the housewife has cooked a chicken and used the carcass to make a stock. It also stands as proof that the French cooks are not the only ones who use cream and eggs to bind a soup. This recipe should serve four.

4	*large onions, sliced very thin*
2	*tbsp butter*
1-1/2	*tbsp flour*
2	*cups chicken stock*
2	*cups milk*
1	*bay leaf*
1/2	*tsp powdered mace*
	salt
	freshly ground pepper
2	*egg yolks*
1/2	*cup heavy cream*

Cook the onions in the butter slowly until transparent, but not browned. Meanwhile steep the bay leaf in the milk as it is brought to a boil. Stir in the flour and mix thoroughly. Add the stock, warmed, to form a smooth sauce. Next add the milk, from which the bay leaf has been discarded. When the liquids are blended and smooth, add the mace (nutmeg can be substituted, but mace is preferred), salt, and freshly ground pepper. Simmer the soup slowly for 20 minutes or until the onions are completely tender. Beat the egg yolks into the cream. When ready to serve, pour the cream into the bottom of a tureen or serving bowl and gradually add the soup, stirring thoroughly. Serve immediately.

SOUPE AU PISTOU

Soupe au pistou is one of the culinary staples of Provence with strong Italian overtones, dating back, no doubt, to the time when Nice and the eastern part of the area belonged to the kingdom of Sardinia. It is a very good vegetable soup into which the diner stirs a spoonful (or more, according to taste) of *pistou,* which is really a variation of the *pesto* sauce the Italians love on pasta. Pasta, *pesto, pistou*—all the ingredients of a tongue twister, but the soup is good. Unfortunately, it can only be made in the warm months when fresh basil is available.

1/2	lb green beans
3	carrots
3	leeks, if available (if not, use a large onion)
2	white turnips
2	zucchini
4	medium potatoes
4	cups stock
4	cups water
2	tsp salt
	freshly ground pepper
2	large tomatoes, peeled, seeded, and chopped
1/2	cup elbow macaroni

Cut all the vegetables except the tomatoes into bite-sized pieces and put them into the combined stock and water. Add about 2 teaspoons of salt and plenty of freshly ground pepper and bring to the boiling point. Cover the pot, turn down the fire, and simmer for 30 minutes. When the carrots and turnips show signs of becoming soft, add the tomatoes and the macaroni and continue to cook until the pasta is to your taste. Meanwhile, prepare the *pistou.*

3	cloves garlic, chopped
1	cup fresh basil, chopped (dried will not do)
	salt
1/4	lb Gruyère or Parmesan cheese, shaved
	olive oil

Put the garlic, basil, and salt into a mortar and pound until crushed. Add the cheese and the oil, alternating until a thick creamy mixture is achieved. You will probably need at least 2 tablespoons of olive oil. Put the *pistou* into a sauce bowl and serve with the soup.

POTAGE TOURANGELLE   *[Loire Vegetable Soup]*

When one visits the Loire Valley to inspect the lovely old châteaux that are scattered from Orléans through Blois and Tours to Angers, he is going to encounter some of France's finest cuisine—as well as the nation's most precise grammarians. When he practices his French along the banks of the Loire, he can expect to be corrected (unless he is more nearly perfect than I) by waiters, waitresses, bellhops, taxi drivers, and shopkeepers. Fortunately, however, they are smart enough to combine good taste with their grammar, and this soup from Tours is ample proof!

2	*tbsp butter*
1/2	*lb lean bacon, diced*
6	*leeks (white part only)*
2	*white turnips, sliced*
1/2	*head cabbage, loosely shredded*
1-1/2	*quarts (6 cups) stock*
1/2	*lb fresh peas, shelled*
about 1	*tsp salt*
	freshly ground pepper
	toast (French-type bread)

Melt the butter in a large saucepan with a lid and cook the bacon until it is transparent. Then lower the fire and cook the leeks (onions are not a good substitute in this recipe), turnips, and the shredded cabbage until heated through, but not browned. Pour in the stock, heated, the salt, and plenty of freshly ground pepper. Cover the pan and cook the soup over a low fire for 1 hour. Taste for seasoning, add the peas, and cook another 30 minutes. Serve to 4 hungry people with slices of toasted bread in the bottom of each soup plate.

BLACK BEAN SOUP

Once upon a time in a great city called New York there was a coffee shop that had only two features to distinguish it from a thousand others. First of all, a lot of my friends at CBS made it their quick-fueling depot and, second, it served the best black bean soup I ever tasted. In an era when the average quick-service restaurant served all of its soups out of cans, it was delightful to find one soup that was the obvious exception. Black bean soup is not a common offering in the ordinary coffee shop, and I tried many times to find a comparable recipe before I discovered this one. It is perfect as it is, but, if you want to improve on perfection, try a tablespoon of Madeira instead of the lemon juice.

> 3   *strips bacon, chopped*
> 2   *tbsp onion, chopped*
> 1   *1-lb can black beans*
> 2   *cups stock*
>   *freshly ground pepper*
>   *salt (taste first)*
> 1   *tbsp lemon juice*
> 1   *egg yolk, hard boiled and grated*

Fry the bacon very crisp. Remove from the skillet and pour off all but 1 tablespoon of the fat. Sauté the onions in this fat and, when they are golden, return the bacon to the pan with 1/2-cup of stock. Heat sufficiently to loosen any bits of bacon and onion that may cling to the sides and bottom. Pour the beans into a blender together with all the stock, heated and unheated, and blend at low speed for 30 seconds, then at high speed for 1 minute until completely smooth. If the soup is very frothy at this point, let it stand for 30 minutes, or longer if you wish. Pour into a covered pan, add 2 twists of ground pepper, heat, and let simmer for 30 minutes. Taste for salt—the bacon and beans may have contributed enough—and add a bit, if necessary. Then add the lemon juice. Stir carefully. Pour into 4 soup plates and garnish with the egg yolk, rubbed through a coarse sieve.

CRÈME DES CHAMPIGNONS [Creamed Mushroom Soup]

In the center of Nice's great covered market, near the Opera, was a stand that specialized in mushrooms—*champignons de Paris*, very much like our cultivated variety; wild mushrooms from the Alps behind the city; and great yellow *cèpes,* fungi that weren't really mushrooms, but were even more succulent. I was a regular customer, and my usual purchase was about 200 grams (close to one-half pound) of whatever was my choice. The dealer never stopped trying to sell me at least a kilo (over two pounds) and a different variety than I selected. It was a game that apparently gave him great pleasure, and I didn't mind because from that stand came the foundations for some fine dishes. This is one of them, geared for four people.

1	*lb fresh mushrooms*
2	*tbsp butter*
1	*tbsp shallots or green onion, minced*
4	*cups chicken stock*
1/2	*tsp salt*
1	*tsp lemon juice*
1	*cup* crème fraîche *(page 282) or heavy cream*
2	*egg yolks*
	fresh parsley, chopped

Wipe the mushrooms with a damp paper towel, chop them finely, and sauté in butter together with the shallots or onion until wilted. Transfer to a blender with 2 cups of the stock and blend until smooth. Pour the blended stock and mushrooms into a deep pan and add the remainder of the stock, the salt, and lemon juice. Bring the mixture to a boil, then lower the fire and simmer, uncovered, very slowly for 30 minutes. Meanwhile, stir the egg yolks into the *crème fraîche* or cream. Remove the soup from the heat and blend in the cream mixture. Return to the fire and reheat. Serve with a generous sprinkling of chopped fresh parsley on each helping.

A BRACE OF PEA SOUPS

It has been my experience that dried peas, green or split, are better foundations for soup than fresh peas, and I also give a tip of the hat to canned peas over the fresh variety for the purpose of potage! Accordingly, I am presenting herewith two versions of pea soup of which I am quite enamored. Both are European recipes, but the end results are very different. The first is a northern European formula and the second, the *potage Saint-Germain*, is a French classic.

POLISH PEA SOUP

1	*1-lb can green peas*
4	*cups stock*
3	*strips bacon, chopped finely*
1	*medium onion, sliced*
1	*clove garlic, crushed*
1	*tbsp flour*
1/2	*tsp thyme or marjoram*
	salt
	freshly ground pepper

CROUTONS

3   *slices stale bread, cut into cubes and fried in butter*

Puree the peas in a blender and add to 3-1/2 cups of the stock, reserving 1/2 cup. Allow the liquid to simmer while you fry the bacon over a low fire until it is crisp, but not burned. Add the sliced onion to the bacon and, when it is golden, add the crushed garlic. When the garlic has cooked for a moment or two without scorching (it must be watched), stir in the flour and cook for about 3 minutes, stirring almost constantly. Now add the remaining 1/2 cup of stock and stir the mixture until smooth. Pour this into the blender for a moment until the onion is pureed, then add to the soup. Now add the salt, pepper, and herb, cover, and let simmer 20 minutes over a very low fire. Serve with fresh croutons.

POTAGE SAINT-GERMAIN   *[Split Pea Soup]*

Potage Saint-Germain—like *boeuf bourguignon, blanquette de veau,* and *coq au vin*— is a traditionally French dish that is basically the same, but different, wherever you happen to encounter it. I am not certain who Saint-Germain was or how he achieved his apparent monopoly on split peas, but his soups are universally excellent and this recipe is the best I have found.

2	*cups split peas*
	cold water
2	*slices bacon*
1	*onion, sliced*
1	*rib celery, chopped*
2	*small carrots, chunked*
1	*small ham bone*
6	*cups stock*
1/2	*tsp salt*
	freshly ground pepper
2	*tbsp butter*
1/2	*cup* crème fraîche *(page 282) or whipping cream*

Wash the peas carefully, put them in just enough water to cover, and bring to a boil. Remove from the fire immediately and allow to stand for 1 hour.

Chop the bacon coarsely and fry until the fat is released, then discard the meat. Sauté the onion in the bacon fat until soft, then add the celery and chunked carrots, and cook another 5 minutes. Heat the stock and put into it the soaked peas, drained, the ham bone, onions, celery, carrots, about 1/2 teaspoon salt, and several grinds of fresh pepper. Bring the soup to a boil, then lower the fire as far as possible, and simmer the soup for 1-1/2 to 2 hours or until the peas are tender. Remove the ham bone and, if it still has any lean meat adhering to it, cut off the meat and return to the soup. Discard the bone. Force the soup through a food mill or put it through the blender, a little at a time. Taste for salt and reheat. Then stir in the butter and the cream and serve immediately.

ZUPPA DI VERDURA [Green Soup]

Zuppa di verdura is a simple Italian vegetable soup, unique in that it includes almost none of the usual soup vegetables. The exception may be celery, but there isn't enough of that to underwrite an argument. The Italian housewife would force this soup through a large sieve, but your blender will do the job just as well and a lot quicker. This recipe is for four persons.

> 2 cups spinach, chopped
> 1 head Boston lettuce, shredded
> 2 stalks celery, chopped
> 4 cups chicken stock
> salt
> freshly ground pepper
> Parmesan cheese, freshly grated

Put the chopped and shredded vegetables into the chicken stock, heated, add a pinch of salt and freshly ground pepper, and bring to the boiling point. Lower the fire and simmer, covered, for 30 minutes. Put the vegetables through a food mill, sieve, or blender, reheat, and serve with grated Parmesan cheese on the side.

POTAGE AU CHOU-FLEUR   [Cauliflower Soup]

Potage au chou-fleur is not a cream soup, although it does have cream in it. It follows an old French custom (and a good one) of binding a soup with egg yolks and cream just before serving. The French also add chicken or light veal stock to soups like this one, very often in order to enrich them.

> 1   *medium cauliflower, cut into flowerets*
> 6   *cups water, boiling*
> 2   *tbsp butter*
> 2   *tbsp flour*
>   *salt*
>   *freshly ground pepper*
> 2   *cups chicken stock*
> 3   *tbsp heavy cream*
> 2   *egg yolks*

Put the cauliflower flowerets into the boiling water, salted. Turn the fire down and continue to boil lightly, uncovered, for 20 minutes or until the cauliflower is tender. Drain and keep the liquid hot. Set aside a number of the smallest flowerets and put the rest through a food mill or puree them in the blender with 1 tablespoon of liquid. Melt the butter in a saucepan and cook the flour in it for 2 minutes, being careful not to let it brown. Add 2 cups of the cooking liquid, boiling hot, to the roux all at once and stir until smooth. Add a pinch of salt and several grinds of pepper. Now add the stock and the pureed cauliflower. Mix thoroughly and simmer for 10 minutes. Meanwhile, mix the egg yolks with the cream and, just before serving, remove the soup from the fire and stir the cream into it. Divide the little flowerets, previously reserved, between 4 soup plates and pour the hot soup over them.

SOUPE AUX POISSONS [Fish Soup]

Soupe aux poissons is a Mediterranean recipe, but it will produce a great soup with whatever fish your dealer has available. I prefer fish with firm white flesh, and there should be at least two different types. You can vary the flavor of this soup by using different fish in its preparation and, if you are a real fish lover, you may enjoy trying the same recipe with various combinations of fish. This recipe is for at least six people, as it is not practical to make fish soup in smaller quantities. Have the dealer clean and bone the fish, then cut the fillets into one-inch squares. Save the heads, bones, and fins for the stock. In fact, you will probably need to ask your dealer for some other leavings in order to get approximately three pounds for the stock (page 56).

4	tbsp butter
2	leeks, chopped
2	medium onions, chopped
2	stalks celery, chopped
1/2	tsp salt
	freshly ground pepper
2	quarts fish stock (page 56)
4	potatoes, peeled and cut into 1/2-inch cubes
3	lb fish fillets, cut into 1-inch squares
2	cups milk
1/2	tsp thyme
1	tbsp sherry
1	cup heavy cream (crème fraîche *recommended*)
	parsley or chives, chopped

Melt the butter in the bottom of a pan and sauté the leeks, onions, and celery until almost, but not quite, browned. This requires watchfulness and frequent stirring! Add salt and some freshly ground pepper, then pour in the fish stock and the potatoes. Keep the fire moderate and cook until the potatoes begin to get tender—about 15 minutes. Now add the milk, the fish fillets, and the thyme. Cook, still over moderate fire, another 10 minutes or until the fish is tender to the fork. Stir in the sherry, then add the cream—off the fire—and heat just to the boiling point, but without actually boiling. Serve with chopped parsley or chives on top of each serving.

SOUPE NORMANDE   [Normandy Vegetable Soup]

Soupe Normande is a white vegetable soup that originated in Normandy, the land of calvados and fine cheeses. It follows the French custom of binding a soup with cream and butter, and it is regarded as a *blanc* because it contains neither tomatoes nor carrots—ingredients in most vegetable soups. Onions may be substituted for the leeks, but they will change the flavor.

> 4 *tbsp butter*
> 4 *leeks, sliced thinly*
> 3 *small turnips, sliced thinly*
> 3 *medium potatoes, sliced thinly*
> 6 *cups stock*
> 1/2 *cup fresh lima beans*
>   *salt*
>   *freshly ground pepper*
> 1-1/2 *cups milk*
> 2 *tbsp heavy cream*
> 1 *tbsp butter*

Melt the 4 tbsp butter in a heavy 3- or 4-quart pan and cook the leeks, turnips, and potatoes for about 10 minutes over a very low fire, making sure not to brown them. Add the stock and, when it starts to boil, add the beans, salt, and freshly ground pepper. Simmer over a low fire for a few minutes, then add the milk, warmed, and continue to simmer until the vegetables are tender. Just before serving, stir in the heavy cream and the final tbsp butter. The French like to pour this soup over bread that has been dried—but not toasted—in the oven.

CLARIFIED STOCK

Clarified stock, technically speaking, is not consommé but there is no denying the fact that a good stock, properly seasoned and laced, perhaps, with a bit of sherry or Madeira, can be a very acceptable substitute. (Genuine consommé is made by simmering stock with additional beef or chicken, depending on the type of stock, before clarifying.)

There are a couple of important things to remember in the clarifying of stock for whatever purpose. First, the stock must be well seasoned before the process is begun. Second, it must be completely free from grease; not difficult if your stock has jellied and the fat congealed. Finally, you must realize that the stock will lose about a third of its volume in the simmering so you can only count on something more than a pint of clarified stock from the quart you start with.

I have keyed this recipe to a single quart of stock but the amount can easily be increased by the addition of another egg for each additional quart of stock. Remember, too, that white chicken stock will be lighter in color after clarification than the darker all-purpose stock.

> 1   *quart stock (jellied preferred)*
>   *salt*
> 1   *egg shell*
> 1   *egg white*
> 1   *tbsp sherry or Madeira (optional)*

Degrease the stock thoroughly and if it is jellied, beat it with a wire whip until liquified. Taste for seasoning and add salt as needed. Beat the egg white and the shell together, lightly, and add about three tbsps of the cold stock, mixing thoroughly. Pour the mixture into the cold stock, put it on a high flame and bring to a boil, stirring gently but constantly. When the stock starts to boil, lower the flame until the stock is barely simmering and continue for 20 minutes. If wine is to be added put it in about two minutes before the simmering is ended. Strain the stock through four layers of wet cheesecloth. If it still shows particles, strain it a second time. It may now be served hot or chilled overnight and served in jellied form.

CRÈME DE CRESSON [Cream of Watercress]

Cresson de fontaine is found in some excellent dishes in France, not the least of which is cream of watercress soup. It is easy to prepare, but you should always be sure to blanch the cress or it will impart a slightly bitter taste. Also be careful to cut out the thick stems, as they are hard to blanch and do not puree easily. Your vegetable dealer sells watercress in bunches, usually just the right size for this soup.

4	leeks
2	tbsp butter
3	medium potatoes, sliced thinly
3	cups stock (chicken stock preferred)
1	tsp salt
	white pepper (optional)
1	cup light cream
2	tbsp Madeira or sherry
1	bunch watercress

Clean the leeks carefully, pulling the leaves apart to detect any sand, then chop coarsely, and sauté in butter until soft. Add the potatoes, the stock, and the salt. Pepper is optional, and white pepper is preferred. Cook slowly for 30 minutes until the potatoes are very tender, then force through a food mill or blend in a blender. While the soup is cooking, clean the cress thoroughly. Save a bit for garnish, then blanch the remainder in boiling water for a few seconds until it wilts. Drain thoroughly, chop, and put into the blender with 2 tablespoons of stock, and liquify. Add the liquid cress to the soup, then stir in the cream and the wine. If it is to be served hot, the soup should be heated to the boiling point, but not allowed to bubble. If it is to be served cold, the soup should be chilled in the freezing compartment of the refrigerator for at least 1-1/2 hours before serving. Hot or cold, top each serving with chopped cress.

CRÈME DU POTIRON FROID [Cold Cream of Pumpkin Soup]

Crème du potiron froid is an easy-to-make cold soup that is somewhat different from most and especially refreshing for a luncheon on a hot day. It is easier to prepare in the United States than in France, where it is almost impossible to buy canned pumpkin. This soup could make four people forget about vichyssoise!

    1   cup cold cooked rice
    3/4 cup light cream
    1/2 cup canned pumpkin
    2   cups chicken stock
    2   tbsp lemon juice
    2   tbsp sugar
         salt to taste

Put the rice and about half the cream into a blender at slow speed until smooth. Add the remainder of the ingredients and blend at high speed for 30 seconds. Taste for salt. If salt is added, blend another 15 seconds or until the soup is creamy. Chill in the freezing compartment of the refrigerator for at least 1 hour before serving.

VICHYSSOISE [Cold Leek—Potato Soup]

I have never eaten vichyssoise in a French restaurant on the Continent, although I understand it is now served in several Parisian establishments. But I know of few soups I would characterize as more typically French than this one. The late Louis Diat is credited with its creation while masterminding the kitchens of the also late Ritz Carlton Hotel. It is, without any doubt, a refinement of his French mother's own leek and potato soup—a potage that is indeed well known in France. Vichyssoise is my favorite of the cold soups, and this recipe should serve six.

6	leeks, about 3/4-inch thick
2	large or 3 medium potatoes
1/4	cup butter
4	cups chicken stock
1	tsp salt
1	cup light cream
1	cup heavy cream
6	tsp chives, chopped

Cut the root stems from the leeks and remove the green tops. Pull the leaves apart and wash carefully. Cut into 1/2-inch pieces and sauté in the butter, melted, until golden—not browned. Add the potatoes, let them steep in the butter for a moment or two, and then add the stock and about 1 teaspoon of salt. Cover the pot and simmer slowly for 30 minutes or until the potatoes are very tender. Taste for seasoning, then put the mixture through a fine food mill or into a blender until completely smooth. Stir in the light cream and refrigerate for at least 1 hour. When ready to serve, stir in the heavy cream, ice cold, and pour 1 teaspoon of freshly chopped chives on each serving.

POTAGE SOFIA

Potage sofia is one of the simplest to make of the typically French soups, yet it is sure to excite comment. The chicken stock should be well seasoned at the start, and the remainder of the ingredients will blend with no further ado. It takes no more than ten minutes to put this soup, piping hot, on soup plates for four people.

5	cups chicken stock
2	whole eggs
3	tbsp Parmesan cheese, grated
1/4	cup bread crumbs, very fine
	fresh nutmeg, grated
1	tsp chives, chopped (optional)

Put the stock into a large saucepan and bring to a boil. In the meantime beat the eggs lightly, add the grated cheese, bread crumbs, and a generous pinch of freshly ground nutmeg. When the stock starts to boil, remove the pan from the fire, stir the egg mixture into the soup, mix well, and then simmer over a low fire for 5 minutes. Remove from the fire, beat for a full minute, then pour into the soup plates, and serve. This potage can be garnished with 1 teaspoon of chopped chives, if desired.

JELLIED CUCUMBER SOUP

Jellied cucumber soup is a grand warm weather soup, but its success depends on the availability of good chicken stock that has jelled of its own richness. To put gelatin into this soup—and it should not be necessary if you use jellied stock, well seasoned—would be a sacrilege. This recipe is for four persons.

1	large cucumber
1	tbsp onion, grated
1/2	cup parsley, finely chopped
1-1/2	tbsp lemon juice
4	cups jellied chicken stock
	salt
	freshly ground pepper
	parsley, for garnish

Peel the cucumber and cut it in half lengthwise. Remove the heavier seeds and grate the remainder very finely. Mix in the grated onion, parsley, and lemon juice and blend them together. Put the cold chicken stock into a blender and liquify it, then add the cucumber mixture, and blend until completely integrated. Taste for seasoning and add a bit of salt and freshly ground pepper. Chill until the soup jells, and then serve in iced consommé cups. Garnish with parsley.

CHAPTER III

Fish and Seafood

*Fish, in the hands of a skilled cook, can be
an inexhaustible source of endless enjoyment.*

BRILLAT-SAVARIN, 1825

Of all the potential foods placed on this sphere by the bounty of the Almighty, probably none exists in an unlimited abundance and incredible diversity as the fishes of the sea and streams.

Beef is beef (in varying degrees of tenderness, of course) wherever you encounter it. The lamb and goat are known in every part of the world. Porkers thrust their inquisitive snouts into the soil of the most remote corners of the globe, and even the edible fowl—game and domestic—has a fairly traceable international pattern.

But the sea turns out food forms that vary astonishingly from section to section, many of them really impossible to approximate outside their native waters. The Mediterranean, as a case in point, has many fish that just do not exist anywhere else in the world. The rascasse, *around which Marseilles builds its famous* bouillabaisse, *isn't known in other waters. The* loup, *the* chapon, *the* Saint-Pierre, *and scores of others appear regularly in the Mediterranean fish stalls and, while some of them look a bit familiar, most of them are different in varying degrees from the fish of other seas.*

This, of course, is one of the problems of compiling an international cookbook. Beef may be tougher in some parts of the world than it is in others, but it is still beef and can be treated as such. But what about the ayu, *the* susuki, *or the* tai *of Japan; the* lapu lapu, *the* bacalao *or the* apahap *of the Philippines; the* red bream, *the* schnapper, *or the* John Dory *of Australia—or even the Dover sole of the English Channel? Some of them—in fact, most of them—can be approximated in the United States (the American sole is actually a flounder, but good!), but they have no exact replicas outside their native waters.*

For that reason I have limited my choice of recipes to those that can be produced in this country without loss of flavor. After all, the first and absolute requisite for seafood is that it be fresh. This is more important with fish than with any other type of food, anywhere in the world. A really stale fish usually speaks for itself, of course, but there is an in-between period when the fish is neither stale enough to be offensive nor fresh enough to have its promised flavor—or to be absolutely safe for human consumption. I have often suspected that this situation is responsible for the fact that so many people are allergic to seafood.

The best guarantee of the quality of the fish you buy is the integrity of your dealer and his pride in the reputation of his shop. If you can find a fish dealer who takes pride in his profession—and they still exist—you won't have to worry about the quality of your purchases.

Tante Marie, the legendary housewife who authored one of France's oldest cookbooks, specifically warns her followers to beware of the fishmonger who smears the gills of his fish with lamb's blood to simulate freshness. I doubt that many American fish dealers have ever thought of that particular subterfuge, but the warning does serve to illustrate the three points that traditionally denote freshness in a fish, viz: bright, protruding eyes, firm flesh, and color around the gills. When the eyes of a fish turn dull and sink in their sockets, when the flesh holds the imprint of your probing finger, or when the gills are dry and colorless, the chances are that that particular fish would be better suited to a nongastronomical career.

COURT BOUILLON

Court bouillon varies even more widely in its makeup than stock, because the term can include all liquids that are boiled for only a short *(court)* time with various seasonings for use as the liquid in which to cook other foods. A court bouillon can be as simple as water with a little vinegar or wine, or it can be a complicated mélange of vegetables, herbs, and spices. Here we are concerned only with fish cookery, and I have found that simple court bouillons are ideal for the average kitchen, easy to make, and low in cost.

There are two very important things to remember in the use of court bouillon. First, the liquid should always be very hot when the fish is placed in it and, even more important, it must never be allowed to boil while the fish is cooking. The barest simmer is sufficient and will prevent the fish from going to pieces in the water. Court bouillon may be strained or not, as preferred.

Here are three basic recipes, each of which will produce slightly more than one quart of liquid.

COURT BOUILLON WITH VINEGAR

4-1/2   cups water
1/4   cup vinegar
1   medium onion, sliced
1   medium carrot, chunked
2   cloves
1   tsp salt
6   peppercorns
    sprig of parsley

Mix all the ingredients and boil for a minute or two. It is now ready for use.

COURT BOUILLON WITH WHITE WINE

> *4-1/2   cups water*
> *1   cup dry white wine*
> *1   medium onion, sliced*
> *1   carrot, chunked*
> *1   bay leaf*
> *1   tsp salt*
> *2   sprigs parsley*
> *pinch of thyme*
> *freshly ground pepper*

Prepare exactly as directed for court bouillon with vinegar.

COURT BOUILLON WITH RED WINE

This court bouillon is used for fish that have a very pronounced flavor. Prepare as directed for court bouillon with white wine, substituting red wine, in the same proportion, for white.

FISH STOCK [Fumet]

The French call fish stock *fumet*, which should not be confused with court bouillon. Fish stock, as the name implies, is a stock used in the preparation of many fish dishes and sauces. It is never as heavy as meat or chicken stock. It is quick and easy to prepare and so low in cost that it is hardly worthwhile to save it from one cooking session to the next, although it will keep up to a week under refrigeration. Your fish dealer should be willing to toss in the necessary fish heads, bones, and trimmings without cost. (If he doesn't, get yourself another fishmonger!) The only other ingredient of material value is a cup of white wine. This recipe, like any other for stock, is only an approximation and the herbs and vegetables can be varied. For instance, mushroom stems can be added or substituted for the carrot. Celery can be added. Vinegar can replace the lemon juice (although I don't particularly advise it), and dry red wine can be substituted for white when you cook a fish of pronounced flavor. This recipe should make a little more than one quart of *fumet*.

3	*lb heads, bones, and trimmings of mild fish, such as whiting or flounder*
4	*cups water*
1	*cup dry white wine*
1	*medium carrot, chopped*
1	*onion, sliced*
4	*sprigs fresh parsley*
1	*small bay leaf*
12	*pepper corns*
1	*tsp lemon juice*
	salt
	pinch of thyme

Put all the ingredients into a medium-sized stockpot and bring to a boil. Reduce the flame and simmer very slowly for 30 minutes. Strain through a cloth and discard all the solids. Keep refrigerated until used.

ESCABECHE FILIPINAS   *[Sweet-Sour Fish]*

In Spain *escabeche* describes a sort of marinade, but in the Philippines, where this recipe originated, it is a method of preparing fish—and a delicious method! In Manila this dish is prepared with the *lapu lapu*, a native fish named for the Visayan chieftain who killed Magellan, but any firm-fleshed fish may be used successfully.

1	*fish (about 3 lb) filleted*
	flour
4	*tbsp oil or lard*
1	*large onion, diced*
1	*bell pepper (preferably red), sliced thinly*
2	*cloves garlic, minced*
2	*cups stock*
4	*tbsp sugar*
4	*tbsp vinegar*
3	*tbsp soy sauce*
	salt
	freshly ground pepper
2	*tbsp cornstarch, dissolved in water*

Fillet the fish or have your dealer do it for you. Season the fillets and flour them lightly, then fry in 1/2 the oil or lard (the latter is preferred in the Philippines) until lightly browned on both sides—about 10 minutes. While the fish is browning, sauté the onion and bell pepper in the rest of the shortening until the onion is just golden. Add the minced garlic and continue cooking until the garlic starts to brown. Add the stock immediately, together with the sugar, vinegar, and soy sauce. Continue cooking until the mixture starts to boil.

If the fish starts to brown too much while the sauce is being prepared, move the skillet off the fire, but don't remove the fillets from the skillet. When the sauce starts to bubble, thicken it with the cornstarch and water, pour over the fish, and let simmer, covered, another 10 minutes. Remove the fish from the sauce and place on a previously warmed platter. Pour the sauce over the fish and serve with boiled rice.

TRUITE AMANDINE [Trout with Almonds]

One of my fondest memories of France will always be of driving through the Maritime Alps and stopping at tiny mountain inns for *truite amandine* or trout prepared in any one of several other ways. Some of these little *auberges* kept live trout in a nearby tank; others relied on the day's catch. I never knew one to store the fish for any period of time, which meant their offerings were always superlative. In this recipe I am specifying one trout per person, but the quantity can be altered to meet the appetites of the consumers and the size of the trout.

4	*fresh trout*
1	*tbsp flour*
1/2	*tsp salt*
	freshly ground pepper
4	*oz butter*
1/4	*lb almonds, slivered*
1/2	*cup stock*
3	*tbsp dry vermouth*
1	*tbsp lemon juice*
	parsley, chopped

For this method of preparing trout I prefer to leave the heads and tails intact. Clean the fish carefully and wipe them with a damp cloth. Roll them in the flour, with which the salt and some freshly ground pepper have been mixed. Melt about 1/2 the butter in a frying pan large enough to hold the fish, side by side. Put the slivered almonds into the butter and fry until browned, but not burned. Remove the nuts and reserve them. Add the remainder of the butter to the pan and, when hot, fry the fish, turning once, about 5 minutes to a side. Test them with a fork; when they flake easily, remove them to a hot serving platter. Add the stock and vermouth, combined and heated, to the cooking pan and scrape the sides and bottom well. Turn the fire up very high and reduce the liquid by about one-half. Add 1/2 the browned nuts and the lemon juice, stir, and pour the sauce over the fish. Sprinkle the rest of the nuts over the whole and garnish with the chopped parsley.

KEDGEREE [Salmon with Rice]

It is sometimes interesting to note marked similarities between cuisines from widely separated corners of the world when you would normally expect complete contrast. Although it was originally, according to my research, a product of the subcontinent of India, *kedgeree* closely resembles the Italian *risottos* (chapter eight). It is not necessary to use salmon in *kedgeree* (haddock or any fish of firm flesh will serve as well), but I prefer salmon because its color presents a pleasing contrast to the rice. Besides, salmon is one of my favorite fish. This recipe has four persons in mind.

2	cups stock
1	cup raw rice
1	tbsp parsley, chopped
1-1/2	lb fresh salmon
2	cups water, boiling
1	tbsp lemon juice
2	tsp salt
1/4	cup butter, melted
3	eggs, hard boiled and chopped
3/4	tsp dry mustard or 1-1/2 tsp Dijon-type mustard
3/4	cup heavy cream
	freshly ground pepper
	paprika

Pour the cold stock (it may be warmed to the melting point, if jelled) over the rice and chopped parsley, mixed. Cover the pan and put over maximum heat until it starts to boil. Lower the fire, put a doubled sheet of aluminum foil between the pan and the flame, and cook as slowly as possible until the stock is absorbed—about 20 minutes.

Put the salmon into a large saucepan and cover with the boiling water, into which the salt and lemon juice have been mixed. Turn the fire down and cook slowly about 20 minutes or until the fish flakes easily. Remove all skin and bones from the salmon and flake into bite-sized pieces. Mix the rice, melted butter, and chopped eggs; then stir in the cream, warmed, and the mustard and several grinds of fresh pepper. Finally, fold in the salmon, taking care not to crumple it too fine. Sprinkle generously with paprika, put into a 400° oven for 10 minutes and serve immediately.

SALMON IN CREAM

I would present this recipe for salmon in cream as an original, except for the conviction that no one can actually come up with a formula for preparing food that some venturesome person, down through the ages, hasn't already tried. So I will merely say that I have no idea who thought of it first. As long as I can prepare it for my own enjoyment, anyone can take the bows. The salmon steaks specified here should be of a size sufficient for one person.

4	*salmon steaks, 1-inch thick*
1/2	*cup white wine*
1/2	*cup stock*
1/2	*tsp dillweed*
	salt
1	*cup sour cream*
1	*tbsp fresh parsley, chopped*

Preheat the oven to 350°. Put the steaks in an oven-proof casserole. Combine the wine and stock, heat, and pour over the steaks. Sprinkle with the dillweed and just a pinch of salt. Place in the oven and bake, basting frequently, for 20 to 25 minutes or until the steaks flake to the fork. Remove the salmon to a hot serving plate and rinse the baking dish with the hot stock, scraping all the browned bits into a saucepan. Reduce the liquid over a hot flame to about 3/4 cup. Then, off the fire, add the sour cream and mix thoroughly. Return to a low fire and heat the sauce, but *do not let it bubble*! Pour the sauce over the steaks and sprinkle with parsley.

SOLE CATHERINE

Sole Catherine is a practical adaptation of France's famous *truite Amandine,* born of a hunger for the original dish at a time when no fresh trout were available. Accordingly, my wife adapted the almonds to fresh sole, and the result was so successful it has been a standard item in our menu planning ever since. I gave the dish the name of its creator.

> 3/4   *cup almonds, blanched*
>   4   *tbsp butter*
>   2   *heaping tbsp shallots or*
>   *green onions, minced*
> 1/2   *cup dry white wine*
> 1/2   *cup stock*
>   *nutmeg*
>   *salt*
>   *freshly ground pepper*
>
>   4   *medium soles (1 for each serving)*
>   *flour*
>   2   *tbsp oil*

Slice the almonds thinly and divide into 2 equal portions. Fry 1/2 of them in 1 tablespoon of butter until golden, remove to a paper towel with a slotted spoon, then cook the shallots or onions in the same butter until soft, but not browned. Add the wine and bring to a boil, then add the stock, the unfried almonds, a pinch of nutmeg, salt, and freshly ground pepper. Reduce the liquid by at least one-half over a very hot fire.

Lightly flour the soles, which have been skinned, and put them into a large frying pan with 3 tablespoons of butter and the oil, heated almost to the smoking stage. (The fish may be fried 2 at a time, if the skillet is too small.) Brown the fish quickly on one side, turn, lower the fire, and cook gently for 10 minutes.

When they are cooked, arrange the fish on a serving platter, browned side up, and pour the sauce over them. Sprinkle with the toasted almonds and serve at once.

FILLETS OF SOLE FLORENTINE

Fillets of sole Florentine, a delectable dish, requires about two cups of fish stock, which can be made in only a few minutes before you prepare the fish. When you buy your fillets, ask your dealer for a couple of pounds of trimmings—heads, tails, and bones—and proceed as on page 56. This is one way I like spinach, and I bless the Florentines for being so adept at concealing the vegetable in the depths of so many tasty dishes.

1-1/2	tbsp butter
1-1/2	tbsp flour
2	cups fish stock
	salt
	freshly ground pepper
4	sole or flounder fillets
1	tbsp lemon juice
5	oz frozen spinach (1/2 of a 10-oz package)
1/4	cup Parmesan or Swiss cheese, grated

Preheat the oven to 350°. Melt the butter in a saucepan, stir in the flour, and sauté for at least 2 minutes, stirring constantly. Pour in 1 cup of fish stock, boiling hot, and stir until creamy. Add a pinch of salt and 2 grinds of pepper and set the sauce aside.

Fold the fillets double and arrange on the bottom of a baking dish, sprinkle with the lemon juice, and pour the remainder of the fish stock around them. Cover with foil and put into the oven for 12 minutes. While the fillets are cooking, prepare the 1/2 package of spinach according to the directions. When it is cooked, drain the spinach and add 1 tablespoon of the liquid to the *velouté* sauce. Discard the remainder of the liquid. When they have cooked for 12 minutes, take the fillets from the oven and remove almost all the stock from the pan. Divide the cooked spinach over the 4 fillets and then pour the *velouté* sauce over the whole. Sprinkle with the grated cheese and return to the oven, advanced to 400°, and bake another 8 minutes or until the cheese is browned. Serve with boiled potatoes.

BAKED SEA BASS

About the closest thing we had to sea bass along the shores of the Mediterranean was the *loup* (or, more accurately, *loup-de-mer* because the *loup,* unqualified, is really a wolf—hardly a substitute for sea bass). This is also an excellent method for preparing red snapper, if you can find one in your market as small as three pounds.

1	*3-lb sea bass (or equivalent)*
2	*large onions, sliced*
4	*stalks celery, cut into 1-inch lengths*
4	*tomatoes, peeled, seeded, and wedged*
4	*tbsp parsley, chopped*
1/2	*cup stock*
1/2	*cup dry white wine*
1	*bay leaf*
	pinch of tarragon
	salt
	freshly ground pepper
	paprika
	lemon wedges

Preheat the oven to 350°. Have the fish cleaned as you wish, but not filleted. (You will probably want to remove the head of the fish, although any European—or Asian, for that matter—will sneer at you for "letting the juices escape.") Put it in a shallow oven-proof baking dish or pan and surround it with the onions, celery, and tomato wedges. Sprinkle with parsley, then pour in the combined wine and stock. Add the bay leaf, tarragon, salt, and pepper and bake in the oven for about 35 to 40 minutes or until the fish flakes to the fork and the vegetables are tender. Sprinkle generously with paprika and serve from the baking dish with the lemon wedges. Boiled potatoes drenched in plenty of butter are superb with this dish.

STUFFED WHITING

This is a simple and delicious method for preparing whiting or any comparable fish of mild flavor and firm flesh. In this recipe one fish is regarded as a portion for one person, based on the usual size of the whiting available on the East Coast of the United States.

> 4   *whiting (about 12 oz each)*
> 4   *tbsp onion, chopped*
> 4   *tbsp celery, chopped*
> 2   *tsp lemon juice*
>   *basil*
>   *thyme*
>   *salt*
>   *freshly ground pepper*
>
> 1/4   *cup stock*
> 3   *tbsp vermouth*
> 2   *tbsp butter*
>   *lemon wedges*

Preheat the oven to 350°. Clean the fish and wipe them dry with a paper towel, including the interior of the cavity. Prepare the stuffing by mixing the onion, celery, and lemon juice with just a pinch each of thyme and basil. Salt and pepper the cavities and put 1/4 of the stuffing in each. Combine the stock, vermouth, and butter, and heat until the butter melts. Pour into the bottom of an oven-proof casserole or baking dish with cover, large enough to hold the fish side by side. Position the fish in the casserole and baste with the liquid. Cover and put into the oven for 10 minutes. Remove the cover, turn the fish gently, baste again, and complete the cooking, uncovered, until the fish is easily flaked with a fork. Remove the fish to a serving platter, pour the pan juices over them, and serve with lemon wedges.

FILETS DE SOLE À LA MORNAY *[Sole with Cheese Sauce]*

Filets de sole à la Mornay is a very simple and a very delicious way to prepare sole (flounder, probably) that is at the same time appealing to the eye. Have the Mornay sauce made in advance (page 226), using either the plain stock or fish stock as a base for the *velouté.* I prefer the latter, but either is good. Have your dealer fillet the soles if you are not experienced at the art. Unless the soles are very small, the two fillets from a single fish should serve two people.

> 2   *medium soles, filleted*
> 1   *quart court bouillon with white wine (page 56)*
> 1   *cup Mornay sauce*
>   *paprika*

Roll the fillets and fasten them with a wooden toothpick. Heat the court bouillon to the boiling point, place the sole in it, and immediately reduce the flame until the bouillon barely simmers. Continue to simmer for 5 minutes.

Remove the fillets from the liquid and arrange them in an oven-proof baking dish. Cover them with the Mornay sauce, sprinkle generously with paprika, and place them under a broiler until the sauce is lightly browned. Serve at once.

COQUILLES SAINT-JACQUES À LA PARISIENNE
[Scallops and Mushrooms in Wine]

Scallops in France are usually sold complete with shell and often with delicious pink coral that can add both to the flavor and the eye appeal of *coquilles Saint-Jacques à la Parisienne.* Also, the shells can be used—and generally are—as serving dishes for this *plat.* Unfortunately, however, the scallops on this side of the Atlantic develop no coral, and they are not sold in their shells. It is almost impossible to get them in their shells unless you harvest them yourself. Consequently, scallop shells are not as common here as in France, but this recipe can be beautifully prepared in a shallow baking dish or a glass pie pan. If you do happen to have the shells (try a gourmet cooking wares store), this should fill four of them.

1-1/2   lb bay or sea scallops
3/4   cup stock
3/4   cup dry vermouth
2   tbsp shallots, chopped
1   bay leaf

Bay scallops are preferred when available, but, if the larger sea scallops are used, cut them into somewhat smaller pieces. Wash the scallops carefully and drain. Put all the ingredients into a covered pan and bring to the boil, then turn down the fire, and simmer, covered, for 5 minutes. Remove the scallops from the liquid. Strain the liquid and discard the solids.

3   tbsp butter
1   cup mushrooms, sliced about 1/4-inch thick

While the scallops are simmering, sauté the mushrooms in the butter for about 3 minutes. Do not let them wilt. Remove the mushrooms with a slotted spoon and save the butter for use in the sauce.

about 3   tbsp butter
3   tbsp flour
1-1/2   cup liquid from the scallops
1   cup heavy cream
2   egg yolks
salt (if needed)
1/4   cup Parmesan cheese, grated
1/4   cup Swiss cheese (Emmenthaler), grated

Using the same pan in which the mushrooms were sautéed, add enough butter to equal 3 tablespoons, heat, and add the flour, cooking for about 3 minutes. Be sure the liquid in which the scallops were poached is still hot, then add it to the flour, stirring to achieve a smooth cream. Taste for salt, which may not be needed. Meanwhile, stir the egg yolks into the cream and, off the fire, stir the cream into the sauce. When thoroughly blended, return the scallops and mushrooms to the sauce, mix, and divide between the 4 shells or pour into the baking dish. Sprinkle the cheese over the top and place under a broiler until the cheese is browned and the sauce is bubbly.

BAKED SEA PERCH

This recipe for baked sea perch was developed specifically to put flavor into the frozen packaged fish on sale at every supermarket. We have used it often with sea perch, but any packaged frozen fish fillets could be substituted. It is important to allow the fish to thaw completely before separating the fillets or they are likely to crumble. My wife and I usually consume a one-pound package of fish thus prepared; this recipe calls for two one-pound packages, in case we have company!

2	*packages (2 lb) frozen sea perch*
1/2	*cup stock*
4	*tbsp butter*
2	*tsp dried parsley*
2	*tsp lemon juice*
1/2	*tsp tarragon*
	garlic powder
1-1/2	*tbsp onion, grated (including juice)*
	salt
	freshly ground pepper

Thaw the frozen fish slowly and thoroughly and separate into fillets. Warm the stock and mix all the other ingredients into it, using just a pinch of both the garlic powder and salt. Let stand until the herbs are well moistened, then pour into a flat oven-proof casserole. Preheat the oven to 425°. Put the fish fillets into the liquid and turn until each one is coated, then bake them in the oven for about 20 minutes or until the fish flakes easily to the fork. Baste frequently with the liquid. To serve, pour the liquid over the fish and over boiled potatoes.

SHRIMP JAMBALAYA

Shrimp jambalaya is one of Louisiana's traditional dishes which, like all traditional dishes, can be cooked in half a hundred different ways, all of them authentic. This recipe is my favorite because it includes ham as a meat additive to the shrimp. (My limited researches have convinced me that *jambalaya* actually is derived from the French *jambon* [ham] so I believe all authentic jambalaya should include ham.) However, I have sampled some excellent jambalayas that were as free from ham as cornflakes and milk are from bacon. Try this one on yourself and three friends.

1/2	*lb ham in one piece (about 1/2-inch thick)*
2	*tbsp butter*
1	*tbsp oil*
1	*large onion, chopped*
1	*green pepper, chopped*
1	*clove garlic, chopped*
1	*cup raw rice*
1	*cup stock (chicken preferred)*
1	*1-lb can tomatoes*
1/2	*tsp tarragon*
about 1-1/2	*tsp salt*
	freshly ground pepper
1-1/2	*lb shrimp, cooked and deveined (about 2 lb raw shrimp)*
1	*quart water*

Sauté the ham in the combined oil and butter until browned, then remove, and keep warm. Cook the onion and pepper in the same fat over a moderate fire until soft, then add the chopped garlic. Pour in the rice and stir well until all grains are coated with oil. Cook for 5 minutes, then pour in the stock and tomatoes. Add the tarragon, about 1/2 teaspoon of salt, and several grinds of fresh pepper. Cube the ham and return to the pan. Cover and simmer until the rice is cooked and most of the liquid absorbed. To cook the shrimp, bring 1 quart of water to the boil and put the raw shrimp into it with 1 teaspoon salt. Keep the fire constant until the water starts to boil again, then pour the water off the shrimp, using the lid as a strainer. Cover the pan tightly and let stand for 10 minutes so that the shrimp can steam. Shell and devein the shrimp, add to the rice, and heat for 5 minutes before serving.

HAMANABE [Japanese Shrimp]

If it were the product of a continental restaurant, *hamanabe* would undoubtedly be called shrimp Florentine because it features spinach as a background for the shrimp. Actually the dish came to me from Japan by way of Manila and a friend whose husband spent the war years as a guest of the Japanese without being served anything half so delicious! As with most oriental dishes, it is important that *hamanabe* not be overcooked.

3	tbsp oil
1	small onion, minced
1-1/2	lb spinach, coarsely torn
3/4	lb mushrooms, sliced
1/4	cup soy sauce (imported)
1/2	cup stock (chicken preferred)
1	tsp sugar
1-1/2	lb fresh raw shrimp

Heat the oil, add the onion, and let soften. Put in the spinach, mushrooms, soy sauce (either Chinese or Japanese is preferred to domestic), and the stock mixed with the sugar. Simmer over a low fire until the vegetables start to wilt, then add the shrimp, peeled and deveined. Cook over a low fire for about 10 minutes or until the shrimp are cooked.

SHRIMP THERMIDOR

For years I enjoyed shrimp Thermidor secure in the belief that the word thermidor had something to do with thermal designations of heat. Then I became curious and began a bit of research. I discovered that Thermidor was the eleventh month in the French Revolution's calendar, and the term refers specifically to the boisterous lads who relegated Robespierre to the guillotine on 29 July, 1794! (The month Thermidor extended from July 20 to August 18.) Thus shrimp Thermidor really is a revolutionary dish—just the thing to eat before you set out to upset a government!

1-1/2	lb medium shrimp, cooked and deveined
4	tbsp butter
3/4	cup mushrooms, sliced
2	tbsp shallots or green onions, sliced
2	tbsp flour
1/2	tsp dry mustard
1/2	cup chicken stock
1	cup crème fraîche (page 282) or sour cream
	salt
2	tbsp Madeira or sherry
2	dashes tabasco
	cayenne pepper
1/4	cup Emmenthaler or Gruyère cheese, grated
1/4	cup Parmesan cheese, grated
	paprika

Heat the butter in a heavy pan and sauté the mushrooms until lightly browned. Remove the mushrooms from the pan and reserve. Add the shallots or onions and cook until soft. Stir in the flour and dry mustard until you have a smooth roux. Add the stock, heated, and continue to stir the sauce to smoothness. Remove the pan from the fire and stir in the cream. Return to the fire and cook over a low fire, stirring constantly, until the sauce starts to thicken. If sour cream is used *do not allow it to boil*. Salt to taste. Several minutes before serving, add the shrimp, the wine, 2 dashes of tabasco and a small pinch of cayenne. Mix well. Pour into an oven-proof casserole and cover with the combined cheeses and sprinkle generously with paprika. Bake in a pre-heated 400°oven until the cheese is brown and bubbly—about 10 minutes—then serve at once with rice.

SHRIMP CREOLE

Shrimp creole is as American as cherry pie on George Washington's birthday. It is not only 100 percent American but almost impossible to duplicate overseas because our peerless Gulf Coast shrimp just don't propagate in foreign waters. The *crevette grise* of the Mediterranean, an excellent shellfish under most conditions, doesn't match our native shrimp when a creole is planned. This recipe might be termed a conglomerate because it combines the best features, in my opinion, of a dozen recipes in my possession. Note carefully the preference for plain boiled rice.

    1   *tbsp butter*
    3   *tbsp oil*
    2   *medium onions, chopped*
 1/2   *cup green pepper, chopped*
 1/2   *cup celery, chopped*
    3   *medium tomatoes, peeled, seeded, and chopped*
    1   *clove garlic, crushed*

       3   tbsp tomato paste
       1   cup stock
       1   tbsp Worcestershire sauce
       1   tsp lemon juice
       1   bay leaf
           pinch of sugar (about 1/4 tsp)
     1/2   tsp thyme
       3   whole cloves
           salt
           freshly ground pepper
     1/2   small eggplant, unpeeled and cut into 1/2-inch cubes
       2   cups shrimp, cooked, peeled, and deveined
           parsley, chopped

Heat the butter and 1 tablespoon of the oil in a large saucepan or skillet and sauté the onion, pepper, and celery until soft, but not browned. Add the tomatoes and the clove of garlic. Stir in the tomato paste, then add the stock, heated, and season with the Worcestershire sauce, lemon juice, bay leaf, sugar, thyme, and cloves. Add the salt and a few good grinds of pepper, cover the pan, and simmer for 30 minutes. Sauté the eggplant cubes in the remaining 2 tablespoons of oil until lightly browned. Add this to the sauce after it has simmered for 30 minutes and cook another 10 minutes, still over a low fire. Now add the shrimp and continue simmering until the shrimp are thoroughly heated—about 10 minutes. Pour the whole into a warmed serving casserole and sprinkle with the chopped parsley. Serve with plain boiled rice; this dish has enough flavor to carry the plain rice, and a highly seasoned rice might provoke a taste conflict.

CHAPTER IV

Poultry

*Je veux que le dimanche chaque paysan
ait le poule au pot.*

HENRI IV, 1598

The late President Herbert Hoover is generally credited with authorship of the "chicken in every pot" ploy in one of his campaign speeches back in 1928. In truth, however, Henri IV (Henry of Navarre) predated Hoover by nearly three and one-third centuries. Henri's utterance is said to have highlighted his coronation at Reims and was happily received even though it did limit his good wishes to peasants on the Sabbath.

It is highly improbable that either of these statesmen could foresee the day when the esteemed chicken would become the most plentiful and reasonably priced meat in both France and the United States, possibly excepting some of the cheaper types of fish. Nevertheless, if there is any meat today that the indigent American or the European peasant can afford to toss in his pot, it certainly must be the chicken.

In this department the United States leads the world. Nowhere is chicken as plentiful or as cheap as in this country, although some of the production-line fryers, broilers, and even roasters can be a bit tasteless if not cooked in a manner to stimulate their natural flavor. Although there is no question of their nutritive value (science has taken care of that very well), there is some doubt as to whether the flesh of the chicken bred and reared in captivity, permitted only the most scientifically perfect diet, can really match flavor with a farmyard pullet that lives on kitchen scraps and whatever other food it can forage for itself.

This is not my own theory, although I have had ample opportunity to test it. During my years in Italy, particularly in fertile Tuscany—the province of magnificent veal, fine fruits, vegetables, and the only authentic Chianti in the world—I quickly learned that the average Italian is willing to pay twice as much, and sometimes more, for a chicken of the barnyard variety in preference to the feathered product of science.

Personally, I settled for the more scientific and lower-priced birds, relying on cooking techniques to bring them to their peak of flavor. This paid off in one important respect particularly; there is no denying that the production-line pullet is invariably more tender. No chicken can spend its life running around a farmyard or open pen, grubbing for food and fighting for its fair share, without developing some husky muscles right where the best eating ought to be.

When buying a chicken (capon and fowl excepted), you usually have a choice of the fryer-broiler or the roaster. In reality about the only differences are the size and price. The smallest chickens can be roasted if you wish, and the largest on sale in the average market can usually be fried. A second choice is between a whole bird and a cut-up one. The latter is always more expensive and, when you buy individual parts, the price is still higher. Prime examples are the breasts.

When you buy a pair of boned breasts, you generally pay just about the cost of the entire chicken intact. At the present writing, a pair of breasts from a three-pound chicken, boned and ready to cook, will cost over $1.00 unless you have an amazing poulterer. The whole chicken at that weight shouldn't cost more than $1.35, often less.

For this reason it pays handsomely to learn to cut up a chicken yourself, carving out the pieces you want to use immediately and freezing the others for later attention. Contrary to what you may have been told, a chicken loses very little flavor or food value in the quick-freezing process. I learned this fact beyond question during the dozen-plus years I lived in the tropical temperatures of the Philippines. If it had not been for the boon of quick freezing, the storage of meats of all kinds, including chicken, would have been a constant health hazard.

As a result of the knowledge gained during those years, our freezer today always holds one to four chickens, whole or in parts, and no one has ever remarked a deterioration of flavor when the chickens were cooked.

So, to realize the maximum from your poultry dollar, always buy the entire bird and carve it yourself. Anyone who has ever carved a chicken or turkey at the table can just as easily cut up the bird before it is cooked. First, of course, the thigh and leg are removed from each side. With a little practice you can learn to remove, as part of the thigh, the treasured oyster from its concavity in the lower back. Next comes each wing, cut to include a generous one-half-inch slice of the breast to give a little more meat, making it a more desirable morsel. Because its meat content is negligible, the third joint (tip) of the wing should be removed for inclusion in the stockpot.

Now, cut the carcass lengthwise through the rib cage into two parts, dividing the breast from the back, the latter of which is, together with the neck, also marked for the stockpot. Finally, carefully remove the skin from the breast section. With a very sharp knife make a cut on one side of the breast bone, as close to the peak of the ridge as possible, and carefully work the meat away from the bone, continuing on down the rib cage until the breast fillet is freed. Repeat this on the other side of the breast bone. You will wind up with two large and two small fillets of firm, moist breast, ready for cooking or refrigeration. The larger fillets will each have a thin, white sinew running along the edge under the skin. Remove this with the point of a sharp knife, and the process is complete. You will be in possession of fillets that would cost you almost the entire price of the chicken if you had bought them individually. And the legs, thighs, wings, and carcass are yours free!

Your first attempt will not be as easy as I have made it sound, but after your second or third try you will be nearly as adept as your poulterer and you'll be realizing at least double on your poultry dollar.

One final tip for the stockpot cook. If you buy your chickens from a dealer who specializes in freshness, the chances are the chicken in his market will still have the feet attached to the drumsticks. And just as probably, he will cut them off and throw them away if you don't protest in advance. No part of a chicken belongs in the stockpot any more than the feet, which have a high percentage of gelatin that will help give any stock—chicken or multi-purpose—an excellent consistency.

To prepare the feet for the stockpot, cut off the claws with a sharp knife or poultry shears. Then drop them into boiling water for a couple of minutes, after which the dry, scaly skin should peel off easily, leaving the valuable bones and tendons. (If you have any trouble removing the outer skin after two minutes of scalding, drop the feet back in the water for another minute or so. Just don't boil them longer than necessary.) If you are not ready to make stock, wrap them in plastic and put them in the freezer. Just be sure the dealer doesn't throw them away—or appropriate them for his own stockpot!

PAPRIKÁSCSIRKE [Chicken Paprika]

The closest I've ever been to Budapest is Vienna, but during my residence
in Nice and San Remo one of my good friends was a Hungarian called
Pishta, apparently a nickname for Stefan. Pishta didn't leave Hungary of
his own will, and he never lost his desire to return. When his nostalgia got
a bit rough, he used to retire to his kitchen and prepare some of the
Hungarian dishes he had learned from his mother. Chicken paprika was
typical. In any part of the world it is a delicious way to eat chicken, but
to Pishta it was a momentary return to Budapest.

4	*tbsp butter*
3	*onions, chopped*
1-1/2	*tbsp Hungarian paprika*
2	*2-lb frying chickens, quartered*
	salt
	freshly ground pepper
1-1/2	*cups chicken stock*
1	*cup heavy cream (*crème fraîche *preferred)*

Melt the butter in a large skillet and sauté the onions until they are
transparent, but not browned. Stir in the paprika and, when well blended,
remove the onions with a slotted spoon, leaving as much fat as possible in

the skillet. Salt and pepper the chicken quarters and sauté them in the fat for about 10 minutes, turning them so they are completely browned. Meanwhile, put the onions through a food mill or puree them in the blender with a little stock. When the chickens are browned, return the onions to the skillet and add the stock, heated. Cover the pan and simmer slowly for 30 minutes or less if the chicken seems too tender. Remove the chicken from the sauce and, off the fire, stir in the cream, adding more paprika if desired. Bring the sauce to a slow boil until it thickens a bit. Pour the sauce over the chicken and serve with *galuska.*

GALUSKA [Soft Dumplings]

Galuska might be called the Hungarian version of *gnocchi* except that it has no potatoes in it. *Galuska* are not noodles and for that reason they must be mixed in a bowl so that they are not stiffened with flour. Actually, the original Hungarian recipe was evolved by cooks who never heard of baking powder but I have found that the baking powder lightens the *Galuska* considerably.

1-1/2	cups flour
1	tsp baking powder
1	tsp salt
1	egg
1/2	cup milk
3	quarts boiling water
1	tbsp butter

Blend the flour, baking powder, salt, egg and milk thoroughly to achieve a soft dough that can be spooned. Heat the water in a wide-bottom pan and melt the butter in it. When the water comes to a rolling boil drop the dumpling dough into it, a teaspoon—or the equivalent—at a time. Cover the pan and boil over a moderate fire for 15 minutes. Remove the *Galuska* with a slotted spoon and serve with the *paprikáscsirke.* Galuska are also excellent with other stews and ragouts.

POULET ROTI À LA CANEBIÈRE [*Roast Chicken à la Canebière*]

Some ten years ago in a tiny hotel on Marseilles' famous *la Canebière,* my wife and I first learned how good plain roast chicken could be when properly prepared (which, to me, means without stuffing). Most people who have spent any time in Marseilles remember the *bouillabaisse* and with good reason. But I never think of that exotic port without being reminded of the roast chicken.

> 1   *roasting chicken (3 to 4 lb)*
>   *salt*
>   *freshly ground pepper*
> 1   *tsp ground tarragon*
> 2   *tbsp butter*
> 1   *large onion, peeled*
>   *olive oil*
>
> 1/3 *cup stock*
> 1/3 *cup dry white wine*
> 1   *tsp beurre manié (page 280)*

Preheat the oven to 350°. Wipe the chicken clean and sprinkle the inside of the cavity with salt, freshly ground pepper, and 1/2 teaspoon of tarragon. Put 1 tablespoon of the butter into the cavity, followed by the onion and the second tablespoon of butter. Truss the bird with cord and coat it completely with oil, using a brush or clean cloth. Sprinkle 1/2 teaspoon of tarragon over the bird and place it on its back in an open roasting pan. Roast for 1 hour or until tender, basting occasionally.

Remove the chicken from the oven and drain the cavity into the juices in the pan. Add the stock and wine, combined and warmed, and boil vigorously until reduced by about one-third. Add the *beurre manié* bit by bit and, when the sauce thickens slightly, pour into a serving boat.

Tour de chef: The bones of this bird—all of them—can be simmered with the remaining carcass, the original onion, a chopped carrot, some diced celery, salt, pepper, and thyme to produce the finest chicken stock or soup you can imagine!

POULET À L'ESTRAGON [Chicken with Tarragon]

There are some herbs that seem to have been created for a particular meat, as undoubtedly tarragon mates perfectly with chicken (see *poulet rôti*, page 82). *Poulet à l'estragon* is a recipe I found in Paris and have used for years. It is the tarragon that lifts this dish out of the realm of ordinary creamed chicken. A three-pound roaster should serve four persons.

> 1   *3-lb chicken, cut into serving pieces*
>   *salt*
>   *freshly ground pepper*
> 2   *tbsp butter*
> 1   *generous tsp tarragon*
> 1   *tbsp shallots or green onions, minced*
> 1   *cup stock*
> 1/2 *cup dry white wine*
> 1   *tbsp brandy (cognac preferred)*
> 1   *cup* crème fraîche *(page 282) or sour cream*

Salt and pepper the chicken pieces and brown them quickly in the butter. When the chicken is golden, add the shallots or onions and sauté until transparent. Stir in the tarragon and mix thoroughly with the chicken. Cover the pan tightly and cook the chicken over a low flame for 10 minutes, shaking the pan often to prevent sticking. Meanwhile pour the stock into a pan and reduce it by one-half over a very hot flame. Add the wine and keep warm. After the chicken has cooked for about 10 minutes, add the brandy and ignite it. When the flame dies, add the combined stock and wine, cover, and simmer until the chicken is tender. There should now be about 1/2 cup of liquid in the pan; add more plain stock if necessary. *Remove the chicken from the fire* and stir in the *crème fraîche* or sour cream. (If *crème fraîche* is used, the sauce can be cooked to the proper consistency; if sour cream is used, extreme care must be taken not to allow it to bubble or it will disintegrate. If this should happen, a bit of *beurre manié* [page 280] can be added.)

When the sauce is thick and creamy, pour over the chicken and serve with boiled rice or mashed potatoes.

POULET DU PRINTEMPS [Chicken and Spring Vegetables]

Poulet du printemps could easily be translated "spring chicken", but the reference here is to the vegetables (although the chicken shouldn't escape the spring classification by too wide a margin). This is a magnificent dish with which to celebrate the advent of new potatoes, baby carrots, little white onions that are not too blasé, and green beans fresh off the vine.

I am not sure where most urban dwellers can locate all these vegetables at the same time, but it is a goal to pursue. Afterwards we approximate!

1	*3-lb roasting chicken*
	salt
	freshly ground pepper
	fresh parsley
3	*oz butter (clarified preferred, page 281)*
1/4	*cup cognac*
1	*lb baby carrots*
16	*small white onions*
1	*lb new potatoes*
1/2	*cup stock*
1/2	*cup dry white wine*
	pinch of rosemary
1/2	*lb fresh green beans, cut into 1-1/2-inch lengths*

Clean the chicken and wipe carefully. Salt and pepper the cavity and insert a small bunch of fresh parsley. Truss the bird as if for roasting. Melt the butter in a Dutch oven-type pan with a tight lid (clarified butter will not burn as readily). Brown the chicken on all sides. When the chicken is nicely browned, warm the cognac carefully in a small pan and light it. Pour it over the chicken while still burning and baste the chicken well, even after the flame has died. Cut all the vegetables into bite-sized pieces. If they are tiny, the new potatoes can be used without peeling. So that they will not lose their shape in cooking, the onions should be peeled and a thin slice cut from the root end, which is then pierced with the tip of the knife. A French cook will usually round the edges of the carrot lengths to improve their appearance. Put all the vegetables except the green beans into the pot with the chicken and baste well with the butter and cognac. Add the stock and wine, combined and heated, and a pinch of rosemary. Cover the pot tightly and put it into an oven preheated to 325° for 1 hour, basting every 15 minutes with the juices in the pan. After 1 hour add the green beans to the pot and cook until they are tender—about 20 minutes. Remove the chicken from the casserole, carve, and arrange on a warmed serving platter. Surround with the vegetables and pour the cooking juices over the whole. Serve with a green salad.

POULET CITRONNÉ [Chicken with Lemon]

Cooks for many years have been combining ducks and ducklings with fruit—notably oranges—with marked success. Here is a recipe for chicken cooked with lemon that I consider comparable to any of the others. It is particularly good with wild rice on the side, but plain boiled rice also is delicious. I like to depart from the usual three-pound chicken in this recipe and substitute one leg and one thigh for each celebrant.

4	chicken legs and thighs, disjointed
	salt
	freshly ground pepper
3	tbsp butter
2	tbsp oil
1	medium onion, thinly sliced
2	tbsp flour
2	cups chicken stock
2	lemons, sliced
1	tsp sugar
1/2	tsp marjoram

Preheat the oven to 375°. Salt and pepper the chicken parts and sauté in the combined oil and butter until browned, then remove to a covered casserole. Add the onion to the skillet and cook until transparent. Stir in the flour and cook for at least 3 minutes, stirring constantly to prevent scorching. Heat the stock and pour it into the flour all at once. Stir until smooth. Slice the 2 lemons without peeling them and discard the heavy end pieces, leaving the equivalent of 1-1/2 whole ones. Discard the seeds and add the slices to the sauce, together with the sugar and marjoram. Cook for another minute, then taste for seasoning and pour the sauce over the chicken. Cover the casserole and cook the chicken in the oven for about 30 minutes, then remove the cover and cook another 15 minutes, basting every few minutes, until the chicken is tender and browned. Add more chicken stock if needed. Serve with your choice of rice.

BOUCHÉES À LA REINE [Creamed Chicken in Patty Shells]

The preparation of puff pastry, a highly intriguing but also somewhat complicated branch of the culinary science, certainly has no place in a book dedicated to the glories of stock. Puff pastry shells in the form of frozen dough are, however, now available in many American markets. These shells, which compare very favorably with the product of a master pastry chef, are easy to prepare and are utterly delicious when filled with this superb creamed chicken preparation.

This recipe can be made with leftover chicken by using a roux prepared with two tablespoons of butter in place of the pan juices, but I believe the improved end result makes the use of fresh chicken, as here specified, well worthwhile and not much more trouble.

8	*chicken thighs*
4	*tbsp butter*
12	*medium mushrooms*
2	*tbsp flour*
3/4	*cup stock*

3/4   *cup light cream*
  2   *tbsp mushroom liquid*
      salt
      freshly ground pepper
1/2   *cup Gruyère or Emmenthaler, grated*
1/2   *cup Parmesan, grated*
  2   *tbsp Madeira or sherry*
1/2   *cup cooked peas*

  8   *patty shells*

Remove the skin from the chicken thighs, sauté the thighs in 2 tablespoons of butter until lightly browned, then cover the skillet, and simmer until tender—about 30 minutes.

While the chicken is cooking, wipe the mushrooms clean, cut off the stems just below the caps, and slice the caps thinly. Simmer the stems in 1/2 cup of water for 5 minutes, reserve 2 tablespoons of the liquid, and discard the rest. Sauté the mushroom slices in the remaining 2 tablespoons of butter and set aside.

When the chicken is tender, remove from the skillet, bone, and cut into 1/2-inch chunks. Keep warm. Prepare a roux by cooking the 2 tablespoons of flour in the juices remaining the pan for about 2 minutes, stirring often so that the flour cooks without browning. Put the combined stock and cream in a saucepan on a hot fire. As soon as they start to boil, pour the stock and cream into the roux and stir with a wire whip or spoon until a smooth sauce is achieved. Season lightly. Add the 2 tablespoons of mushroom liquid, then the grated cheese. When blended, return the chicken to the sauce, add the sautéed mushrooms, the peas, and finally the Madeira. Stir again and then simmer, covered, over a very low fire for 5 minutes.

Taste for seasoning. Then fill the freshly baked patty shells, garnish with the pastry caps, and divide the remainder of the sauce among the 4 servings. The sauce can be prepared in advance and heated for immediate service.

COQ AU VIN [Chicken in Red Wine]

Coq au vin is another of France's traditional recipes, property of every French housewife in some form and varying widely, not only from region to region but from kitchen to kitchen. Coq au vin is the poultry counterpart to boeuf bourguignon and just as excellent. Strictly speaking, a coq is exactly what it sounds like, but few French roosters have to submit themselves to such indignities today. Originally created to make the cock edible after years of ruling the barnyard with iron spurs, coq au vin now is aimed at making an ordinary chicken extraordinarily delicious—and it succeeds admirably! This is the recipe I have found the most rewarding.

1	3-lb roasting chicken, cut into serving pieces
2	tbsp butter
2	tbsp oil
1	clove garlic, crushed
1	cup dry red wine
3/4	cup stock
	thyme
	marjoram
	bay leaf
	salt
	freshly ground pepper
24	small white onions (for preparation see page 121)
1/2	lb mushrooms, sliced
about 1	tbsp beurre manié (page 280)

Brown the chicken in 1 tablespoon of oil and 1 tablespoon of butter, mixed. When golden, add the crushed garlic, the wine and stock, combined and warmed, a pinch each of thyme and marjoram, a bay leaf, salt, and freshly ground pepper. Once the liquid comes to a boil, set the fire very low and simmer, covered, for 45 minutes.

In a separate skillet heat the rest of the oil and butter and sauté the onions on all sides until lightly browned. Remove the onions to a lidded pan with only the oil that clings to them and steam over a very low fire for about 20 minutes. Put the sliced mushrooms in the same oil the onions were sautéed in and brown lightly.

When it is tender, remove the chicken from the liquid and thicken the juice with 1 tablespoon *beurre manié* or more if necessary. (One tablespoon of flour dissolved in water may be substituted for the *beurre manié*, but the latter is certain not to produce lumps and floured water can be treacherous.) Remove the pan from the fire and stir constantly while the thickening is added.

When smooth, return the chicken to the sauce together with the onions and mushrooms. Simmer another 5 to 8 minutes and serve with boiled potatoes.

ARROZ À LA VALENCIANA [Chicken with Spanish Rice]

In spite of the Spanish name and the fact that this dish might well be described as *paella* without seafood, I first tasted *arroz à la valenciana* in the Philippines and it was Lydia, our *maîtresse de la maison* for many years who prepared it for us—Lydia, a Filipino who spoke no Spanish! Where she obtained her recipe I never learned, but by watching her at work I came up with this approximation. First she made a sauce.

    3   *cups chicken stock*
1-1/2 *cups tomato puree*
       salt
       freshly ground pepper
    1   *stalk celery, chopped*
    1   *large carrot, chunked*
    1   *onion, chopped*
       thyme
    1   *bay leaf*

Combine all the ingredients, including a generous pinch of salt and a little less thyme, and bring them to a boil. Then reduce the fire and simmer, covered, for at least 45 minutes. After the simmering period remove the bay leaf and force the sauce, including the vegetables, through a food mill or put it through a blender. Keep the sauce warm.

2	*3-lb fryers, cut up*
about 1/2	*cup olive oil*
2	*onions, chopped finely*
1	*clove garlic, minced*
2	*cups rice*
1/2	*lb mushrooms, sliced*
1	*green pepper, sliced*
2	*stalks celery, chopped*
2	*canned sweet pimientos*
3	*green onions, chopped*
	saffron
	paprika
1	*medium-can white asparagus*
	salt
	freshly ground pepper

For this dish you need a large (about 6-quart) pot with a tight-fitting lid (stainless steel preferred). Fry the chickens in the oil until browned on all sides, then remove from the pan, and keep warm. Add the 2 onions and sauté until golden, then add the minced garlic, and cook another 2 minutes. If at this time the oil seems low, add another 2 tablespoons. Pour the dry rice into the hot oil and onions and stir until it turns golden, watching carefully to avoid sticking. When the rice starts to turn golden, remove the pot from the fire and add the sliced mushrooms, sliced pepper, the celery, one pimiento, cut in strips, and the green onions. Stir in the saffron—as big a pinch as your pocketbook will stand, for it can be expensive—and about 1/2 tablespoon of paprika. If your saffron supply is low, cut it down and increase the paprika. The rice must be golden. Add a pinch of salt and several grinds of fresh pepper.

Meanwhile preheat the oven to 350° and heat the sauce to the boiling point. Now add it to the rice, stirring well to prevent the rice from caking. When the mixture is complete, return the chicken to the rice, cover tightly, and place in the oven for 45 minutes. When the rice is tender and the liquid absorbed, the dish is ready.

There are several ways of serving this dish, but my favorite is to place it on a large platter and garnish with the second pimiento, cut into 1/2-inch-wide strips, and the white asparagus stalks, heated in their own juice.

POULET À LA MOSELLE [Chicken in Moselle Wine]

One of the most delightful of Europe's white wines is Moselle, which really isn't white at all but a pale green that seems to symbolize in advance the refreshing qualities that make it a world favorite. I obtained this recipe in Luxembourg, where the Moselle doesn't produce quite as fine as further down the river beyond Trier, but any Moselle is guaranteed to make any chicken taste better. This simple recipe, which serves four, can, of course, be made with any dry white wine, but I still prefer Moselle when available.

1	*3-lb chicken, cut up*
4	*tbsp butter or margarine*
1	*small onion, minced*
1	*clove garlic, crushed*
1	*cup stock*
1	*cup Moselle or other dry white wine*
6	*medium mushrooms, sliced*
	pinch of thyme
	salt
	freshly ground pepper
	beurre manié *(page 280)*
1	*tsp lemon rind, grated*

Brown the chicken in 3 tablespoons of butter, remove from the skillet, and keep warm. Sauté the onion in the same butter and, when transparent, return the chicken to the pan and add the crushed garlic. Add the stock, wine, thyme, salt, and pepper. Cover tightly and let simmer until the chicken is tender. Sauté the mushrooms in the remaining tablespoon of butter. Grate the lemon rind. When it is tender, remove the chicken from the pan and add the *beurre manié* to the liquid a little at a time, stirring constantly. When the sauce begins to thicken, return the chicken, add the mushrooms and grated lemon rind, and simmer another 5 minutes.

Serve with rice or mashed potatoes.

UNFORGOTTEN CHICKEN

Unforgotten chicken is a dish contrived particularly to take care of that cold leftover chicken in the refrigerator that might otherwise be forgotten and allowed to deteriorate or spoil. It is also an excellent means of making delightful the remains of that turkey carcass a couple of days after Thanksgiving or Christmas. Even the crust is simple to prepare.

    4   tbsp butter
    3   oz. cream cheese
    1/2 cup flour
         pinch of salt

Allow the butter to soften without melting, then combine all the ingredients in a mixing bowl, and work into a smooth dough. Allow to chill, covered, in the refrigerator for 1 hour.

    1-1/2 cups leftover chicken or turkey, cold
    1   10-oz package frozen mixed vegetables, plain

salt
freshly ground pepper
nutmeg

1-1/2	*cups plus 2 tbsp chicken stock, hot*
1/4	*lb mushrooms, sliced*
3	*tbsp butter*
3	*tbsp green onion, minced*
2-1/2	*tbsp flour*
1/2	*cup milk*
2	*tbsp Madeira or dry sherry*

While the dough is chilling, cut the chicken into bite-sized pieces and set aside. Sprinkle the mixed vegetables, which have been allowed to thaw naturally, with a pinch of salt, several grinds of fresh pepper and a pinch of nutmeg. Pour 2 tablespoons of hot stock over them and set them aside also. (One word of warning: be sure the mixed vegetables you buy are just that—no sauce.)

Melt the butter in a skillet and sauté the green onion lightly, then add the flour, and cook for 3 or 4 minutes, stirring constantly so it doesn't brown. Pour in the 1-1/2 cups of hot stock and stir until the *velouté* sauce starts to thicken smoothly. Next add the milk and the Madeira and, when that is blended, a pinch of salt and 2 grinds of fresh pepper. Now pour the vegetables onto the bottom of a 1-1/2-quart baking dish and pour half the sauce over them. Put the chicken and the mushrooms into the remainder of the sauce and add to the casserole.

Preheat the oven to 375°. Lightly flour a sheet of waxed paper, put the chilled dough on it, and pat it out with your hand until roughly the shape of the baking dish. Flour the top of the dough, put another sheet of waxed paper over it, and roll very lightly until the dough is about 1/4-inch thick. Cut the dough to fit the top of the baking dish and cut about 4 3/4-inch slashes in it to let steam escape.

Put the dough on top of the casserole, handling it very carefully because it will be soft. Bake in the oven for 45 minutes or until the crust is golden brown.

WATERZOÏ [Belgian Chicken Fricassée]

Waterzoï is a traditional Flemish dish that, strangely perhaps, is often compared with *bouillabaisse* and *poule-au-pot*, two completely contrasting dishes, because *waterzoï* is the only national dish I ever heard of that is equally authentic when made with chicken or fish. I suppose *waterzoï* could be classified as a soup, but because it is a complete meal in itself I believe it deserves different definition. I have never tasted *waterzoï* made with fish on any of my trips to Belgium, so I am staying with the chicken. Some recipes specify a fowl, but I prefer a large roaster because it cooks quicker and the meat is never dry.

1	*4-lb roasting chicken*
	salt
	freshly ground pepper
2	*tbsp oil*
6	*cups chicken or multi-purpose stock*
2	*leeks (white stems only)*
2	*ribs celery*
1	*carrot*
1	*medium onion*
1	*tbsp parsley, chopped*
1	*bay leaf*
	thyme
	marjoram
1/2	*lb mushrooms, sliced*
2	*egg yolks*
2/3	*cup* crème fraîche *(page 282)*

Wipe the chicken and season the cavity with salt and freshly ground pepper. Heat the oil in a large skillet and brown the bird well on all sides. Transfer the chicken to a large Dutch oven-type pan and pour the stock, heated, over it. Turn the fire very low and simmer the chicken, covered, for 15 minutes. Meanwhile, cut the leeks, celery, and carrot into 1-inch lengths and chop the onion coarsely. After 15 minutes add the vegetables to the chicken with the parsley, bay leaf, a pinch each of thyme and marjoram, and 1/2 teaspoon of salt. Recover the pan and continue to simmer. At the end of 30 minutes add the mushrooms and cook until the chicken is very tender. Remove the chicken from the pot and cut it up. Discard the bay leaf. Put the egg yolks and *crème fraîche,* well blended, in the bottom of a large soup tureen or similar serving dish. Add the hot broth and vegetables and mix well, then add the chicken. Serve in soup plates.

POLLO ALLA CACCIATORE [Chicken, Hunter Style]

Pollo alla cacciatore might be termed the *coq au vin* of Italy, or perhaps it would be just as well to call *coq au vin* the *pollo alla cacciatore* of France. The point is that this is an extremely popular peasant dish for which there is really no definitive recipe. Fundamentally, you must consider Hunter Style as meaning "cooked in tomatoes and wine with herbs." From that base you can actually ad-lib your own formula, but this is truly one of the best recipes I have tried and I recommend it if you don't feel utterly creative. When augmented with vegetables and a bit of salad, it produces about what four hungry people would require.

1	*3-lb chicken, cut up*
2	*tbsp olive oil*
2	*tbsp butter*
2	*medium onions, sliced*
1	*clove garlic, minced*
1	*oz Italian brandy or equivalent*
3	*large tomatoes, peeled, seeded, and chopped*
1	*cup stock*
1/2	*cup Soave or other dry white wine*
1	*tbsp tomato paste*
1	*tsp oregano*
	pinch of tarragon
	salt
	freshly ground pepper
1/4	*lb fresh mushrooms, sliced coarsely*

No Italian cook would ever think of preparing this dish with anything but a whole chicken cut into serving pieces, but few Italians can go down to the *gran marcata* and buy chicken legs, thighs, and wings. If he could, I believe he would do so, because these are the parts of the chicken that best lend themselves to *pollo alla cacciatore*. Chicken backs have no meat and the breasts in liquid invariably come up tough and hard.

Regardless of what parts of the chicken you choose, use the equivalent of a 3-pound chicken and sauté it in a skillet that has a lid in the combined oil and butter until well browned on all sides. Move the chicken to the side of the pan and cook the onions in the same fat until golden. Add the minced garlic just before the onions are cooked, then pour in the brandy, warmed, and ignite it. Keep the lid of the skillet handy to extinguish the flame after about 15 seconds. Add the chopped tomatoes and stir briefly before pouring in the combined wine and stock, heated. Stir in the tomato paste and seasonings and, when blended, cook, uncovered, over a low flame until the chicken is tender and the liquid has all but evaporated. There should be not more than 1/2 cup. Add the sliced mushrooms at this time and let the whole simmer, this time covered, for 5 minutes. Serve from the pan, if desired, with boiled potatoes or *risotto* (page 261).

POULET AU DIABLE [Chicken in Hot Sauce]

Poulet au diable is a *plat* I have insisted on preparing with chicken thighs ever since my return from Europe—first, because thighs are really my favorite part of the bird; second, because the sauce can be rather overpowering for the delicate flavor of chicken breasts; and, third, because I can buy chicken thighs by themselves in this country, and that can be difficult in most of Europe!

The beauty of *poulet au diable* is that you can regulate the piquancy of the sauce by altering the amount of cayenne and Tabasco. That's why I have not specified definite amounts of either. Try a generous pinch of cayenne first, then taste the sauce once before adding the Tabasco and again after each dash. The strength of these condiments, as well as individual tastes, can vary widely. Two thighs should serve one average eater, which makes this an ideal dish for four people.

       8   *chicken thighs*
       5   *tbsp butter*
       1   *tbsp shallots or green onion, chopped*
     3/4   *cup stock*
     3/4   *cup dry white wine*
       2   *tbsp tomato paste*
           basil
           thyme
           cayenne
           salt
       1   *cup mushrooms, sliced*
       1   *cup sour cream*
           Tabasco

Sauté the thighs until golden in 3 tablespoons of butter. Add the shallots or onions and cook until transparent. Pour in the stock and wine, combined and heated, then stir in the tomato paste and a pinch each of basil, thyme, and salt. Add a generous pinch of cayenne. When the liquids are completely blended, bring them to a boil, then lower the fire and simmer the chicken, covered, until tender—about 40 minutes.

Meanwhile, sauté the mushrooms in the remaining 2 tablespoons of butter until lightly browned, but not cooked down. Drain and keep warm. When the chicken is tender, remove to a serving dish and keep warm. Turn up the flame all the way and reduce the remaining liquid to about 1/2 cup. *Off the fire* add the sour cream and stir thoroughly into the pan juices. Add the sautéed mushrooms and return to a low fire. Heat very slowly, making sure the cream doesn't boil. Add Tabasco, a dash at a time, tasting regularly until you achieve a sauce that is piquant according to your own standard. Serve immediately with plain boiled rice. (This dish is also good made with chicken wings or legs—or both!)

POULET AU CHAMPAGNE [Chicken in Champagne]

I first encountered *poulet au champagne* in France's Champagne region where I was assured it had to be prepared with champagne in order to be authentic. That premise is certainly valid as far as authenticity is concerned, but I have since learned that the substitution of any good dry white wine will produce excellent results. Inasmuch as champagne is not as cheap in most parts of the world as in the vicinity of Reims and Epernay (and the bubbles disappear instantly), I confess that I substitute on a habitual basis in the preparation of this dish!

1	*roasting chicken*
2	*tbsp butter*
6	*medium mushrooms, sliced*
about 3	*tbsp water*
1	*tbsp flour*
1	*clove garlic, crushed*
1	*cup champagne or dry white wine*
1	*cup stock*
1	*tbsp shallots or green onions, chopped*
	thyme
	rosemary
	salt
	freshly ground pepper
3	*tbsp* crème fraîche *(page 282) or sour cream*
2	*egg yolks*
1	*tbsp unsalted butter*
	juice of 1 small lemon

Section the chicken, season, and brown in the butter in a pan large enough for each piece to lie flat. Put the mushrooms in about 3 tablespoons of water and let simmer for about 10 minutes. Sprinkle the browned chicken with flour and add the crushed garlic. Mix well. Add the champagne or wine, stock, and 1 tablespoon of the mushroom liquid (reserve the drained mushrooms). If necessary, add water to cover the chicken. Now add the shallots or onions and the herbs. Cook covered until the chicken is tender—about 45 minutes.

Remove the chicken from the pan and reduce the liquid by one-half over a very hot flame. *Remove the pan from the fire* and stir in the *crème fraîche* or sour cream, egg yolks, and butter, mixed. Add the lemon juice and mushrooms. Reheat, but do not boil. Correct the seasoning and pour over the chicken on a serving platter.

POLYNESIAN CHICKEN

The inspiration for Polynesian chicken was sparked during a trip my wife and I made some years ago from Hong Kong through the Philippines, the Solomons, and the New Hebrides to Australia. Although our ship flew the Swedish flag, its crew was Chinese and we were enthralled by our cook's use of Pacific island spices. Ginger is Polynesian, but it is also East Indian and Chinese. Most of the ginger we use in the United States today comes from Jamaica in the West Indies. If you can buy dried ginger and grate it yourself, the flavor will be heightened.

1	*3-lb chicken*
1	*medium onion*
4	*cloves*
	salt
	freshly ground pepper
2	*tbsp butter*
3/4	*cup stock (chicken preferred)*
1/2	*tsp freshly ground ginger*
about 2	*tbsp cornstarch, dissolved in water*

Preheat the oven to 350°. Clean the chicken and dry it thoroughly with a paper towel. Stud the onion with the cloves, salt and pepper the cavity, and put the onion inside. Truss the bird with string and rub a little salt on the skin. Put the stock and butter into a pan and warm together, then pour into a baking dish large enough to hold the chicken. Put the chicken in the stock, breast up, and sprinkle with the ginger. Place in the oven and, when it starts to brown, baste the chicken with the stock. Roast the chicken for 1 hour, basting every 10 minutes. If the stock gets low, add more a little at a time. The juices of the chicken will contribute, but the amount will vary according to the bird. When it is tender and well browned, remove the chicken to a serving platter and keep warm. If it is oven-proof, put the baking dish on top of the stove to prepare the sauce; if not, pour the juices into a saucepan, being careful to include all the brown bits. Thicken the remaining liquid (there should be about 1 cup) with the cornstarch mixed with very little water. You should not need all the cornstarch mixture, so add a little at a time until you achieve the desired consistency. Carve the chicken at the table and serve the sauce on the side.

CHICKEN POT PIE *[With a Chicken Stock Bonus]*

This chicken pot pie is a Hoosier recipe my wife brought with her when she left Bedford, Indiana, quite some years ago to marry a youthful New York sportswriter. The recipe is unusual in that it not only leads the way to a magnificent chicken dish but also results in at least a quart of fine chicken stock, as fine as was ever produced, for future use.

This recipe has withstood the test of years, and the only major alteration in the original basic formula is the addition of a soupçon of dry white wine, a *tour de chef* my wife picked up during our years in Europe. If any Hoosier feels this innovation has in any way marred the quality, a quarter cup of stock can be reinstated. The original recipe was intended to serve six people, but I recommend it be held to four. Someone is sure to want seconds.

1   *chicken, about 3 lb*
1/2   *medium onion, chopped*
1   *carrot, chunked*
2   *leeks, if available, or 6 green onions*
1   *bay leaf*
6   *quarts of water*
     salt
     freshly ground pepper

Cut up the chicken and place it, with the onion and carrot, in the water. Cut the root stems and green tops off the leeks or green onions, clean them very carefully, and cut into 1-inch slices. Add the leeks or green onions, bay leaf, salt, and freshly ground pepper to the pot. Bring to a boil, then lower the fire, and simmer, covered, for 45 minutes or until the chicken is very tender. Remove the chicken from the pot, take the meat off the bones, and return the bones to the pot, together with the skin. Then cut the chicken meat into bite-size pieces and keep warm.

3   *tbsp butter*
4   *tbsp flour*
2   *cups stock (above)*
     salt
     freshly ground pepper
1/4   *cup dry white wine*
1   *tsp lemon juice*
1/4   *cup heavy cream*
1   *cup frozen peas*

Cook the flour in the butter for 2 or 3 minutes, stirring to prevent browning. Strain off 2 cups of the stock in which the chicken was simmered and add, boiling hot, to the flour and butter. (Replace the liquid with 2 cups of water in the stockpot.) Stir until smooth and, when the sauce starts to thicken, add several grinds of fresh pepper, the wine, then the lemon juice. Finally, *off the fire,* stir in the heavy cream and taste the sauce for salt. Return the chicken to the sauce and add the peas. Pour the mixture into an oven-proof baking dish (9-inch glass skillet is excellent) and top with freshly cut, unbaked biscuits.

BASIC BISCUITS

1-1/2	*cup flour*
1	*tsp salt*
2	*tsp baking powder*
4	*tbsp vegetable shortening*
1/2	*cup milk (more if needed to make a manageable dough)*
	butter, melted

Mix the dry ingredients with the shortening prior to making the pot pie and store in the refrigerator. Preheat the oven to 375°. When ready to put the "crust" on the pie, add the milk to the other ingredients and mix to obtain a soft but firm dough. Roll out the dough on a floured board to a thickness of about 1/2 inch and cut with a 2-inch biscuit cutter. Place the biscuits on top of the chicken to cover the entire surface loosely with a single layer and brush with a little melted butter. Put the casserole in the oven and bake until the biscuits are nicely browned. Serve immediately, perhaps with a little mashed potatoes.

STOCK

During all this time the liquid in the pot in which the chicken was cooked should be simmering very slowly. Let it continue, keeping the water level at about a quart, for an overall total of about 2-1/2 hours. Then let it cool, strain, and store, covered, in the refrigerator.

CHICKEN CALYPSO

Dominica is a hospitable little island in the eastern Caribbean that is noted for, among other things, "mountain chicken"—a variety of frog that thrives in the island's rain forests, grows to astounding proportions, and is a culinary favorite of the Dominicans. Fortunately for many Americans who prefer their chickens with feathers, chicken calypso, although a Dominican dish (at least I got it from Dominica!), does feature the familiar barnyard bird. This recipe should satisfy four people.

1	3-lb chicken, cut up
1/4	cup oil
	salt
	freshly ground pepper
1-1/4	cups dry rice
1	medium onion, diced
1/2	green pepper, diced
1/2	tsp saffron
2-1/2	cups chicken stock
12	mushrooms, sliced
2	oz light rum
	angostura bitters

Sauté the chicken in the oil until golden brown, sprinkle with about 1/2 teaspoon of salt and several grinds of fresh pepper, cover the pan, and cook slowly for 25 minutes. Remove the chicken and keep warm. Put the rice, together with the onion and green pepper, into the hot oil, then stir in the saffron. (Paprika can be used if saffron is unavailable, but the saffron is preferred.) Next, pour in the stock, warmed, the mushrooms, rum, and a couple of good dashes of angostura. Put the chicken on top of the rice, cover the pan tightly, and simmer over a very low fire for 20 minutes until the rice is tender and has absorbed most of the stock. Correct the seasoning and remove the chicken. Fluff the rice with a spoon and cook another 5 minutes, still very slowly. Pile the rice on a serving platter and arrange the chicken on top.

POULET NIÇOIS   [Chicken, Nice Style]

The four distinguishing components of Provençal cookery are olive oil, tomatoes, garlic, and herbs; virtually every true Provençal or Niçoise dish includes at least three, if not all four. This delicious recipe for *poulet Niçois* from the capital of the Côte d'Azur combines all four with onions and saffron thrown in for good measure. It is as typical of southeastern France as mimosa in April!

1	3-lb chicken, cut up
1	tbsp flour
3	tbsp olive oil
8	small white onions
2	garlic cloves, whole
1	medium onion (yellow)
4	cloves
	salt
	freshly ground pepper
	saffron
1/3	cup stock
1/3	cup dry white wine
4	medium tomatoes, peeled, seeded, and cut into large chunks
	sage
	thyme
	bay leaf
12	black olives, pitted
1/2	tsp lemon juice

Flour the chicken pieces lightly and sauté them in the olive oil with the garlic and onions. (The white onions should be whole; the yellow one quartered and each quarter spiked with a clove.) Salt and pepper lightly and add a pinch of saffron. When the chicken is golden, add the combined stock and wine, heated, then the tomatoes, a pinch of thyme and sage, and a bay leaf.

Cover the skillet and cook over a moderate fire until the chicken is tender—about 45 minutes. Just about 5 minutes before serving, add the olives and remove the garlic and bay leaf. Stir in the lemon juice and serve with boiled rice.

SPEZZATINO DI POLLO CON RISO [Braised Chicken with Rice]

Spezzatino di pollo con riso is a typical Italian dish, flavorful and aromatic, that might be found almost anywhere in the area from Rome north through Tuscany. In this recipe plain boiled rice is specified, but chicken *risotto* (page 261) is equally delicious. Some Italian cooks would add one-half cup of Chianti, Bardolino, or some other dry red wine, but I prefer this just as it is.

1	3-lb chicken, cut up
	flour
1/3	cup olive oil
1	cup onion, chopped
3/4	cup celery, diced
1	clove garlic, minced
1/2	cup stock
1	1-lb can peeled tomatoes
2	tbsp parsley, chopped
1/2	tsp oregano
1/4	tsp basil
	salt
	freshly ground pepper
1-1/4	cups rice
2-1/2	cups cold water
1/2	tsp salt
	Parmesan cheese, freshly grated

Flour the chicken lightly and brown it in the oil, using a large skillet with a lid. When it is browned, remove the chicken and sauté the onion and celery in the same oil until tender, but not browned. Add the minced garlic and cook for another minute or so, then stir in the stock. Mix the parsley, oregano, and basil with the tomatoes (chop the tomatoes a bit if necessary), then add to the skillet. Salt and pepper to taste. Return the chicken, cover the pan, and simmer slowly for 45 minutes.

After 25 minutes put the rice into the cold water and add the salt. Bring the water to a boil, then put a sheet of aluminum foil, folded double, under the pan, cover, and simmer very slowly over lowest heat until the liquid is all gone and the rice tender. Don't worry if the rice scorches a bit at the bottom; just be sure the moisture is gone.

Put the rice on a serving platter with the chicken on top and cover with the sauce. Sprinkle generously with Parmesan and serve more of the cheese on the side.

CHICKEN TETRAZZINI

Luisa Tetrazzini and Dame Nellie Melba came "aria-ing" out of Florence, Italy, and Melbourne, Australia, respectively, late in the last century. For over three decades they vied for honors at La Scala, Covent Garden, the Met—in fact, every major opera house in the world—and with overwhelming success. It seemed certain their golden voices would make them immortal. They achieved immortality, all right, but hardly as they had planned it. Dame Nellie today is best remembered as the gal who gave her name to peach Melba and Melba toast, while Luisa is immortalized by chicken Tetrazzini.

Personally, I feel that Luisa came off with the best of the deal because chicken Tetrazzini is a truly delicious concoction, and this recipe is the best I have found. I must believe, however, that an Italian prima donna would probably have preferred Marsala to the sherry specified herein, but I do not counsel a change. This formula is superb as it stands.

Incidentally, this recipe, which serves six, differs from most in that it provides its own stock as it develops.

1   chicken (about 3 lb), cut up
1   quart cold water
1   medium onion, quartered
1   small carrot, chunked
    salt
    freshly ground pepper
    pinch of thyme
1/2   lb fresh mushrooms, sliced
4   tbsp butter
2   tbsp Parmesan cheese, grated
    dash of paprika (optional)
1/4   lb broad egg noodles

SAUCE

1/4   cup butter
1/3   cup flour
2   cups light cream
1   cup stock (above)
1/4   cup dry sherry
1/2   tsp salt

Put the chicken, onion, carrot, salt, pepper, and thyme into the quart of cold water and bring to a boil. Lower the fire and simmer very slowly for 1 hour or until the chicken comes off the bones easily. Remove the chicken and strain the liquid through a sieve. Discard the solids and reserve the stock (about 3 cups).

To prepare the sauce, cook the flour in the butter for about 2 minutes, stirring frequently to prevent browning. Add 1 cup of the stock in which the chicken was cooked and 2 cups of cream, combined and heated, then the salt. When the sauce starts to thicken, add the sherry and continue to stir until creamy.

While the chicken is cooking, sauté the mushrooms in 2 tablespoons of the butter, but don't let them steam. Remove them with a slotted spoon and pour the butter remaining in the skilled into a shallow baking dish (about 11 inches long by 7 inches) and grease the bottom.

Cook the noodles for 10 minutes in the stock remaining from the chicken (less the cup used in the sauce), then drain well, and pour into the freshly greased baking dish. Sprinkle 1 teaspoon of salt over the noodles plus the remaining 2 tablespoons of butter, melted. Cover the noodles with a cup of sauce.

Next, spread the sautéed mushrooms over the noodles and again cover with sauce. Add the chicken, boned and cut into 2-inch chunks, and season with another good pinch of salt. Pour the rest of the sauce over the chicken and top with the Parmesan cheese. (A dash of paprika may be added.)

At this point the dish may be refrigerated overnight or frozen for later use. If you plan to serve immediately, bake in a preheated 350° oven for 30 minutes, then place under the broiler for 5 minutes to brown. If the dish is chilled overnight or frozen, increase the baking time to 45 minutes and then brown as indicated.

CHICKEN AND ASPARAGUS

There is always something exciting to me about the arrival of a new asparagus season. The appearance of the first batch of these succulent young stems invariably makes a wastrel of me; I often pay more than one dollar for a pound of asparagus, although I know that within only a couple of weeks it will be plentiful and from one-third to one-half that price. Still, I have never lived any place where fresh asparagus is available all year—if, indeed, there is such a place—so the new season is always a thrill.

Here is a dish that does justice to fresh asparagus (it is also excellent with the frozen variety) in combination with leftover cooked chicken:

1-1/2   lb fresh asparagus
2   cups cooked chicken, chunked
3   tbsp butter or oil
3   tbsp flour
1-1/2   cups stock
3/4   cup milk
salt
freshly ground pepper
1/2   cup cheddar cheese
2   pimentos, chopped coarsely

Preheat the oven to 350°. Clean the asparagus thoroughly, cutting off the scales and peeling the lower ends of the stems thinly. Cook in boiling water, salted, for 8 minutes, drain, and dry thoroughly. Cut off the tips about 2 inches from the top and set aside. Cut the remainder of the stalks into 1-inch pieces. At the same time make a roux of the butter and flour, cooking the flour well without scorching. Add the stock and milk, mixed and heated, and stir until thickened. Taste for salt and add several grinds of pepper. Add the cheese and pimientos and mix well. Put the 1-inch asparagus pieces in the bottom of a 1-quart casserole and lay the chicken chunks on top. Pour the sauce over the whole and bake in the oven until browned and bubbly. Five minutes before removing the casserole from the oven, put the asparagus tips into boiling water for two minutes; drain carefully (they are brittle!), then arrange them on top of the cheese, points to the center, and return to the oven for two minutes. Serve with boiled rice or potatoes.

POULET AUX NOUILLES NIÇOISE   [Chicken and Noodles Niçoise]

Poulet aux nouilles Niçoise is one of our favorite recipes for utilising leftover roast chicken. In fact, we have been known to roast a chicken just to have the meat for this dish. Its name reflects the fact that the dish originated in Nice, although there is nothing distinctively Niçoise or Provençal about it. Regardless of its antecedents, *poulet aux nouilles Niçoise* is an excellent entrée.

1/2	*roasted chicken*
1/2	*lb thin egg noodles, 1/8-inch*
1-1/2	*quarts water*
3/4	*cup fresh mushrooms, sliced*
1/2	*cup cheddar cheese, grated*
1	*tbsp shallots or green onion, chopped*
1	*tbsp flour*
1	*tbsp butter*
1/2	*cup stock*
1/2	*cup fresh cream*
2	*tbsp sherry or Madeira*
	salt
	freshly ground pepper

Boil the noodles for 10 minutes in 1-1/2 quarts of salted water; drain and pour into a warm mixing bowl. Cook the shallots or onions in the butter until transparent, then stir in the flour and cook for 2 minutes, stirring constantly. Add the combined stock and cream, heated just to the boiling point, and stir until the sauce is smooth. Season and add the grated cheese, reserving 1 tablespoon, and the mushrooms. Cook together slowly for 5 minutes, then add the wine, and mix well. Pour the sauce into the mixing bowl and mix thoroughly with the noodles.

Preheat the oven to 450°. Bone the chicken and cut the meat into large pieces. Place these pieces on the bottom of a greased baking dish and pour the noodles over them. Sprinkle the rest of the cheese over the top and bake in the oven for 15 minutes. Serve from the casserole.

CHICKEN WITH MUSSELS

In spite of the fact that I was given this recipe in New York by a friend who disclaimed any knowledge it had European roots, I am sure it originated along the Mediterranean. Nowhere else would you encounter the inspiration of combining chicken with mussels!

Regardless of origin, however, this is a magnificent dish in any language. The one thing to remember, if you are not familiar with mussels, is that they must be carefully washed and scrubbed with a stiff brush. Discard any mussels not tightly closed.

1/2	cup olive oil
1	3-lb chicken, cut up
4	cloves, garlic, unpeeled
1/4	tsp oregano
1/4	tsp basil
1/4	tsp powdered rosemary
1	cup dry white wine
1	cup stock
3	medium tomatoes, peeled, seeded, and chopped
1	green pepper, thinly sliced
1/4	cup parsley, chopped
2	lb mussels
	salt
	freshly ground pepper

Heat the oil in a large skillet with a tight-fitting lid. Brown the chicken over high heat, then add the *unpeeled* garlic cloves, the herbs, and the stock and wine (reserving a very little), combined and preheated. Heat the chopped tomatoes and thinly sliced pepper in the small amount of combined stock and wine. Add to the chicken, together with the chopped parsley, cover the skillet, and simmer very slowly for 30 minutes.

Meanwhile, scrub the mussels very carefully under cold running water and, when the chicken is tender, add them to the liquid and cook until all are opened. Remove the chicken and mussels to a large serving platter and keep warm while you reduce the liquid remaining in the skillet by about one-third. Taste for salt and add several grinds of fresh pepper. Pour over the chicken and mussels and serve immediately. If too thin, the liquid may be thickened with a bit of *beurre manié* (page 280).

PIGEONNEAU AU VIN BLANC [Squab in White Wine]

I have never been an all-out fancier of squabs, pigeons, and other small birds so popular in much of Europe, principally because I consider them too much trouble to prepare for cooking and it is difficult to find a poulterer abroad who will do it for you. If you have such a poulterer, however, this recipe from the South of France is rewarding. One squab should be sufficient for one person.

4	*young squabs*
	salt
	freshly ground pepper
6	*tbsp butter*
1	*small carrot*
1	*medium onion*
1	*bay leaf*
1	*cup stock*
1	*cup dry white wine*
1/4	*lb mushrooms*
1	*tbsp flour*
2	*tbsp sherry or Madeira*

Season the squabs inside and out with the salt and plenty of freshly ground pepper, then brown them on all sides in 4 tablespoons of the butter. Chop the carrot and onion coarsely and add to the birds, then pour in the stock and wine, combined and preheated to the boiling point. Add the bay leaf, cover the pot, and cook over a very low flame for 1 hour. Meanwhile, sauté the mushrooms in the remaining 2 tablespoons of butter until lightly browned, then remove with a slotted spoon and reserve the butter. Preheat the oven to 350°. Remove the squabs from the liquid and place in a large oven-proof casserole. Strain the stock and discard the solids. Cook the flour in the mushroom butter for a minute or two, then add the hot stock, and stir until smooth. Stir in the sherry or Madeira, pour the sauce over the squabs, and place them in the oven, uncovered, for 10 minutes, basting often. Serve from the casserole.

ROCK CORNISH HEN TÊTE-À-TÊTE

Members of the Men's Liberation Movement have asked me not to make public this recipe because they feel that any woman who prepares and serves it, tête-à-tête, to the man of her choice will really have him at her mercy. Nevertheless, because I regard this as one of the best recipes I have ever found for two persons, I am ignoring the petition. If a man finds a girl who can turn out food like this, he'd be foolish to let her escape!

1	medium Rock Cornish hen
1/2	lemon
	salt
	freshly ground pepper
2	tbsp flour
2	tbsp butter
1	tbsp oil
2	tbsp green onions, chopped
1/2	tsp thyme
1	tsp tarragon
1	cup stock
1/4	cup dry white wine
1-1/2	tbsp cornstarch

Wipe the hen with a dry cloth. Cut the 1/2 lemon into 2 pieces and rub the bird with one of them, squeezing a few drops into the cavity. Salt and pepper well, inside and out, then flour the hen lightly, and brown on all sides in the combined oil and butter. At the same time sauté the onions until golden. A flame-proof glass Dutch oven-type casserole is perfect for this purpose. Sprinkle the bird with the herbs, then add the stock and wine, combined and preheated. Add the juice from the second lemon quarter, cover the casserole, and simmer very slowly for 1-1/4 to 1-1/2 hours. Turn the bird several times and finally leave it breast up until it is quite tender. Now remove the bird to a carving board and cover with a warm cloth. There should be about a cup of liquid remaining in the casserole when the hen is removed; if not, add a little hot stock. Bring the liquid to a boil and mix the cornstarch with 1/4 cup of the hot liquid. Pour about one-half the cornstarch into the sauce, stirring constantly, turn the heat on high, and let the liquid thicken. If necessary, add more cornstarch solution, a little at a time, until the sauce has the proper consistency. Carve the hen, discarding the wing tips and carcass. Put the legs, thighs, and breast meat into the sauce and simmer another 5 minutes. Serve with wild rice or *risotto*.

CANETON MONTMORENCY [Duck and Cherries]

Montmorency used to be a quiet little village northwest of Paris, noted locally for the quality of its laces and its cherries. Today Paris has all but swallowed up the suburban community, and the cherries are only a memory. But the memory is likely to persist because the term *Montmorency*, applied to any French dish, has come to indicate the use of cherries in its preparation. This recipe, to my personal taste, is the superlative method of preparing duck, and one day I intend to visit Montmorency again to see if the local restaurateurs are really aware of the *plat* that does their community so much honor!

1   *duck, about 5 lb*
     salt
     freshly ground pepper
about 1/2   *tsp thyme*
2   *medium onions*
1   *medium carrot, sliced*

If it is frozen, the duck should be completely thawed before cooking. Wipe the bird with a damp cloth and examine for pin feathers. Salt and pepper the cavity and sprinkle with thyme. Cut a medium onion in two and put both halves in the cavity, then truss the duck with skewers or a string. Place the second onion, chopped, and the sliced carrot on the bottom of a large roasting pan. Put the duck in the pan, preferably on a rack so that it won't founder in the cooking juices, and roast in the oven for 1 hour and 45 minutes—30 minutes less if you prefer the meat rare. As soon as the duck starts to brown, prick the skin to allow the fat to escape and begin basting every few minutes with the following liquid:

1   *1-lb can sour cherries*
1   *tbsp sugar*
1/4   *cup port*

SAUCE

1   *cup stock*
about 2   *tsp cornstarch, dissolved in water*

Drain the cherries and put the juice together with 1 tablespoon of sugar and the wine into a blender. Divide the strained cherries in equal halves and put one-half into the juice. Blend until the cherries are reduced to minute flecks. This will give you about a cup of basting juice, about one-half of which should be reserved for the sauce. Spoon the basting liquid over the duck a little at a time and use the cooking juices in the pan for supplemental basting. When it is done, remove the duck to a hot platter and pour most of the fat out of the roasting pan. Pour in a cup of stock and bring to a boil, scraping the sides and bottom carefully. Pour this liquid into a skillet (for easier handling) and add the remainder of the basting liquid. Bring this to a boil and, off the fire, add the cornstarch dissolved in a bit of water. Return to the fire and boil until thickened. Correct the seasoning and pour some of the sauce over the duck. Position the remainder of the cherries around the duck and serve the rest of the sauce on the side. This sauce goes admirably with mashed potatoes.

ROCK CORNISH HEN TORINO

I have never been certain just what a Rock Cornish hen really is—its antecedents and its history. I never knew it in my youth, and I never encountered it outside the United States. So all I can say of the bird for sure is that it is wonderful eating and lends itself to any number of variations in its preparation. This recipe is actually a method of preparing chicken, which I once came across in Turin. I find it fits the Rock Cornish hen admirably, is simple to prepare, and, above all, provides the foundation for an excellent meal. The hens vary in size, but this recipe was designed for birds weighing about a pound each, one to a customer.

4	*Rock Cornish hens*
1/2	*lemon*
	salt
	freshly ground pepper
1	*tbsp butter, melted*
1-1/2	*cups chicken stock*
1/2	*cup dry vermouth*
1/2	*tsp thyme*
	beurre maniè *(page 280)*

Preheat the oven to 400°. Rub the hens with the lemon and squeeze a few drops into the cavities. Salt and pepper them, inside and out, and brush with the butter. Combine and heat the stock and wine, meanwhile arranging the hens on a rack in a large roasting pan. Pour the hot liquid over them, sprinkle with thyme, and put them in the oven for about 45 minutes, basting regularly with the liquid. When they are done, remove the hens to a serving platter and thicken the sauce with a bit of *beurre maniè*. Serve the sauce on the side.

CHAPTER V

Meat

God sends meat and the devil sends cooks.

JOHN TAYLOR, 1630

There can be no doubt that the Almighty is the provider of meat—one of the greatest boons he grants this hungry world—but I am not prepared to concede that all cooks are emissaries of Satan—despite the observation of the poet, John Taylor, more than one-third of a millenium ago. Taylor, who seems to have been remembered more as an eccentric than as a bard, lived in England during the seventeenth century, and there is nothing in history to indicate that those years, particularly in the land of the Stuarts, were culinary milestones. Actually, there may have been some foundation for Taylor's indictment at the time it was leveled, but today I really believe the worst charge we can make is that the Devil allows too many presumed cooks to remain at large, probably because he doesn't want them in his own domain.

There is no reason for anyone to be a bad cook in these days of modern conveinences, good instruction, and the finest ingredients in history. And there is nothing easier to cook well than meat, providing you have an interest and are blessed with even the least amount of patience.

It is important that every aspiring cook master the art of meat cookery first and foremost because meat is America's principal food, more so than in any other nation. Twenty-five cents out of every dollar you spend for food goes to provide your table with meat. This is not true of any other country in the world with the possible exception of Australia, where there is a big difference in the way that twenty-five cents is spent In the United States the biggest part by far will be spent for beef; in Australia it will be spent for lamb.

For this reason it isn't strange that the United States produces the world's finest beef—and by a wide margin. Argentina, Australia, and Scotland are all noted for their fine beef, but, in all honesty, none of them produce beef in quantity as properly fed and as adequately aged as the United States. The Japanese produce Kobe. beef, a premium meat from specially fed steers that are not allowed to exercise and are said to be massaged daily(!) to produce tenderness. But Kobe beef is both rare and expensive and will never be mistaken for United States Prime.

American pork, too, is one of the finest meats anywhere, but comparable pork can be found in other countries, notably those of northern Europe and Australia. Hams vary greatly in the way they are cured, and preference usually depends on individual taste. The American precooked, oven-ready ham is by far the great favorite in this country, but the distinctive Smithfields of Virginia and the Italian Prosciutto crudo *(the dry, dark ham that is served tissue thin) are the choice of millions.*

There is probably no country in the world that produces lamb to equal that of Australia, and here, again, the reason lies in the Australian's preference for that meat. Lamb is easier to grow than beef because sheep can thrive on herbage that would starve a steer. Australia has always suffered from too little rainfall—often long droughts of two, three, or more years in duration. Consequently, nature's forage is better suited to the raising of sheep than cattle, and the early settlers adopted lamb as their primary staple. That situation has remained throughout the years, although great tracts of cattle land have opened in the past half-century.

Southern Europe is supreme in the production, as well as in the preparation and serving, of veal. Milk-fed veal, common in Italy (although expensive, even by United States standards), is almost unknown in this country. In fact, a great percentage of the meat sold as veal by butchers in the United States is more nearly baby beef.

Veal has two qualities that render it unique among meats. First of all, it is much more filling than most meats, particularly beef. The trencherman who thinks nothing of packing away a full-pound steak would be hard pressed to consume two-thirds the same weight in veal. For this reason veal is not as expensive in comparison with other meats as a direct matching of prices might indicate.

Veal's second quality is inherent tenderness—and here I refer to the genuine veal, not baby beef—which reduces the necessary cooking time and makes it possible to retain the delicate flavor of the meat. This is particularly important because the delicacy of veal is like that of a chicken breast; hard cooking will ruin it.

Its delicate flavor makes veal quite amenable to the stimulation of a good sauce, and stock, fortified either by Marsala (Italian) or Madeira

(Portuguese and preferred by the French), is often the base for such sauce—quick and easy to prepare.

China is one country where a single meat predominates without attaining superiority. In that vast segment of Asia pork is the most common meat—when meat is available. Due to the overpopulation and the resultant poverty that has gripped China for centuries, however, most of the pork produced in that country has never matched that of more affluent nations in quality or quantity. Today the average person among six or eight hundred million Chinese in Asia exists on a rice diet to which the sayings of Mao Tse-tung are a more likely adjunct than meat of any type.

Even so, the Chinese in centuries past have managed to surmount almost unsurmountable difficulties in developing a cuisine—or cuisines—that ranks with the world's finest. And the lowly pig has been a major contributing factor. The Chinese, of course, aren't the only people who excel in the preparation of pork. Only in the Middle East and in parts of the Indian subcontinent, where various religions forbid its use, is pork anything but an important part of man's daily life. And the methods of preparing it, either fresh or cured, are as varied as the people who eat it.

These, then, are the principal meats on which this great world lives from day to day. The recipes that follow reflect my quarter-century of traveling around and about this world, always curious and always hungry!

ESTOUFFADE PROVENÇALE *[Provençal beef stew]*

This peasant beef stew from my favorite part of France, Provence, is a frequent choice of mine for two very excellent reasons. First and most important, my guests always praise it to the good of my vanity and, second, its preparation can be very conveniently interrupted for predinner conviviality. Assuming you don't want to spend the cocktail hour in the kitchen, just start early in the day with:

> 2   lb shin beef or chuck, cut into 2-inch cubes
> 3   medium onions, sliced
> 2   carrots, shredded
> 2   cloves garlic, crushed
> 1   cup dry white wine
> 1   cup stock
> 2   heaping tbsp tomato paste
> 2   tbsp butter
> 2   tbsp oil (olive oil preferred)
> 1   heaping tbsp flour
> 1   bay leaf
>   pinch of oregano
>   pinch of thyme
>   salt
>   freshly ground pepper
>
> 1/2   lb fresh mushrooms
> 24   green olives, pitted and blanched in boiling water

Use a heavy pot with a tight-fitting lid, large enough for the meat to lie flat on the bottom. Brown the meat in the combined butter and oil, then add the carrots and onions, and sauté until the onions are golden. Add the flour and mix thoroughly; then add the wine, stock, tomato paste, bay leaf, oregano, thyme, salt, and pepper. Bring the mixture to a boil, then cover tightly, and lowering the fire, simmer slowly for 1-1/2 hours. When it is tender, remove the meat and keep warm while you puree the liquid in a blender or through a collander. Return the meat and sauce to the pot.

At this point you can set the stew aside, overnight if desired, until about 20 minutes before serving. (Add an extra 5 minutes if it is allowed to get cold). Reheat to the boiling point, then add the mushrooms and olives, lower the fire, and cook another 10 minutes. Serve from the pot on boiled potatoes, by preference.

RAGOÛT AU VIN BLANC [Beef Stew in White Wine]

Ragout au vin blanc is one of the easiest French ragouts to prepare and is an excellent contrast to the traditional *boeuf bourguignon*, best known of the peasant ragouts. On the theory that the potatoes add nothing to the overall flavor of the dish, some cooks believe they are better when cooked separately and served with the finished stew. Most French stews are cooked without potatoes, but this recipe was an exception and I have never tried to change it. It serves four people.

2   *lb beef shin, cut in 2-inch cubes*
1   *tbsp oil (olive oil preferred)*
1   *large onion, thickly sliced*
1   *clove garlic, minced*
1   *tbsp flour*
1   *cup stock*
1   *cup dry white wine (the original recipe*
     specified Muscadet)
1   bouquet garni *consisting of 1 bay leaf, 1 strip*
     lemon peel, and 1 small branch celery
3   *medium carrots, chunked*
3   *small turnips, chunked*
     salt
     freshly ground pepper
4   *medium potatoes, halved*

Heat the oil in a deep pot with a lid (a cast iron or stainless Dutch oven is ideal) and brown the meat on all sides. Add the onion and brown without scorching, add the garlic, then stir in the flour and mix thoroughly. Add the stock and wine, combined and preheated, the *bouquet garni*, the carrots, and the turnips. Season lightly.

As soon as the mixture reaches the boiling point, lower the fire, cover the pot tightly, and simmer as slowly as possible for 2 hours. About 30 minutes before serving, add the potatoes and cook another 25 minutes or until the potatoes are done. Remove the *bouquet garni* and serve from the pot.

BOEUF BOURGUIGNON [Burgundy Beef Stew]

Boeuf bourguignon is the classic of all French beef stews and a favorite throughout France. More often than not, it is made with almost any dry red wine in preference to Burgundy; the reason, of course, is economic. No French housewife is going to pay extra for real Burgundy to lubricate her Sunday stew when she knows the local *vin du pays* will serve the same purpose. Only in Burgundy itself, where the *vin du pays* is Burgundy, are you likely to find this recipe living up to its name. But, whether made with *Chambertin, Margaux, Côte de Provence,* or California *Zinfandel, boeuf bourguignon* still ranks in my estimation as the greatest example of how delicious peasant cooking can be. The *cordon bleus* should have it so good!

Boeuf bourguignon is one dish that needs meat of inferior quality. If made from *prime* beef, it will cook to pieces before its flavors have melded together. Even *choice* can be too tender, as this stew was designed, ages ago, to conquer tough, unaged country beef. For this reason I recommend *good* or *standard* grades (if you can find them) so that your stew can simmer sufficiently and still maintain its breed.

This recipe is the result of more than a dozen years of experimentation with a score of *boeuf bourguignon* recipes. There is no authentic recipe for *boeuf bourguignon*—most housewives in France never use a formal recipe—but this one will succeed admirably with the ingredients available in the United States.

2   *lb rump- or chuck-grade beef, cut in 2-inch cubes*
4   *tbsp olive oil*
2   *medium onions, sliced*
1   *tbsp flour*
2   *cloves garlic, crushed*
1/2 *cup salt pork, diced finely*
1   *cup stock*
1   *cup dry red wine*
1   *bay leaf*
    thyme
    oregano
    salt
    freshly ground pepper
1   *cup fresh mushrooms, sliced*
24 *white baby onions (optional)*
    parsley, chopped

Brown the beef in a large Dutch oven-type pot, preferably cast iron or stainless steel, using 3 tablespoons of the oil (one-half salad oil and one-half butter may be substituted). Remove to a warm plate. Sauté the sliced onions in the same oil and, when golden, return the meat (plus any juice) to the pot, add the flour and the crushed garlic, and mix thoroughly.

While the beef and onions are browning, sauté the salt pork in a separate skillet until deep golden brown. Drain well and add to the pot together with the stock and wine, slightly warmed, the herbs, and seasoning. Bring the mixture to a boil, then lower the flame and simmer slowly until the meat is tender. The time, which should be close to 2 hours, will vary according to the grade of beef.

Once the meat starts to simmer, wipe the mushrooms with a damp cloth, remove most of the stem, and cut the tops into 1/4-inch slices. Sauté the mushrooms in the remaining tablespoon of oil or the same amount of butter. (Or they may be added to the pot, uncooked, about 30 minutes before serving.)

If you use the baby onions—and I always do—peel them, trim the tops, and cut a thin slice from the root end. Pierce this end with the point of a knife so the onion will hold its shape, and sauté in the same oil or butter you used for the mushrooms. When the onions are browned on all sides, cover the pan and let them steam over a very low flame for 20 minutes.

Add the sautéed mushrooms and onions to the pot about 15 minutes before removing from the fire. Sprinkle with chopped parsley and serve with boiled potatoes.

If I am making a *bourguignon* in advance, to be served several hours later or even the next day, I empty the stew into a large ovenware casserole (earthen) and put the onions and mushrooms on top. About 30 minutes before serving I put the casserole, covered, into a 350° oven, sprinkle with parsley when done, and serve from the casserole.

BOEUF HONGROIS [Hungarian Beef]

Boeuf Hongrois, a very flavorful dish, can be offered as proof absolute that the Hungarians actually don't serve all their meat as goulash. Or perhaps someone will step up and claim that this actually *is* a form of goulash. All I know for certain is that the Hungarian who gave me this recipe didn't call it goulash. And what's the difference? *Boeuf Hongrois* is delicious under any name! This recipe should serve four people with perhaps a little left over.

3	lb lean beef (round is good), cut into 1-inch cubes
1/4	cup butter
1/4	cup oil
1	medium onion, chopped
5	tbsp sweet Hungarian paprika
1	rounded tbsp tomato paste
1/2	cup stock
1/2	cup red wine
	salt
	freshly ground pepper
1-1/2	cups sour cream
1/4	cup fresh dill, chopped, or 1 tsp dried dillweed

Heat the oil and butter in a heavy pan and brown the meat on all sides. Push the meat to the side of the pan and cook the onion in the same fat until soft, but not browned. Add the paprika and blend; then add the tomato paste and blend, making sure each piece of meat is well coated. Next add the stock and wine, combined and preheated, cover the pan, and cook slowly until the meat is tender, about an hour and a half. When ready to serve, add the sour cream and dill. Heat but do not allow to boil. Correct the seasoning and serve, preferably over broad noodles.

CARBONNADES À LA FLAMANDE *[Flemish Beef Stew]*

Carbonnades à la Flamande is famous in continental culinary circles because it is one of the few dishes in which beer elbows wine into obscurity. It really ranks as the *boeuf bourguignon* of Belgium, where it originated. Although *carbonnades à la Flamande* require a minimum of three hours for preparation—probably longer—most of that time is spent with the stew in the oven, which makes it an ideal dish for company. Once taken from the oven, it will remain hot enough for serving for at least thirty minutes. This recipe is tailored for four persons.

2	lb beef, rump or chuck
3	slices raw ham or Canadian bacon
3	tbsps oil
1	onion, thinly sliced
2	tbsp flour
1	cup stock
1	cup beer, warm
1	tbsp sugar
	thyme
	rosemary
1	clove garlic, crushed
	salt
2	carrots, chunked
1	tbsp wine vinegar

Cut the beef into 1-inch cubes and the ham or bacon into 1-inch squares. Heat the oil in a large skillet and brown the beef and ham or bacon together. Remove the meat and sauté the onions in the same fat until soft. Stir the flour into the fat and onions and cook for about 3 minutes, stirring regularly to prevent the roux from burning. Add the heated stock and stir until smooth. Add the warm beer and stir in the sugar, herbs and crushed garlic but don't try to thicken the sauce. Taste for salt. Preheat the oven to 350°. Cut the carrots into 1-inch chunks. Cover the bottom of an oven-proof casserole with sauce, add the meat, top with carrots, and cover with the remainder of the sauce. If there is not sufficient liquid to cover the meat add more beer. Cover the casserole tightly and place in the 350° oven for 2-1/4 hours or until the meat is tender. Stir in the wine vinegar about five minutes before serving.

BEEF À LA MODE

Beef à la mode is another pot roast with a French accent—one that is easy to assemble and almost foolproof in production. Either rump or round beef can be used with equal success.

1	*pot roast, about 3 lb*
2	*tbsp oil*
1	*cup stock*
1	*cup dry white wine*
2	*tbsp cognac*
1	*bay leaf*
	pinch of thyme
	salt
	freshly ground pepper
4	*carrots, cut into 1-inch chunks*
12	*small white onions*
2	*tbsp parsley, chopped*

Trim the roast of excess fat and brown in the oil in a deep, covered, Dutch oven-type pot. Add the stock and wine, warmed, and bring to a boil; then turn the flame low and simmer for 1 hour. Add the cognac, bay leaf, thyme, salt, and pepper and simmer for another thirty minutes. Clean the onions and puncture the root base of each with the tip of a knife, so they won't lose their shape. After the roast has simmered 1-1/2 hours, add the carrot chunks; then after 15 minutes add the whole onions.

Continue cooking, slowly, until the carrots are tender. Remove the roast to a serving platter, slice the vegetables, and arrange them around the roast. If necessary, thicken the sauce slightly by boiling it briskly to the desired consistency. If desired, a bit of *beurre manié* (page 280) may be added. Pour the sauce over the sliced meat and sprinkle with the chopped parsley.

POLISH POT ROAST

Polish pot roast comes very close to being a Polish version of German *sauerbraten*, although the final flavor is quite different. It cannot be prepared on the spur of the moment because of its prolonged marination period, but, once the meat has been treated, the final preparation compares with any pot roast and provides an admirable accompaniment for egg noodles.

        1   cup stock
        1   medium onion, sliced
      1/2   cup wine vinegar
      1/2   tsp dillweed
        8   peppercorns
about 1/4   tsp salt
        1   3-lb pot roast

            flour
        3   tbsp oil
            stock (if needed)
        1   cup sour cream

Wipe the pot roast dry and put it in a large bowl. Make a marinade by combining the stock, onion, vinegar, dillweed, peppercorns, and salt. Pour the marinade over the roast, turn so that it is thoroughly covered, fasten a piece of plastic over the bowl, and refrigerate for at least 48 hours. When ready to prepare it, remove the meat from the marinade and dry with paper towels. Strain the marinade and reserve the liquid and onions. Flour the meat well and brown in the oil on all sides using a Dutch oven-type pan. Add the onions, then the strained liquid from the marinade. Bring to a boil, then lower the fire, and simmer slowly for about 1-1/2 to 2 hours until the meat is tender. There should always be at least 1/2 cup of liquid, so add more stock as needed. When the meat is done, reduce the liquid to about 1/2 cup if necessary. Slice the meat and arrange on a platter. Remove the liquid from the fire and stir in the sour cream, blending well. Heat the sauce but do not let it bubble, not even a trifle. Pour the sauce over the meat and serve with egg noodles or boiled potatoes.

BIFTECK AU POIVRE [Pepper Steak]

My first encounter with pepper steak, French style, came quite some years ago in Paris when the late arrival of a plane delayed our dinner long past the hour Frenchmen normally dine. Our only recourse was a huge *brasserie* on the boulevard des Italiens, complete with an orchestra. Our guest was Gladys Slaughter Savary, an American married in France who once operated in Manila the finest French restaurant in the Far East. Madame Savary had an innate horror of restaurants that served entertainment in addition to food ("You can't do both things well!"), so she studied the menu with a jaundiced eye. Her recommendation was that I try the *bifteck au poivre* and I demurred. The phrase *pepper steak* conjured for me visions of stewed beef and green peppers. Not at all, she insisted; this is something quite different. It was!

I have been a *bifteck au poivre* addict ever since and have eaten it all over France with a score of different sauces (the crusted peppercorns demand a sauce of some type). Here are two very different recipes that I consider outstanding.

BIFTECK AU POIVRE JOSÉPHINE [Pepper Steak Josephine]

Amiens is noted first of all for its magnificent thirteenth century Gothic cathedral, a magnet that attracts beauty-lovers from all over the world. It is also noted, in my book, for several outstanding restaurants, not the least of which is Joséphine, a quiet little establishment with an attraction of its own. I once drove from Ghent, in Belgium, some 200 kilometers to Amiens just to enjoy again one of the best pepper steaks I have ever tasted. This recipe is the result of that trip.

2	*thick steaks (tenderloins are ideal)*
3	*tbsp peppercorns, crushed*
5	*tbsp butter*
1	*tbsp oil*
1	*oz brandy (cognac preferred)*
1/2	*cup stock*
1	*tsp Dijon-type mustard*
1/2	*lemon*
3/4	*cup* crème fraîche *(page 282) or sour cream*

Crush the peppercorns coarsely (I use a mortar and pestle) and crust the steaks on both sides with them. Cook the steak in 2 tablespoons of the butter and the oil. About 2 minutes on each side should be sufficient unless you want them very well done; they will continue to cook to some degree on the very hot plate to which you remove them while you make the sauce.

Have a lid ready for the skillet. Lace the cooking juices with the brandy, slightly warmed, and light for an instant only, using the lid to snuff the flame before the brandy burns out. Add the remainder of the butter and, when it is melted, add the stock, previously warmed, and the mustard. Mix well so that the mustard doesn't lump. Squeeze in the juice of the half lemon; then, over a very hot fire, boil the liquid until it is reduced by at least one-third. Now, *take the pan off the fire,* stir in the *crème fraîche* or sour cream, and continue stirring over the fire until you achieve a thick, creamy sauce. (If you use sour cream, be sure not to let it boil after stirring into the stock or it will liquefy.) When the sauce has a satisfactory consistency, return the steaks to the pan. Let them simmer for 1 minute, then remove to heated serving plates, and divide the sauce between them.

BIFTECK D'APHRODITE [Pepper Steak in Port Wine]

Bifteck d'Aphrodite had its inception in a comfortable little restaurant on the Left Bank, not far from les Invalides, called *Chez les Anges.* The angels from which the restaurant takes its name are dainty little white marble (perhaps) seraphims, whose connection with Aphrodite was never clear to me. But the connection of *Chez les Anges* with a delicious pepper steak was immediate. I have visited the place many times without ever exploring any other part of what I am sure is an excellent menu.

> 2   *thick steaks*
> 3   *tbsp peppercorns, crushed*
> 5   *tbsp butter*
> 1/2   *cup port wine (ruby)*
> 1/4   *cup stock*

Crust the steaks with the peppercorns and cook them in 3 tablespoons of the butter, as for *bifteck au poivre Joséphine.* Then remove to a hot plate and keep warm. Pour the port into the cooking juices, being careful that it does not ignite. Over a very hot fire reduce the wine by one-half, stirring constantly; then add the stock and reduce further by about one-third. Now add the remainder of the butter, a little at a time, letting the sauce boil briskly, but continuing to stir until the sauce is thick and satiny. Pour the sauce over the steaks and serve immediately. This is another steak that is handcrafted for mashed potatoes!

ESTOFADO DE VACA [Spanish Beef Stew]

The *estofado de vaca* I discovered in Barcelona is like no other beef stew I've ever tasted. It is delicious in a completely unique way; the idea of including fruit in a meat dish is not new, but this is the only ragout recipe I know that calls for nuts as well. Like so many from all parts of Europe, this stew undoubtedly originated in a peasant kitchen, with its main purpose to make tough beef edible. The continental recipe specified several hours of cooking to achieve tenderness, but American-grade chuck will probably be ready to fall apart after one and one-half hours. This recipe is for four, but my wife and I often make the full recipe and keep half in the refrigerator for three or four days. The second meal is usually better than the first.

2	lb chuck, cut in 2-inch cubes
1/3	cup olive oil
1	large onion, sliced
2	cloves garlic, minced
1	large tomato, peeled, seeded, and cut into eighths
1	oz Spanish brandy
2	tbsp flour
1/2	cup dry white wine
1	cup stock
1/2	tsp paprika
1	small bay leaf
1/2	tsp thyme
	pinch of cinnamon
	salt
	freshly ground pepper
1/2	lb prunes
1/2	cup pine nuts (pignoli)

Brown the meat in the olive oil and remove to a casserole (a 10-inch glass skillet is perfect). Sauté the onion and garlic in the same oil until browned, but not scorched. Remove to the same casserole and add the tomato. (The original recipe called for a whole tomato as is—seeds, peeling, and all. But I have never found anything tasteful in either tomato peeling or seeds, so I always peel the tomato and cut it in two horizontally to remove the seeds. Then I cut each half into quarters for this dish.) There should be about 2 tablespoons of oil remaining in the skillet at this time. If not, add the difference and heat. Next add the brandy (cognac won't hurt this stew!) and light. When the flame dies, add the flour to the oil and cook until brown, stirring constantly. Now add the wine and stock, combined and warmed, and stir until you get a smooth sauce. Add the paprika, bay leaf, thyme, cinnamon, freshly ground pepper, and salt to taste. When it is completely blended, pour the sauce over the meat and vegetables, cover the casserole, and simmer for 1-1/2 hours. Keep watch on the liquid, adding a bit more stock if it gets too low. While the meat is simmering, cook the prunes in a little water until tender. When the meat is tender, drain the prunes and add them together with the pine nuts to the stew. (Incidentally, pine nuts can usually be purchased at any Italian market under the name *pignoli*.) Simmer another 10 minutes and serve from the pan with boiled potatoes.

BEEF STROGANOFF

The first time I encountered beef stroganoff—in Shanghai some months before Pearl Harbor—it seemed to me the most exotic dish I had ever experienced. Today I find it on menus of midwestern lunchrooms and New York coffee shops, and I sometimes wonder why I ever considered it outstanding. Then I remember the words of a friend: "If you ever tire of Beethoven, it can't be his fault. No matter how poorly he is performed or how often you hear his music, the fact remains that it is still Beethoven and, properly presented, Beethoven is incomparable." The same might be said of beef stroganoff. Properly prepared, it is still a marvelous dish and this is my favorite recipe for four.

> 1-1/2   *lb lean beef*
>   1   *tbsp Dijon-type (hot) mustard*
> about 1/2   *tsp salt*
>   *freshly ground pepper*
>   2   *tbsp butter*

Cut the beef (select one of the more tender cuts) into 2-inch strips about 1/4-inch wide, removing all fat and gristle. Put the meat in a mixing bowl and stir the mustard into it, making sure the individual pieces are coated. Sprinkle in the salt and several grinds of pepper. Then let the meat stand for 2 hours in a cool place—not the refrigerator. About 30 minutes before you are ready to serve, sauté the meat in the butter, as hot as possible without burning—(this is a good time for clarified butter, page 00). If liquid forms in the pan, cook it away. As soon as it starts to brown just a little, remove the meat from the pan and keep warm.

>   2   *tbsp butter*
>   1   *large onion, sliced thinly*
>   2   *tbsp flour*
> 1-1/2   *cups stock*
>   2   *tbsp tomato paste (optional)*
>   *thyme*
>   2   *tbsp Madeira or sherry*
>   1   *cup sour cream*

Add the butter to the pan in which the beef was sautéed and cook the onion until golden, but not browned. Stir in the flour and blend well; then pour in the stock, heated to the boiling point, and stir until smooth. (This is where a wire whip comes in handy!) Now you face a decision that only you can make. One international school of Stroganoff devotees passionately condemns the inclusion of tomato paste, while an equally vociferous contigent, to which I belong, believes the tomato paste is essential. Take your choice. If you include it, stir the paste well into the liquid. In any event, add a touch of thyme and return the meat to the sauce. Simmer over a very low flame for 20 minutes or until the meat is tender. This will vary by several minutes according to the quality of the beef. When the meat is tender, add the Madeira or sherry and continue to simmer for another 5 minutes. Now remove from the fire and stir in the sour cream thoroughly. Return to the stove and heat very gently, making sure that the liquid does not bubble. Serve with boiled rice, by preference, or with egg noodles.

Tour de chef: I often sauté 1/4 pound of mushrooms, sliced, in 1 tablespoon of butter and add them to the Stroganoff at the same time as the wine.

ASADO PICANTE [Spiced Pot Roast]

This recipe for *asado picante* was given to me by a friend who brought it from Mexico, or so he said. Actually, the distinct chili flavor imparted by the cumin reminds me more of San Antonio or El Paso. Whatever its generic roots, however, it is a highly recommended method for bestowing lasting enthusiasm on a prosaic rump or chuck roast. Four people who want to enjoy *asado picante* to the utmost will prefer it with plain boiled rice, although potatoes are not off limits.

1	4-lb pot roast
3	tbsp flour
1/2	tsp salt
	freshly ground pepper
3	tbsp oil
1	large onion, sliced
1	clove garlic, crushed
1	tsp ground cumin
1/2	tsp red pepper flakes
3	medium tomatoes, peeled, seeded, and cut into eighths
1	cup stock
3	medium carrots, chunked
	beurre manié *(page 280)*

Wipe the meat with a paper towel and coat it generously with the flour, mixed with the salt and several good grinds of fresh pepper. Heat the oil in a large Dutch oven-type pan and then brown the meat well on all sides. Remove the meat and sauté the onion in the same oil until golden, then add the crushed garlic, the cumin, and the red pepper flakes. Mix thoroughly, return the meat to the pan, and turn it in the onion mixture several times. Peel the tomatoes, cut them in half horizontally and remove the seeds. Cut each half into quarters and add to the pot. Pour the stock, heated, over the meat, cover the pan, and cook over a very low fire for 1-1/2 hours, adding more stock if necessary to maintain the liquid at about a cup. Then add the carrots and cook over a very moderate fire until the meat is tender—probably another hour—still watching the liquid level. When it is tender, remove the meat to a warm platter and thicken the sauce with a bit of *beurre manié*. Serve with rice or potatoes.

MANZO A CHIANTI [Beef in Chianti]

Just across the border from France's Provence is Italy's exquisite *Riviera dei Fiori* (Riviera of the Flowers), perched precariously on the slopes of the Ligurian Alps where they tumble directly into the Mediterranean. It was there I found a way to cook Toscano beef with the gusty red wine of the Riviera—*Rossesse*—with a result that was, and still is, superb. Neither *Rossesse* (roh-say-say) nor Tuscany beef can be found in this country, to my knowledge, but Tuscany's famous Chianti can be combined with American beef with complete success:

MARINADE

1   cup Chianti or other dry red wine
1   medium onion, sliced thinly
3   cloves garlic, minced
1   tsp oregano

> 1   *3- to 4-lb pot roast (round preferred)*
> 1   *large onion, sliced*
> 1/4 *lb salt pork, diced*
> 2   *tbsp olive oil*
> 1/2 *cup stock*
>   *flour*
>   *salt*
>   *freshly ground pepper*

Combine the wine, onion, garlic, and oregano and marinate the roast at least 4 hours, turning every hour and piling the onion slices on top each time. When ready to cook, strain the marinade and discard the solids. Wipe the meat dry with paper towels (the wine will ruin cloth towels) and dredge it with flour. Put the oil into a large pot with a tight cover, brown the onion and salt pork, and then brown the floured meat on all sides.

Add the strained marinade liquid to the pot together with the stock, salt, and pepper. Simmer over a low fire for 3 hours, covered, or until the meat is tender, adding more water if necessary. When it is done, remove the meat and boil the remaining liquid until it thickens slightly. Slice the meat and serve with the sauce on the side. This dish is excellent with boiled potatoes.

BOEUF EN MIROTON

Boeuf en miroton is a simple and delicious method for lifting cold roast beef well above the level of ordinary leftovers. This is, in fact, the last act for any standing rib roast in our family and can be equally effective with other types of cold beef. We have even adapted it to cold roast lamb by making the brown sauce with lamb bits instead of beef. This recipe is known to every French housewife and varies only in the way the *sauce brune* is prepared.

cold beef, sliced
brown sauce

There is an excellent recipe for brown sauce on page 227, but for *boeuf en miroton* I alter the formula slightly to make full use of the browned bits of beef that always result from a roast. This is my favorite.

2	*tbsp butter or oil*
1	*medium onion, chopped*
2	*tbsp browned bits of beef*
2	*tbsp flour*
1-1/2	*cups stock*
1/4	*cup dry white wine*
1	*tbsp tomato paste*
	thyme
	oregano
	salt
	freshly ground pepper

Put the butter in a hot skillet. Sauté the onion and browned bits of beef (these can come from an outside cut or from the fall-out of carving, and you can use as much as you have handy) until the onion is well browned, but not burned. Remove the onion and beef bits and save. Stir the flour into the fat and cook over a medium flame, stirring constantly, until the flour too is well browned. Now add the stock, prewarmed, and stir to achieve a smooth sauce. Add the wine and tomato paste, a pinch each of thyme and oregano, salt, and freshly ground pepper. When thoroughly mixed, cover the pan and simmer slowly for 20 minutes. Correct the seasoning, strain the stock, and discard the solids. Preheat the oven to 400°. Pour a little sauce into the bottom of an ovenware casserole and cover with a layer of beef, sliced. Add more sauce and beef, alternating until all is used. Be sure to save enough sauce to cover the top. Put the casserole, uncovered, into a 400° oven for 15 minutes. Serve from the casserole.

KÖNIGSBERGER KLOPS [German Meat Balls]

Poor old Königsberg, once the proud capital of East Prussia, is no more. Where it once reigned over an important part of the Continent now stands Kaliningrad, a city of Russians for the past quarter century and not likely to change. Consequently, one must contemplate *Königsberger klops* with a special regard. They not only represent a superlative method of preparing meat balls, in any language, but also carry in their spherical being the last vestiges of the circumstance that once was vested in a great capital city. This dish has been a classic in Germany for scores of years, but proof of its international renown is that I first encountered *Königsberger klops* in Manila's New Europe restaurant nearly twenty years ago. It is a grand dish in any hemisphere.

3/4	*lb ground beef*
1/2	*lb ground pork*
1/4	*lb ground veal*
1	*hard roll*
	milk
1	*medium onion, diced*
1	*tbsp butter*
4	*anchovy fillets, minced finely*
2	*eggs*
about 1/2	*tsp salt*
	freshly ground pepper
1	*tbsp lemon juice*
1/4	*tsp marjoram*
3	*cups stock*
2/3	*cup dry white wine*

SAUCE

2	*tbsp butter*
2	*tbsp flour*
1	*tsp Dijon-type mustard*

2   *cups stock (above)*
1   *egg yolk*
2   *tbsp capers*
    cayenne pepper

If you do not have a meat grinder, have your butcher put the three meats, together, through his grinder twice, so that they will be chopped as finely as possible. Break up the roll and soak it in as little milk as possible for about 15 minutes. Dice the onion and sauté it in the butter until transparent. Mince the anchovy fillets finely. In a large mixing bowl combine the meat, the bread (with as much milk pressed out of it as possible), the onion, and the anchovy fillets and mix thoroughly. Beat the eggs lightly; then mix them into the meat, together with the salt, several good grinds of fresh pepper, the lemon juice, and marjoram. Beat this mixture with a wooden spoon until it is completely blended. With a large spoon lift out enough meat to form a ball the size of a walnut or golf ball when rolled in the hand. Place it on waxed paper and repeat until all the meat is transformed into balls.

Combine the stock and wine and heat to the boiling point, using a large bottom pan—10 or 12 inches in diameter. Place the meat balls in the stock very carefully so that they do not crowd each other and continue boiling until the balls come to the surface. Now turn the fire as low as possible and simmer the balls for at least 15 minutes. It is almost impossible to overcook them, and the pork should be completely done. When they are done, remove the meat balls from the liquid with a slotted spoon and place in a heated serving dish. Strain the stock in which the balls were simmered and save the liquid.

In a medium saucepan or skillet heat the butter and cook the flour until a golden roux is achieved. Pour 2 cups of the strained stock, boiling hot, into the roux. Stir with a wire whip or a wooden spoon until smooth. Stir in the mustard. Beat the egg yolk lightly and add about 1 tablespoon of the hot sauce, stirring constantly. Remove the saucepan from the fire and stir the egg mixture into it. Mix thoroughly; then return the pan to the fire. Add the capers and taste for seasoning. Add a good dash of cayenne pepper and pour the sauce over the meatballs. Serve preferably with small noodles (page 261) or boiled potatoes.

BORSCHT *[Russian Vegetable Soup]*

It has been suggested that *borscht* might more properly belong in that section of this tome reserved for soups. Several years ago the Manila Overseas Press Club had its kitchen supervised by a Russian lady with a French name, Madame Dupont, whose *borscht*—a Russian dish prepared with French skill—was a complete and memorable meal in itself. I have tried to approximate her recipe here. Try it and I'm sure you'll agree it's a meal rather than just a soup. This formula is styled for four hungry persons.

2	*lb brisket of beef*
1-1/2	*quarts stock*
1-1/2	*quarts water*
1	*tsp peppercorns*
1	*clove garlic*
1	*large onion, quartered*
1	*large bay leaf*
1	*tsp salt*
4	*medium beets, peeled*
2	*cups cabbage, shredded*
1/4	*tsp dried dillweed (1/4 cup fresh dill preferred, if available)*
2	*tbsp lemon juice*

sour cream
sour cream and horseradish sauce (1 tbsp horseradish and 2 tbsp sour cream, mixed)

Put the meat, the combined stock and water, peppercorns, garlic, onion, bay leaf, and salt into a large pot. Bring to a boil (skim if necessary); then turn the fire low, cover, and simmer for 2 hours. Add the whole beets and simmer another hour. Remove the meat and the beets from the liquid, strain, and discard the other solids. Return the liquid to the pot, add the cabbage and the beets (which you have just shredded), and simmer together until the cabbage is crisply tender—about 20-25 minutes. When ready to serve, add the dillweed, lemon juice, and more salt if needed. Serve the soup with sour cream on the side. Slice the brisket and serve with the sour cream and horseradish sauce and with fresh pumpernickel.

BRAISED BEEF WITH GINGER

Many long years ago, as the story tellers would have said, there was no such thing as refrigeration against summer temperatures, and even the best cuts of meat had a disconcerting habit of getting a little high if not cooked and consumed immediately. The answer, if you were wealthy, was the use of spices literally to smother the adverse aroma of the meat and to make it edible, if not particularly alluring. The use of ginger in this recipe has none of those connotations. It is used to give first-class meat an aroma and a flavor that is just a bit different—and delicious. This dish, which is really a pot roast, should be more than enough to feed four persons.

> 1   *tbsp oil*
> 1   *3-lb pot roast, rump or chuck*
> 1   *onion, minced*
> 2   *tomatoes, peeled, seeded, and chopped*
> 1   *clove garlic, crushed*
> 1/2   *tsp powdered ginger*
> 1   *cup stock*
> 1   *bouquet garni, consisting of 1 small rib celery,*
>   *1 bay leaf, and a zest of orange peel, tied together*
>   *sugar, a pinch*
>   *salt*
>   *freshly ground pepper*
> 1   *tbsp dry sherry*

Heat the oil in a Dutch oven-type pan and brown the meat well on all sides. When the meat is browned, add the minced onion to the fat and cook until golden; then put in the chopped tomatoes and the crushed garlic. Cook for 5 minutes, then stir in the ginger (freshly grated whole ginger root preferred), and mix well. Heat the stock to the boiling point and add to the pot together with the *bouquet garni*, sugar, a pinch of salt, and several grinds of fresh pepper. Cover the pot and cook over a very low fire for about 3 hours or until the meat is tender to the fork. Remove the meat and add the sherry to the sauce. If it is too thin, reduce the sauce by boiling with the lid removed; if too thick, add a bit of stock. Serve with boiled potatoes.

BOEUF AU RAIFORT [Beef and Horseradish]

Boeuf au raifort is another flavorful way to lift leftover beef from the "warmed-up" class to the status of a full-fledged *pièce de résistance*. This is more or less a type of *miroton*, but it will never be mistaken for the *boeuf en miroton* previously presented. With a sauce as piquant as this will prove to be, mashed potatoes are recommended for the four participants.

2	*lb cooked beef sliced*
1	*4-oz jar prepared horseradish*
1	*tbsp flour*
1	*tbsp oil*
1	*cup stock*
1	*tbsp Dijon-type mustard or 1/2 tsp dry mustard*
about 1/4	*tsp salt*
	freshly ground pepper

Place the sliced beef in a baking dish and pour the entire jar of horseradish over it. Let it marinate for at least 1 hour, turning the meat two or three times and piling the horseradish on top. Preheat the oven to 450°. Make a roux by cooking the flour in the oil for 2 or 3 minutes, stirring to keep the flour from scorching. Add the stock and stir with a wooden spoon or wire whip until smooth. Add the salt and several grinds of fresh pepper, then blend in the mustard smoothly. Pour the sauce over the meat and horseradish and bake in a 450° oven for 30 minutes.

Tour de chef: I find that 1/4 cup of Parmesan, sprinkled over the top before the casserole goes into the oven, provides both flavor and color.

SHORT RIBS BAKED IN RED WINE

I have never yet discovered what the French do with short ribs; I have never seen them in a *boucherie* or on a menu in France. But since our return to the United States, we have had a lot of fun applying French cooking techniques to a typically American cut of meat, and the results have been most gratifying. Short ribs baked in red wine is one dish we have found reminiscent of France, although you won't find it in any compendium of *la grande cuisine*. Be sure to choose ribs with plenty of meat on them. Also, because you are dealing with bones, select a large skillet or braising pan.

3	*lb short ribs*
2	*tbsp oil*
	garlic salt
4	*medium carrots*
2	*medium onions*
3	*stalks celery*
1/2	*cups red dry wine*
1-1/2	*cups stock*
1/2	*tsp basil*
1/2	*tsp thyme*
	salt
	freshly ground pepper

Brown the ribs on all sides in the oil and sprinkle with just a pinch of garlic salt. Chop the carrots, onions, and celery into fairly small pieces and put them in the bottom of a flame-proof casserole. Place the browned ribs in the middle of the vegetables and pour the wine and stock, combined, over the whole. Stir in the thyme, basil, a pinch of salt, and plenty of freshly ground pepper. Cover the casserole and, over a moderate fire, bring to a boil. Meanwhile, preheat the oven to 350°. When the liquid starts to boil, transfer the casserole to the oven and cook, covered, for 1 hour. Remove the lid and cook at the same heat for another 30 minutes. The liquid will boil down, but don't let it boil away completely. There should be more than 1/2 cup at all times. Add more stock (heated) in small quantities if needed. Without thickening the sauce, serve with boiled potatoes.

SPICED SHORT RIBS

Many persons will find spiced short ribs reminiscent of chili, perhaps or Hungarian goulash soup. Actually they are as American as hominy grits and owe their trace of the exotic to cumin (which is, incidentally, the spice that gives chili powder its distinctive flavor).

A large pot with a tight-fitting lid is your first requisite for this culinary exercise. A ten-inch skillet, also with fitted lid, is ideal if you decide to halve the recipe for two persons.

3	lb meaty short ribs, cut in chunks
2	tbsp oil
2	medium onion, sliced
1	clove garlic, crushed
3/4	cup stock
3/4	cup tomato puree
1/2	cup dry white wine
1	tbsp tomato paste
1	tsp ground cumin
1/2	tsp dry mustard or 1 tsp Dijon-type mustard
1	bay leaf
	salt
	freshly ground pepper

Brown the meat on all sides in the oil, remove from the pan, and sauté the onions in the same fat until golden. Meanwhile, mix the stock, tomato puree, and wine and warm slightly. When the onions are transparent, crush the garlic into them and return the meat. Pour in the warmed liquids and heat until they start to bubble. Now stir in the tomato paste, cumin, and mustard. Salt and pepper to taste and add the bay leaf. Cover tightly and allow to simmer over a low flame for 45 minutes. Test the meat for tenderness and continue simmering until ready to serve, preferably with boiled potatoes or wide egg noodles.

BRAISED SHORT RIBS

This good old American recipe, braised short ribs, has a dollop of vermouth added because we think it improves the flavor. Plain white wine can be substituted or an extra one-fourth cup of stock used instead. The important thing is to be sure that your short ribs have plenty of meat on them. Three pounds of bones augmented by the vegetables should be sufficient for four persons.

3	*lb short ribs*
	flour
3	*tbsp oil*
1-1/4	*cups onions, chopped*
1	*cup celery, chopped*
3	*carrots*
1	*small eggplant*
3	*medium tomatoes, peeled and seeded*
1	*cup stock*
1/4	*cup dry vermouth*
1/2	*tsp basil*
1/2	*tsp thyme*
	salt
	freshly ground pepper

Heat the oil in a skillet, meanwhile dredging the bones in sufficient flour to cover them completely. Brown the ribs on all sides, then remove to an oven-proof casserole, and keep warm. Add the onions and celery to the oil. When the onions are golden, add the carrots, cut in half lengthwise, then in thirds; the tomatoes, chopped; and the eggplant, peeled and cut in 3/4-inch cubes. Preheat the oven to 350°. Meanwhile, heat the combined stock and vermouth, pour over the vegetables, and stir in the basil, thyme, salt, and pepper. Let simmer for about 5 minutes until the browned bits of meat and flour are loosened. Pour the entire mixture over the ribs. Cover the casserole, put it in a 350° oven, and bake for 1-1/2 hours. If you leave it in longer, reduce the fire and add another 1/2 cup of stock. This dish can be served with potatoes on the side or with a salad only.

OSSO BUCO MILANESE [Braised Veal Shanks]

Osso buco is as typical of Italy as *fettucini*, but this recipe for *osso buco Milanese* comes from France—from Nice, not far from the Italian border, where Italian foods are prepared with a French accent. Nice, which was, of course, once part of the kingdom of Sardinia (now Italy), has become almost entirely French in the past century, but souvenirs of the Italian kitchens still persist, together with scores of Italian family names attached to families that today speak only French.

Ask your butcher to cut the veal shin for you in three-inch lengths, making sure there is plenty of meat on each bone and plenty of marrow inside. And care must be taken during the cooking to be certain that the marrow does not escape the bone. Marrow is one of the best reasons for enjoying this delicacy.

4	*veal shin marrow bones, 3 inches long*
2	*tbsp butter*
2	*tbsp olive oil*
1	*carrot, grated*
1	*medium onion, minced*
1/3	*cup celery, chopped*
1	*cup stock*
1	*cup dry white wine*
2	*tbsp tomato paste*
1	*clove garlic, crushed*
	rosemary
	oregano
	salt
	freshly ground pepper

GREMOLATA

1	*clove garlic, minced*
2	*tbsp parsley, chopped finely*
	grated rind of 1 small lemon

Brown the veal shin on all sides in the combined oil and butter. If desired, the shins may be tied with twine first to prevent the meat from coming off the bones. Use a lidded pan large enough for the four shins to stand alone. When the meat is browned, add the carrot, onion, and celery and simmer about 10 minutes, stirring occasionally. Now add the wine and stock, warmed, the tomato paste, crushed garlic, rosemary, oregano, salt and fresh pepper. Bring the mixture to the verge of a boil, then lower the flame, and simmer slowly for 1 hour or until the veal is tender. If the sauce seems too thin at this time—it should have the consistency of a gravy—thicken it with a bit of *beurre manié* (page 280) or with 1 tablespoon of flour dissolved in water.

Mix the minced garlic, chopped parsley, and grated lemon rind to form the *gremolata*. About 5 minutes before serving, add the *gremolata* to the sauce. Serve with boiled rice, boiled potatoes, or egg noodles.

VITELLO TORINO [Veal with Vermouth]

Turin is probably the world's largest producer of dry vermouth, so it is only natural that cooks in that very attractive city should use dry vermouth quite extensively. This recipe for *vitello Torino* can convert raw veal into an excellent dinner for four people in a matter of minutes.

1-1/2	*lb veal scallops, pounded thin*
	flour
4	*tbsp butter*
	salt
	freshly ground pepper
1/2	*cup dry vermouth*
1/4	*cup stock*
1/4	*cup mushroom liquid (page 283)*
1/2	*lb mushrooms, sliced*

Dredge the scallops well in the flour and sprinkle with salt and freshly ground pepper. Sauté in 3 tablespoons of the butter until well browned. Add the vermouth and, without lowering the fire, cook until almost all evaporated. Next add the stock and mushroom liquid, combined and heated, cover the pan, and simmer for 15 minutes. Meanwhile, sauté the sliced mushrooms in the remaining tablespoon of butter. When the meat has simmered for 15 minutes, add the mushrooms to the pan. Cook slowly for 5 minutes and serve with a good *risotto* (page 261).

VITELLO CON PISELLI [Veal with Peas]

In Italy we always made *vitello con piselli* with fresh garden peas—quick frozen vegetables still are not common outside Italy's larger cities—but in the United States I have found that the frozen variety produces the same excellent results and is, of course, infinitely easier to handle.

1   *medium onion, sliced thinly*
3   *tbsp butter*
1   *tbsp oil*
2   *lb stewing veal, cut into 1-inch pieces*
2   *tbsp flour*
1/2 *cup dry white wine*
1   *cup stock*
1   *clove garlic, crushed*
    thyme
    salt
    freshly ground pepper
2   *10-oz packages frozen green peas*
2   *tbsp fresh parsley, chopped*

Sauté the onion in the butter until golden, then remove with a slotted spoon, and reserve. Dust the veal with the flour (a paper bag is excellent) and brown in the same butter, to which the 1 tablespoon of oil has been added. Return the onion and add the wine. Cook over a high heat until the wine is almost evaporated. Add the stock, crushed garlic, a generous pinch of thyme, salt, and freshly ground pepper. Cover the skillet tightly and simmer over a low fire for at least 1 hour, adding more stock or water if needed.

Remove the peas from the freezer as soon as you start browning the onions and allow them to thaw naturally. When the veal is tender, add the peas to the broth and simmer another 5 to 7 minutes until the peas are cooked. Sprinkle with the chopped parsley and serve with potatoes or rice. Tiny new potatoes, when available, are superb with *vitello con piselli*.

SAUTÉ DE VEAU BASQUAIS [Veal Stew, Basque Style]

I have spent very little time in the so-called Basque country, which straddles the French-Spanish border at its western extremity, but I do know that the Basques love sweet peppers and use them in cooking with a lot of imagination. *Sauté de veau Basquaise* is a good example. When it is properly produced, this dish combines the two qualities that contribute so much to the enjoyment of food—flavor and eye appeal. In order to do this dish justice, it really is necessary to combine the red and green peppers, so hold this recipe in reserve when the sweet red peppers are off the market.

2	lb shoulder of veal
2	tbsp olive oil
about 1/4	tsp salt
	freshly ground pepper
3	tomatoes, peeled and seeded
1	red pepper
1	green pepper
1	onion, chopped
1	clove garlic, crushed
1/2	tsp thyme
1/2	cup stock
1/2	cup dry white wine
	parsley, chopped

Cut the veal into strips about 1/2 inch by 2 inches and sauté them in the oil until lightly browned. Sprinkle with the salt and several grinds of fresh pepper. Add the tomatoes, peeled, seeded, and cut into quarters, and the peppers, seeded and cut into strips about the size of the pieces of meat. Also add the chopped onion, thyme, and the crushed garlic and let the ingredients cook over a moderate fire for 2 minutes. Then pour in the stock and wine, combined and heated. Cover the casserole and cook over a low fire for 45 minutes. Then remove the lid and cook another 30 minutes or until the meat is tender and the liquid has reduced to about 1/2 cup. Serve with boiled rice or your favorite *risotto*. Sprinkle with parsley.

VEAL CHOPS IN SOUR CREAM

Veal chops in sour cream is an adaptation of a recipe I got in Zurich some years ago which has been a favorite in our home ever since. The major difference from the original is the substitution of sour cream for yoghurt. I find that yoghurt is just a bit too tart for the delicate flavor of the veal. This recipe is based on one generous veal chop per person.

```
  4   large veal chops
  2   tbsp butter
  1   tbsp oil
  2   tbsp shallots or green onions, chopped finely
1/4   cup dry vermouth
1/2   cup stock
      pinch of thyme
      marjoram
      salt
      freshly ground pepper

  8   medium mushrooms, sliced
1/2   cup sour cream
```

Sauté the chops in the butter and oil until lightly browned; then add the shallots or green onions and cook until golden, but not browned. Add the stock and vermouth, combined and warmed, together with the thyme, marjoram, salt, and freshly ground pepper. Cover the pan, lower the fire, and simmer slowly for about 35 minutes or until the veal feels tender to a fork. Now add the mushrooms and simmer another 5 minutes, still covered. Remove the chops to a hot serving plate and keep warm. Remove the mushrooms from the liquid with a slotted spoon and put them on top of the chops. Over a very hot flame boil down the liquid in the skillet until only about 2 tablespoons remain. *Take the skillet off the fire* and stir in the sour cream. When blended, return the skillet to a very low flame and warm, being careful not to let the sauce boil. When it is warm, pour over the chops and mushrooms and serve immediately. A bit of paprika or a sprinkle of chopped parsley will add to the appearance of the *plat*.

VITELLO PARMIGIANA [Veal with Parmesan Cheese]

For some reason I have never understood, most Italian restaurants in this country insist on smothering Parmesan cheese dishes with mozzarella, a cheese of considerable merit but guaranteed to overwhelm the delicate flavor of Parmesan—one of the truly *great* cheeses of the world. The little *trattoria* in Livorno that specialized in *vitello parmigiana* also specialized in breading the chops lightly, so that they were never soggy. Topped with plenty of *parmigiana*—a cheese that doesn't "string"—their offering was not to be forgotten. There's no reason why any careful cook shouldn't do as well. And save the mozzarella for your next pizza. A chop per person is this formula.

4	*rib veal chops*
1	*egg, slightly beaten*
1/2	*tsp salt*
	freshly ground pepper
1/2	*cup very fine bread crumbs*
1/2	*cup oil (olive oil preferred)*
1-1/2	*cups tomato sauce (page 273)*
1/2	*tsp basil*
1	*small clove garlic, crushed*
1	*tbsp butter*
1/2	*cup Parmesan, freshly grated*

Preheat the oven to 350°. Dry the chops with a paper towel and dip them into the lightly beaten egg, to which the salt and pepper have been added. Dip immediately into the bread crumbs, covering all sides, and then into the oil, which has been heated almost to the smoking point in a heavy skillet. Brown the chops on all sides, then place in an oven-proof casserole large enough for all four chops to lie flat.

Add the basil and crushed garlic to the tomato sauce (canned may be used if you have none of your own on hand). When the chops are in the casserole, cover them with the sauce. Divide the Parmesan into four equal parts and concentrate one portion largely on each chop. Bake in a 350° oven for 35 minutes. Believe it or not, the Italians seldom serve this dish with pasta of any type; a vegetable is the better accompaniment.

VITELLO AROMATICO [Veal with Herbs]

The Italians use *vitello aromatico* for veal that is less tender than the milk-fed *scallopini*, which could never stand up to the heavy aromatization of this formula. The sauce, when cooked down until a minimum of liquid remains, is very reminiscent of a number of spaghetti sauces in my experience, and I have no doubt that some Italian somewhere has used it for just that purpose. This should satisfy four people.

1-1/2	lb veal
2	tbsp olive oil
2	medium onions, sliced thinly
1	clove garlic, crushed
1/2	tsp oregano
1/2	tsp basil
1	tbsp fresh parsley
about 1/2	tsp salt
	freshly ground pepper
1	cup Italian bell tomatoes, drained
1/2	cup stock
1/3	cup dry white wine
1/3	lb mushrooms, thinly sliced

Select a large skillet (a glass skillet-casserole is ideal) and sauté the veal in the oil until lightly browned. Remove and keep warm. Add the onions to the oil and cook over a moderate flame until they are transparent. Add the crushed garlic and then stir in the oregano, basil, parsley, salt, and several grinds of fresh pepper. Drain the tomatoes well and chop them a bit if necessary (incidentally, two medium tomatoes, peeled, seeded, and chopped, may be substituted, as may ordinary canned tomatoes); then add to the casserole. Now add the combined stock and wine, heated. Cover the pan and simmer over a low fire until the veal is tender—about 45 minutes. After about 30 minutes add the sliced mushrooms to the casserole. If the sauce is too thin after the veal is cooked, remove the lid and cook over a moderate fire until you achieve the consistency of a rich tomato sauce. Taste for seasoning and serve with mashed potatoes—or egg noodles!

VEAU AUX CHAMPIGNONS [Veal and Mushrooms]

Veau aux champignons is easy to prepare and requires very little time. The basic recipe is used by housewives all over France, each contributing her own variations. Not too many use mushroom liquid as generously as specified here, but I believe the result more than justifies this particular modification.

1/2	lb mushrooms
1-1/2	cups water
1-1/2	lb veal scallops
	flour
4	tbsp butter
2	tbsp oil
2	tbsp shallots or green onions, chopped finely
1/3	cup stock
1/3	cup dry vermouth
	salt
	freshly ground pepper
	pinch of thyme

Wipe the mushrooms clean with a dry cloth and cut the stems at the base of the caps. Cut the caps into 1/4-inch slices and reserve. Put the stems in the water and boil briskly until less than 1 cup of water remains. Strain, reserve the water, and discard the stems.

Pound the scallops very thin, flour generously (use a sack if desired), and brown in 2 tablespoons of the butter and the oil, combined. Add the shallots or green onions and sauté for about 2 minutes; then add the vermouth and stock, warmed. Add the thyme, salt, and pepper and cook until the liquid in the skillet is reduced by at least one-half. Now add 3/4 cup of the mushroom liquid, cover the skillet, and simmer slowly until the meat is tender—about 30 minutes.

While the meat is simmering, sauté the sliced mushroom caps in the 2 remaining tablespoons of butter and add to the veal just before serving.

BLANQUETTE DE VEAU [Creamed Ragout of Veal]

Blanquette de veau is to veal what *boeuf bourguignon* is to beef in the French ménage—a culinary classic known to every housewife. It is a bit more complicated to prepare than its beef counterpart, but not a great deal—certainly not enough to deter it from ranking as one of the top favorites in French homes. As for most classic dishes, every French housewife either has her own recipe for the *blanquette* or, more often, works from instinct. This is the best of many recipes I have tried.

2	lb lean veal (shoulder or breast), cut into 1-1/2-inch cubes
2	cups stock
2	cups water
1	tsp salt
1	large onion, halved
4	cloves
1	large carrot, chunked
1	stalk celery with leaves, chunked
1	clove garlic, whole
	peppercorns
	thyme
1	bay leaf
12	small white onions
1/2	lb fresh mushrooms
6	tbsp butter
2	tbsp flour
2	cups stock, strained (above)
1/2	cup dry white wine
1	cup crème fraîche (page 282) or sour cream
2	egg yolks
1	tsp lemon juice
2	tbsp fresh parsley, chopped

Combine the water and stock, bring to a rolling boil, and add the salt.

Put the veal into the liquid a little at a time, so that the boiling continues. Add the onion halves spiked with the cloves, the carrot, celery, and garlic. Finally, add a few peppercorns, a pinch of thyme, and the bay leaf. Lower the fire, cover the pan, and simmer very slowly for 1-1/2 hours or until the meat is tender. Remove the veal from the stock and keep warm. Strain and reserve the stock, discarding the solids.

Peel the small white onions, trim the tops, and cut a thin slice off the root ends. Pierce this end with the point of a knife, so that the onions will hold their shape. Sauté them in 2 tablespoons of the butter until browned, then cover the skillet, and steam over a very low flame for 30 minutes. Cut the mushrooms into 1/4-inch slices and sauté in 2 tablespoons of the butter until brown, being very careful not to let them steam.

When the veal is tender, prepare a roux from the flour and the 2 remaining tablespoons of butter, stirring constantly over a medium fire until the flour is cooked but not browned. Add 2 cups of the strained stock in which the veal was cooked, still stirring until the sauce is smooth. Next add the wine and continue stirring until slightly thickened. Blend the egg yolks into the cream; then, off the fire, stir the mixture into the sauce. Return to a low fire to cook gently—never boil—until the sauce is thickened. Correct the seasoning and add the lemon juice.

Combine the veal, onions, and mushrooms with the sauce on a serving platter or in a serving dish. Sprinkle with the freshly chopped parsley and serve with boiled rice or mashed potatoes.

JARRET DE VEAU À L'ESTÉREL *[Veal Shanks à l'Estérel]*

The Estérel is a mountainous massif that fronts on the Mediterranean between Cannes and Saint-Raphael—wooded, wild, and beautiful. It was in a little restaurant near Agay, fronting on the sea, that I found *jarret de veau à l'Estérel*, a delicious method for preparing veal shanks. It is something very near to combining them with the wonderful *ratatouille* of Provence, although the mélange of vegetables is not exactly the same. The veal shanks take longer to cook than the vegetables, so start them well in advance.

     4   *veal shanks, 2 inches thick*
     2   *tbsp flour*
     4   *tbsp butter*
     4   *tbsp oil*
   1/2   *cup stock*
     1   *tbsp lemon juice*
   1/2   *tsp salt*
       freshly ground pepper
about 1/4   *tsp oregano*

     1   *small bulb fennel*
     2   *stalks celery*
     2   *zucchini squash*
     1   *medium eggplant*
     4   *very ripe tomatoes*
     2   *onions, sliced*
   16   *green olives, pitted*

Have the butcher cut the veal shanks so that there is plenty of meat on them. Flour them well and brown on all sides in *half* the butter and oil, combined, using a Dutch oven-type pan large enough for all four bones to rest side by side. Pour the stock and lemon juice, combined and heated, over them, add the salt, several grinds of fresh pepper, and the oregano. Cover the pan and cook slowly for 1 hour, adding a bit more stock if needed. The shanks should never cook dry.

Chop the fennel (bulb only) and the celery together rather finely. Wash and dry the zucchini and the eggplant and cut into bite-sized pieces without peeling. Peel and seed the tomatoes and chop coarsely. Blanch the olives in boiling water for 5 minutes and drain.

After the veal has cooked for 45 minutes, heat the rest of the butter and oil, mixed, in a heavy saucepan. Sauté the onions, celery, and fennel until the onions are golden, but not browned. Cover the pan and simmer for 5 minutes; then add the zucchini, eggplant, and tomatoes. Cover again and cook over a slow fire for 8 minutes. When the veal is tender to the fork, pour the vegetables into the same pan, add the olives, and let the whole mixture simmer another 10 minutes.

This is almost a meal in itself, combining meat and vegetables. If you feel the need of potatoes, plain boiled ones are best.

VEAU AGENAIS [Veal Stew with Prunes]

Agen is a quiet little city on the Garonne River about one-half the distance between Bordeaux and Toulouse, noted principally for its prunes and table grapes. (No, ma'am, the French do *not* turn all their grapes into wine!) As a result, the terms *Agenais* and *Agenois* have become France's culinary designation for a dish that includes prunes. Agen is also close to Auch, the capital of the Armagnac country, so the brandy herein specified undoubtedly was Armagnac originally. However, no one will object if you should use cognac or one of the better brandies.

<pre>
1/2   lb prunes
  2   oz brandy
       water

  2   lb veal, cut into 1-inch pieces
  1   tbsp butter
  1   tbsp oil
  3   medium onions, sliced
  3   strips bacon, cut into 1-inch pieces
  1   heaping tbsp flour
  2   cups stock
  2   medium carrots, chunked
  1   bay leaf
about 1/2 tsp salt
       freshly ground pepper
</pre>

Put the prunes in a mixture of the brandy and just enough water to moisten well (they don't have to be covered). Let them marinate overnight, stirring occasionally. Sauté the veal in the butter and oil until brown, using a heavy saucepan; then remove and add the bacon and onions. Cook until the onions are golden. Return the meat, sprinkle with the flour, and mix thoroughly. Pour in the stock, heated; then add the carrots, bay leaf, salt, and several good grinds of fresh pepper. Cover the pan and simmer over a low fire for 1-1/2 hours or until the meat is tender.

Drain the prunes, reserve the juice, and remove the stones. About 20 minutes before serving, add the prunes and the brandy liquid and cook slowly, still covered, until ready to serve. *Veau Agenais* is excellent with buttered boiled potatoes.

VEAU AU RUSSE [Veal with Caviar]

I first encountered *veau au Russe* many years ago in Shanghai, when it was a haven for White Russians and good Russian restaurants were easy to find. The combination of the *smetana* (sour cream) and the caviar is unusual and delicious as long as the caviar doesn't dominate. For this reason I advise against lumpfish caviar, which will bring an end result far from the effect you are trying to achieve. If real caviar is too expensive—and it may well be, as it isn't easy to buy by the tablespoonful—try a tablespoon of tomato paste instead, added just before the cream, for a different but delicious dish.

1-1/2	lb lean veal, cut into 1/4-inch strips
2	tbsp butter
1	tbsp shallots or green onions, minced
3/4	cup dry white wine
1/2	cup stock
	thyme
	salt
	freshly ground pepper
1	tbsp lemon juice
1	cup sour cream
1	tbsp black caviar
or 1	tbsp tomato paste (optional)
2	cups boiled white rice

Brown the meat lightly in the butter, remove it from the pan, and keep warm. Sauté the shallots or onions until golden, then add the wine, and reduce by one-half over a hot flame. Add the stock, a pinch of thyme, salt, and freshly ground pepper. When all is blended, return the meat. Simmer for 35 minutes, covered, until the veal is tender. Make a bed of boiled rice in a serving dish. Remove the veal from the liquid with a slotted spoon, place it on the rice, and cover with a sheet of foil until ready to serve. There should be about 1/2 cup of cooking juices remaining in the pan. If more is needed, add stock; if too much remains, reduce it over a hot flame. *Off the fire* stir in the lemon juice and the sour cream, mixing well. (Add the tomato paste, if used, just before the cream.) Return to a very low fire and heat the cream gently until hot, but *do not let it bubble*! Stir in the caviar and blend smoothly, then pour over the veal and rice. Serve immediately.

VITELLO CON PEPERONI [Veal with Peppers]

No one lives in Italy long without becoming aware of the Italians' love for sweet peppers, which they grow not only in the familiar green bell variety but also in colorful reds and yellows. We do, of course, buy red sweet peppers in the American markets in season—not often enough—but I have never seen the yellow ones this side of the Atlantic. *Vitello con peperoni* can be made with green peppers exclusively, but, if you can include one or two sweet red ones, both the flavor and the eye appeal will be enhanced.

4	*bell peppers*
1	*medium onion, chopped*
4	*tbsp olive oil*
3	*tbsp green olives, chopped*
1	*tbsp capers*
1	*16-oz can peeled tomatoes*
2	*anchovy fillets, mashed*
1	*clove garlic, minced*
	oregano
	freshly ground pepper
	salt

4   *loin veal chops*
2   *tbsp flour*
1/2 *cup stock*
1   *tbsp butter*

Clean and seed the peppers and break them into bite-size bits. Sauté them, together with the onion, in 1 tablespoon of the olive oil for 5 minutes, stirring often. Add the olives, capers, and tomatoes, drained, and cook under cover another 20 minutes or until the peppers are soft.

In another skillet sauté the mashed anchovies and minced garlic in 1 tablespoon of the oil until the garlic is golden, but not browned. Then add to the vegetables and mix well. Add a pinch of oregano and a couple of grindings of fresh pepper. Salt should be used sparingly because of the anchovies. Keep the mixture warm.

Dredge the chops lightly in the flour and cook in the remaining 2 tablespoons of oil until done—about 20 minutes. Remove the chops to a warm serving plate and surround with the vegetables. Pour the stock into the juice from the chops and cook over a high fire, adding the butter bit by bit until slightly thickened. Pour over the chops and serve with rice.

SAUTÉ DE VEAU MARENGO [Braised Veal Marengo]

Back in 1800 Napoleon defeated the Austrians at a tiny crossroads in northern Italy called Marengo. At the same time he launched a culinary legend by telling his orderly he was hungry. Food was in short supply, but the resourceful orderly managed to scrounge a chicken, some mushrooms, a couple of tomatoes, and, of course, some wine—or so the legend tells us. The result was a dish called *poulet Marengo*. Whether the story is true, it certainly gave birth to a bevy of *Marengo* recipes—all featuring wine, tomatoes, and mushrooms—of which this is one. Incidentally, I did not get this recipe in Marengo. Driving from Turin to Genoa one day, I managed to locate the ancient battlefield and paid a visit to the neighborhood *trattoria*. The proprietor had never heard the legend, and I settled for pasta.

2   lb breast or shoulder of veal, cut into 1-1/2-inch cubes
2   tbsp butter
2   tbsp oil
2   large onions, sliced
1   clove garlic, crushed
3   tbsp flour
4   large tomatoes, peeled, seeded, and diced
1   cup stock
1   cup dry white wine
    oregano
    tarragon
    salt
    freshly ground pepper

3/4   cup fresh mushrooms, sliced
2   tbsp parsley, chopped

Brown the meat in the combined oil and butter, using a pan with a tight-fitting lid. When it is brown, remove the meat and sauté the onions in the same oil. Add the crushed garlic, stir in the flour, and blend well, cooking the flour without browning it. Pour in the stock and wine, combined and warmed, then the tomatoes. Return the meat to the liquid with a pinch each of oregano, tarragon, salt, and fresh pepper. Cover and simmer over a slow flame for 1 hour or until the veal is tender. About 15 minutes before serving add the raw mushrooms. Sprinkle with the parsley and serve with boiled or mashed potatoes.

GIGOT AU VIN BLANC [Leg of Lamb with White Wine]

Gigot au vin blanc is one of the simplest and most flavorful ways to roast a leg of lamb I ever encountered. If it is rich, the stock will, in mixture with the wine, impart a slight glaze to the lamb as well as heighten its flavor. It is difficult to give exact measurements for the stock and wine because much will depend on the size and texture of the *gigot*. The important thing is to use your judgment. If the basting juices get too low, add more stock. Unless the meat is particularly fatty, there should be little problem of too much liquid because all the cooking is done in an open pan. This recipe can also be easily adapted for a half leg by reducing the components by perhaps a quarter.

1	*5-lb leg of lamb*
2	*cloves garlic, sliced*
	salt
	freshly ground pepper
1/2	*cup dry white wine*
1	*cup stock*
about 1/2	*tsp thyme*
about 1/2	*tsp marjoram*
1	*tbsp* beurre manié *(page 280)*

Preheat the oven to 325°. Clean the lamb carefully, making sure that it has no fell (fuzzy skin). Make several incisions in the meat with the point of a very sharp knife and insert slivers of the sliced garlic. Rub with salt and sprinkle generously with freshly ground pepper. Combine the stock and wine and pour into the bottom of a roasting pan, sized to fit the *gigot*. Place the lamb in the stock and sprinkle with thyme and marjoram. Put the pan into a 325° oven, uncovered, and roast about 30 minutes to the pound, basting frequently. By the time the meat is done, there should be at least 1 cup of liquid remaining in the pan. If there is too much fat, spoon most of it away and then thicken the remainder with the *beurre manié*. You can increase the amount of sauce by adding 1 cup of hot stock to the pan juices, scraping the pan carefully, and thickening with 1 tablespoon of *beurre manié* to each cup. Correct the seasoning and serve.

AGNEAU À LA POÊLE *[Lamb in a Frying Pan]*

Agneau à la poêle is a deceptive name for this *plat* because the frying pan is used more as a casserole than a skillet. I fell heir to this recipe during my years in France, but I am not sure just where. All I know is that it is to hard to conceive of an easier stew to put together in a short time or a lamb stew that can surpass it in flavor.

I am presenting this as a recipe for two persons because this is the original recipe and the one that my wife and I use for ourselves, usually two or three times a month. It can easily be increased for more persons.

         2   *shoulder lamb chops, 1 inch thick*
         2   *tbsp olive oil*
         1   *clove garlic, split*
         2   *small onions, halved*
         2   *medium white turnips, halved*
         3   *carrots, quartered lengthwise*
         2   *medium potatoes, quartered (optional)*
       1/3   *cup dry vermouth*
       2/3   *cup stock*
             basil
             salt
             freshly ground pepper

Sauté the chops and garlic in the oil, using a heavy skillet with a lid. When the chops are browned on both sides, add the onions, carrots, turnips, and potatoes (if desired) and heat in the oil. Warm the stock and vermouth together and add to the skillet, together with a pinch of basil, salt, and freshly ground pepper. Cover the pan tightly and simmer slowly until the meat is tender—about 1 hour. Remove the lid and allow to boil moderately for another 10 minutes. Correct the seasoning and spoon the remaining liquid over the meat and vegetables as served from the pan.

Incidentally, if someone should eat the garlic by mistake, he would find it quite bland, its power almost entirely eliminated by more than an hour of simmering.

MOUSSAKA [Balkan Lamb Pie]

Moussaka is said to have originated in Romania, but it has spread all through the Balkans and the eastern Mediterranean countries and many people today regard it as Greek. I regard it as delicious. Most *moussaka* recipes call for the cooked lamb to be ground (*moussaka* offers an admirable career for the remains of that leg of lamb!), but I prefer having it cut in small bite-size bits so that all four diners will know they are eating a basically meat dish.

2	*average eggplants, unpeeled*
	olive oil
1-1/2	*lb cooked lamb*
2	*medium onions, thinly sliced*
2	*tbsp butter*
	salt
	freshly ground pepper
1	*cup* velouté *sauce (page 226)*
1/4	*cup milk*
1/2	*cup cheese, grated (Parmesan, Gruyère, or cheddar)*

Preheat the oven to 350°. Wipe the eggplants carefully, discard a thin slice from both ends of each, and cut the remainder into 1/2-inch slices. Coat each slice with olive oil and put them in an open pan. Bake in a 350° oven for about 30 minutes or until the slices are tender. Meanwhile, sauté the onions in the butter until golden and reserve. When the eggplant is done, put 1 tablespoon of oil on the bottom of a 2-quart oven-proof casserole and place a layer of slices on it. Sprinkle with a little salt and freshly ground pepper; then cover with a layer of the lamb and a layer of the onions. Repeat with more eggplant, seasoning, lamb, and onion until all are used. The topmost layer must be of eggplant. Combine the *velouté* sauce with the milk until smooth and pour it over the whole. Then cover with the grated cheese of your choice. (Gruyère and Parmesan in combination are particularly good.) Put the casserole, uncovered, into a 350° oven for 30 minutes or until the cheese is browned and crusty.

AGNEAU MARRAKECH [Moroccan Lamb]

In a little side street off *rue Lamartine* in Nice was a hard-to-find little North African restaurant that specialized in *couscous*—the Algerian-Moroccan-Tunisian national dish—served with a variety of meats (mostly lamb) and sauces, highly spiced and sometimes explosive, but always good. *Agneau Marrakech* undoubtedly was intended to be served with *couscous*. But because the preparation of *couscous*—made from specially processed grain—is so difficult to portray to anyone not acquainted with the end result, I am recommending Moroccan lamb as an accompaniment to rice—or hominy grits!

2	*lb lean lamb, cut into 1-inch cubes*
1/3	*cup oil*
2	*medium onions, chopped*
2	*cloves garlic, crushed*
1/2	*tsp red pepper flakes*
	salt
1/2	*tsp turmeric*
	stock (chicken stock preferred)
3	*medium tomatoes, peeled, seeded, and chopped*
2/3	*cup white raisins*
	dry white wine

Heat the oil in a large Dutch oven-type pan with a good lid. Sauté the lamb until browned, remove, and keep warm. Add the chopped onions to the oil and cook until transparent. Add the crushed garlic, then return the meat, and season with the red pepper flakes, a pinch of salt, and the turmeric. Stir in enough stock, heated, to cover the meat and then add the tomatoes. Turn the fire low and cover the pan. While the meat is simmering, put the raisins in the dry white wine, using just enough to cover them, and let steep for at least 30 minutes. When the meat has simmered about 45 minutes, add the raisins and the wine, return the cover, and simmer another 45 minutes or until the meat is very tender. Taste for seasoning (it should be peppery) and serve with rice or hominy grits.

AGNELLO ALLA ZUCCHINI [Italian Lamb Stew]

Agnello alla zucchini from Tuscany, is typically Italian on two counts—the zucchini and the oregano. And it is delicious on all counts. One of our neighbors in Livorno used to vary this formula by cutting the *brodo* (stock) in half and adding one-half cup of dry white wine. To many this improves the taste and I don't argue, but I do believe this particular *stufatino* can hold its own just as presented here.

    3   medium tomatoes
    2   tbsp olive oil
    2   lb lamb shoulder, cut into 3/4-inch cubes
    2   medium onions, chopped
    1   clove garlic, minced
    1   cup stock
  1/2   tsp oregano
         salt
         freshly ground pepper
    3   medium zucchini

Dip the tomatoes in boiling water for 30 seconds (15 seconds, if very ripe) and peel. Cut each tomato in half horizontally, remove the seeds, and chop coarsely.

Brown the lamb well in the oil and remove to a pot with a tight-fitting lid. Sauté the onions and garlic in the same fat until the onions are transparent, being careful not to let them char. Transfer the onions to the meat pot, pour the stock into the skillet, and bring to a boil, stirring carefully to dislodge all browned bits from the pan. When it is heated, pour the stock over the lamb and onions. Add the chopped tomatoes, oregano, salt, and fresh pepper. Cover the pan and simmer for 1 hour or until the meat is tender.

While the meat is cooking, wash the zucchini, cut off both ends, and slice into 1/2-inch slices. When the meat is tender, arrange the zucchini in a layer on top of the lamb, re-cover, and simmer another 15 minutes. Correct the seasoning and serve over egg noodles.

LAMB PILAF

There's a great affinity between *pilaf* which comes from the eastern Mediterranean countries, and *risotto*, which is as Italian as pasta. The link, of course, is the Mediterranean itself, which has joined the two areas since the dawn of time and provided a medium for the exchange of ideas as well as trade. The Turkish or Greek *pilaf* is usually eaten as a main course and is generally more spicy than its Italian *cugino*. In making a good *pilaf*, you must be sure that nothing is browned and that includes the butter. For that reason I recommend the use of clarified butter, which is less likely to scorch than ordinary butter.

1/2	*lb lean lamb, cut into bite-sized pieces*
1/4	*lb clarified butter (page 281)*
3	*onions, chopped finely*
1	*oz pine nuts* (pignoli *page 136*)
2	*cups rice*
1	*tbsp sugar*
1	*tomato, peeled, seeded, and chopped*
2	*oz white raisins*
1-1/2	*tsp salt*
	sage
	freshly ground pepper
4	*cups stock*

Melt the butter in 4- or 5-quart pan with a tight lid and cook the lamb lightly for about 5 minutes. Remove with a slotted spoon and keep warm. Put the onions in the same butter and sauté until transparent, but not browned; then add the pine nuts and the rice. Cook the rice about 5 minutes, stirring almost constantly to prevent sticking. Then add the sugar, tomato, raisins, salt, a generous pinch of sage, and 6 twists of fresh pepper. Meanwhile, bring the stock to a boil in another pan and add it, boiling hot, to the rice. Return the lamb and cover the pot tightly. Turn the fire as low as possible, put the pot on a sheet of aluminum foil, doubled, and cook until the stock is all absorbed by the rice. Remove the pan from the stove, wrap in a heavy towel, and let stand for 20 minutes before serving.

PORT ROYAL LAMB STEW

Port Royal is situated on a little peninsula that juts from the south of Jamaica into the Caribbean, forming the seawall of Kingston Harbor. In addition to its long history as a pirates' den and a naval base, Port Royal has attained immortality by affixing its name to this lamb stew, which is quite popular in the West Indies. It differs from the average stew in that the stewed meat is incorporated into a white sauce and flavored with orange and angostura. For four people you need the following.

1-1/2	lb lean lamb, cut into 1-inch cubes
	salt
	freshly ground pepper
1	tbsp vinegar
3	cups stock
1	bay leaf
1/4	lb fresh mushrooms, sliced
4	tbsp butter
2	tbsp flour
1	egg yolk, beaten
1	tsp orange peel, grated
	angostura bitters

Salt the lamb lightly and sprinkle with pepper. Place in a bowl and pour the vinegar over it. Let stand for 30 minutes, stirring often to mix the vinegar thoroughly. Heat the stock in a deep saucepan. After it has marinated, put the lamb in the stock, together with bay leaf, cover, and simmer for 1 hour or until the meat is tender. Strain and reserve 2 cups of stock. While the meat is cooking, melt 1/2 of the butter in a skillet and sauté the mushrooms until lightly browned. Remove the mushrooms from the butter with a slotted spoon and reserve. When the meat is tender, add the remaining 2 tablespoons of butter to the mushroom pan, add the flour, and cook for 2 minutes, stirring to prevent browning. Add the hot stock and stir until smooth. Off the fire stir in the beaten egg yolk and stir until the liquid starts to thicken. Add the meat, mushrooms, orange peel, and a good dash of angostura. Heat without boiling and serve with boiled rice.

POITRINE D'AGNEAU AUX PETIT POIS [Breast of Lamb with Peas]

Poitrine d'agneau aux petit pois is a simple, low-cost dish from the south of France that is sure to be a favorite with anyone who likes lamb. For easy handling it is best to have the butcher cut the breast so that the individual bones are no more than three inches in length.

> 3   *lb breast of lamb*
> 2   *tbsp flour*
> 2   *tbsp oil*
> 1   *medium onion, chopped*
> 1   *clove garlic, minced*
> 1/2   *cup dry white wine*
> 1   *cup stock*
> 1/2   *tsp dried mint*
>   *salt*
>   *freshly ground pepper*
> 1   *10-oz package frozen peas*

Cut the lamb into individual pieces according to the bones and dredge well in flour. Heat the oil in a skillet and brown the meat on all sides. Remove the meat to a Dutch oven-type pan with a tight-fitting cover. Sauté the onion and garlic in the same oil until the onion is transparent; then add them to the meat. Pour the combined stock and wine into the skillet and bring to a boil, scraping the pan carefully to dislodge all bits of meat and onion. Pour the liquid over the meat and onion and add the mint, salt, and freshly ground pepper to taste. Then cover the pot and let simmer slowly for at least 1 hour until the meat is tender and starting to pull away from the bones.

While the meat is cooking, allow the peas to thaw naturally. When the meat is tender, add the peas to the pot, stir, and allow to simmer for another 8 minutes. Serve with boiled potatoes or tiny new potatoes, when available.

LAMB CHOPS LYONNAISE

The most reasonably priced lamb chop is the shoulder chop, a good cut of meat for flavor but hardly as tender as the loin and rib chops. For that reason the shoulder chop lends itself well to some type of braising, and this is a method we enjoy very much. Lamb chops lyonnaise is actually my wife's adaptation of a recipe we came across in Europe. It is easy to prepare, flavorful, and not expensive, particularly if you are a martini lover and keep dry vermouth in the house. Choose lean shoulder chops and trim the excess—but not all—fat away. Enough should remain to allow the chops to cook in their own fat after a very light start with the oil.

4	*thick shoulder lamb chops*
1	*tbsp oil*
1	*large onion*
1	*clove garlic, crushed*
	salt
	freshly ground pepper
1/2	*cup stock*
4	*tbsp dry vermouth*

Heat the oil in a lidded skillet large enough for the 4 chops to lie flat. Brown the chops slowly, turning a couple of times. Meanwhile peel the onion, cut it in half horizontally, and then cut each half into 8 pieces. When the chops are brown, add the onion chunks, crushed garlic, a bit of salt, and freshly ground pepper. Cover the pan and sauté for about 15 minutes over a slow fire, making sure the onions are not too browned. Add the stock and wine, combined and heated, cover again, and simmer another 20 minutes until the chops are tender when tested with a fork. Remove the chops to a warm plate. Turn the fire up as high as possible and reduce the sauce to a satiny consistency—about 1/2 cup in volume. Remove the onions from the sauce and divide between the chops; then pour the sauce over the whole. Excellent with buttered boiled potatoes.

NAVARIN [Lamb Stew]

Actually this dish should not be called *navarin* because the name means *mutton stew. Larousse* defines *navarin* as "a ragout of mutton with turnips and, sometimes, potatoes." So if you are a purist, call it *mock navarin* to ease your conscience, but by all means use lamb which, in my book at least, has the better flavor. Shoulder of lamb is excellent and in this quantity should satisfy four hungry people.

2	*lb lamb shoulder, boned and cut into 1-inch cubes*
	salt
	freshly ground pepper
4	*tbsp flour*
4	*tbsp butter*
2	*cups stock*
1/2	*cup dry white wine*
2	*large tomatoes, peeled, seeded, and chopped coarsely*
1	*clove garlic, crushed*
1	*bay leaf*
	pinch of rosemary
8	*small potatoes (new, if available)*
2	*white turnips, quartered*
12	*small white onions, whole (page 245)*

Sprinkle the lamb with a pinch of salt and a few twists of freshly ground pepper. Put half the flour in a sack and shake the lamb chunks in it until uniformly floured; then brown in the butter, using a large skillet or pan with a lid. When the meat is browned on all sides, stir the rest of the flour into the butter and add the stock and wine, combined and boiling hot. Stir until smooth. Add the tomatoes, crushed garlic, bay leaf, and rosemary.

Cover the pan, turn the fire low, and simmer, covered, for 30 minutes. Taste for salt. Add the potatoes, turnips, and onions and more stock if needed. Cook, still covered, for another hour or until the vegetables are done. Correct the seasoning again and serve with a green salad for contrast.

MOUTON AUX OLIVES [Lamb and Olives]

Olive trees are one of the glories of Provence and the Côte d'Azur, so olives and olive oil understandably play an important role in the cuisine of that part of the world. I have never tasted olive ice cream or cream puffs stuffed with the delicious fruit, but I have enjoyed olives in just about any other type of dish you can imagine. *Mouton aux olives* is a favorite method for preparing lamb—or mutton *(mouton)*, if you prefer—with a combination of green and ripe olives. This is for four people who like olives.

2	*tbsp butter*
2	*tbsp olive oil*
2	*onions, sliced*
2	*carrots, sliced thinly*
2	*medium white turnips, sliced*
	thyme
	marjoram
1	*bay leaf*
about 1/4	*tsp salt*
	freshly ground pepper
1-1/2	*lb stewing lamb, cut up*
about 3	*cups stock*
1/2	*cup green olives, pitted*
1/4	*cup ripe olives, pitted*

Heat the butter and oil in a large pan and sauté the onions, carrots, and turnips until they are soft, stirring often. Add the thyme, marjoram, bay leaf, salt, and several grinds of fresh pepper. Cover the meat with the stock, warmed, using just enough to cover. Over a moderate fire cook for 30 minutes, covered; then add the olives, cover again, and let simmer for another hour or until the meat is tender. Remove the meat and the olives from the vegetables; put the rest of the ragout through a food mill, a heavy sieve, or a blender, a little at a time. When the puree is smooth, return the meat and olives and simmer another 15 minutes. Correct the seasoning and serve with boiled potatoes or rice.

LAMB SHANKS PROVENÇAL

For some reason lamb shanks are not too common in either French or Italian cuisine; this is surprising, since neither wastes a whit of the lamb, sheep, calf, steer, porker, or anything else. I have always been fond of shanks when properly cooked, so I was quite pleased when I discovered this recipe in Marseilles several years ago. Originally, the Provençal housewife prepared this dish in an earthenware pot on the kitchen hearth, but I have found that a stainless steel Dutch oven-type pan will do the same job for me right on top of the kitchen range.

2	*tbsp olive oil*
4	*slices bacon, chopped*
4	*lamb shanks*
2	*cloves garlic, sliced thinly*
	salt
	freshly ground pepper
3/4	*cup stock*
3/4	*cup dry white wine*
3	*carrots, cut into 1-inch lengths*
1	*turnip, quartered*
4	*stalks celery, cut into 1-inch lengths*
2	*large tomatoes, peeled, seeded, and chopped*
	basil
	bay leaf
3/4	*cup white beans, precooked*
8	*artichoke hearts (optional)*

Heat the olive oil in the bottom of a pan large enough for the four shanks to lie side by side. Sauté the chopped bacon in the oil until it starts to brown. Clean the shanks carefully, removing any excess fat; then make incisions in them with the point of a knife and insert the very thin slivers of garlic. Salt and pepper the shanks and brown them in the same oil. Heat the stock and wine together and pour over the shanks as soon as they are browned. Add the carrots, turnip, celery, and tomatoes to the pot together with the basil, about 1/2 teaspoon of salt, freshly ground pepper, and the bay leaf. Cover the pot and simmer as slowly as possible for 2-1/2 hours. Try not to open the pot during this time. Meanwhile prepare the beans (page 182) and parboil them until tender.

    After 2-1/2 hours add the drained beans and the artichoke hearts, if desired, to the shanks. (If you decide to use the artichokes, try the canned hearts. The tiny ones used in the original recipe simply do not exist in the United States.) Cover again and simmer another 30 minutes. Serve from the pot, if desired.

LAMB SHANKS À LA GRECQUE

Lamb shanks *à la Grecque* is one dish that can be prepared in an oven-proof earthenware pot, as long as it has a tight-fitting lid, because these shanks really are not braised. In this day of stainless steel and Pyrex, not too many housewives on this side of the Atlantic have such a pot, so I recommend a nine-inch glass skillet as an acceptable substitute.

2	*carrots*
1	*large onion, sliced thinly*
4	*stalks celery*
2	*bay leaves*
1	*tsp oregano*
1/2	*tsp thyme*
1	*clove garlic, minced*
2	*lamb shanks*
	salt
	freshly ground pepper
1/2	*cup tomato sauce*
3/4	*cup stock*
1/4	*cup olive oil*
4	*small potatoes (new, if available)*

Preheat the oven to 350°. Cut the carrots and celery into thin julienne strips about 2-inches long and slice the onion as thinly as possible. Make a bed of these vegetables on the bottom of the cooking pot and sprinkle the bay leaves, the oregano, thyme, and minced garlic over them. Clean the shanks, cut off any excess fat, rub with salt and pepper, and place on top of the vegetables. Combine the stock, tomato sauce, and oil and pour over the shanks and vegetables; then cover tightly and put into a 350° oven. After 1-1/2 hours remove the lid, add the potatoes, and cook another 30 minutes, uncovered, basting the potatoes several times with the juices. Serve from the pot.

AGNELLO ALLA CACCIATORE

Any American who has patronized an Italian-American restaurant anywhere in the United States knows *chicken cacciatore*, but not everyone knows that the Italian cook can prepare almost any type of meat or fowl *hunter style*, and often does. Obviously, the Italian hunters like their ragouts highly seasoned, and who can blame them? *Agnello alla cacciatore* is expected to satisfy four hunters.

2   *lb lamb, cut into bite-size pieces*
2   *tbsp olive oil*
1   *tsp salt*
    freshly ground pepper
1   *clove garlic, crushed*
1/4   *tsp marjoram*
1/4   *tsp oregano*
1   *tbsp flour*
1/2   *cup red wine*
1   *cup stock*
4   *anchovy fillets, minced finely*
    parsley

Sauté the lamb in the olive oil until browned on all sides. Add the salt, a generous amount of freshly ground pepper, then the garlic, marjoram, and oregano. Stir in the flour and add the stock and wine, combined and heated. Cover the pan and simmer for about 45 minutes or until the lamb is tender. Stir the minced anchovy fillets into the sauce. Simmer another 10 minutes, uncovered. Serve with a generous sprinkling of parsley on top.

AGNEAU INDIENNE [Curried Lamb]

Agneau Indienne is a method for preparing lamb with an oriental savor—and a really good way to use some of the cheaper cuts, such as the shank or the shoulder (the stewing cuts). The dish is easy to prepare, and it is tasty, especially with good mango chutney.

2	*lb lean lamb*
1	*tbsp oil*
1	*tbsp butter*
2	*tbsp shallots or green onions, chopped*
1	*clove garlic, crushed*
2	*tbsp Madras curry powder*
	salt
	freshly ground pepper
1	*cup stock*
1/2	*cup dry white wine*
1	*cup sour cream*

Cut the lamb into bite-size pieces and brown in the combined oil and butter, together with the shallots or onions. When they are browned, add the garlic, curry powder, salt, and pepper and mix thoroughly. Add the stock and wine, warmed, cover the skillet tightly, and allow to simmer over a very low fire for 1 hour or until the lamb is tender.

A few minutes before serving remove the lid of the skillet and allow the lamb to simmer, uncovered, until the liquid is reduced to about 1/2 cup. Remove the skillet from the fire and stir in the sour cream, blending well. Return to the fire and heat, but *do not boil*! Serve with boiled white rice and chutney on the side.

CASSOULET À L'AGNEAU *[Beans with Lamb]*

Cassoulet is one of France's traditional dishes—everywhere available, complicated to make (a good *cassoulet* may require two or three days), and always rich. Consequently, I hasten to assure one and all that *cassoulet à l'agneau* is not a real *cassoulet*; it is not difficult to prepare, and it is no richer than any combination of meat and beans. But it is delicious, and that is my reason for including it. This recipe was originally meant for mutton, but I'm a lamb man! It should serve six.

2	*cups dried white beans*
5	*cups water*
1	*large onion*
6	*whole cloves*
1/2	*lb slab bacon, cut into 1/2-inch cubes*
1	*clove garlic, diced*
1-1/2	*tsp salt*
1	*bay leaf*
2-1/2	*lb lean lamb, cut into 1-inch cubes*
2	*tbsp oil*
1	*medium onion, chopped*
2	*tsp Dijon-type (hot) prepared mustard*
1	*large tomato, peeled, seeded, and chopped*
3/4	*cup stock*
about 1/4	*tsp freshly ground pepper*

Wash the beans carefully, discarding broken or discolored ones. Put them into cold water in a large saucepan and bring to a full boil. Reduce the flame and simmer for 20 minutes, then remove from the fire, and let the beans stand for 1 hour. Peel the large onion and stud it with the six cloves. After 1 hour add the studded onion to the beans, together with the raw bacon, garlic, salt, and bay leaf. Cover the pan and simmer for another hour until the beans start to get tender. Meanwhile, brown the lamb in the oil. Remove the lamb and cook the chopped onion in the same oil until golden. Add the mustard and tomato and, when thoroughly warm, add to the beans together with the lamb. Discard the clove-studded onion. Taste the mixture for salt. Add the freshly ground pepper and pour the entire mixture into a large oven-proof casserole. Stir in the stock, heated, and bake in a 325° oven for 1 hour, covered, then 15 minutes, uncovered. Serve from the casserole.

LAMB WITH DILL SAUCE

Lamb with dill sauce is a Swedish method for cooking lamb which I have never encountered outside Scandinavia. The idea of boiling lamb, except for stews, is almost unknown in the United States, and I doubt that I could subscribe to it if it weren't for the dill sauce which lifts this dish from the ordinary to the top rank of taste sensations. This is another recipe that provides its own stock as you proceed. I have remarked that most lamb dishes can be prepared with all-purpose stock, but this sauce definitely needs lamb stock.

1	*3-lb shoulder of lamb, boned*
	bones from the shoulder
	boiling water
1	*bay leaf*
4	*sprigs of fresh dill*
2	*tsp salt*
6	*peppercorns*
6	*whole allspice*

Have the meat rolled and tied as if for roasting, put it in a large pot together with the bones, and pour in enough boiling water to cover both. Continue to boil, skimming the surface of the water until it is clear. Add the remaining ingredients, cover the pot, and simmer slowly until the meat is tender—most of 2 hours. When it is done, remove the meat from the liquid and keep warm. Strain the stock, reserve 2 cups of the liquid, and discard the bones and seasonings.

> 2   *tbsp butter*
> 2   *tbsp flour*
> 2   *cups lamb stock*
> 3   *tbsp fresh dill, chopped*
> 2   *tbsp sugar*
> 1   *tbsp white vinegar*
> 1   *egg yolk, beaten*

Make a roux of the flour and butter and, after it cooks at least 2 minutes, pour in the stock, boiling hot. Stir until smooth and then add the dill, sugar, and vinegar, off the fire. While it is still off the fire, stir 2 teaspoons of the sauce into the beaten egg yolk; when blended, stir into the sauce. Return to the fire and heat gently, stirring almost continuously until the sauce is thickened. Meanwhile, cut the meat into 1/2-inch slices and arrange on a hot platter. Pour about half the sauce over the meat and serve the remainder on the side. This dish was just made for little new potatoes boiled in their jackets, but ordinary boiled potatoes or plain boiled rice will serve admirably.

BISTECCA DI MAIALE SICILIANO [Sicilian Pork Chops]

This recipe for *bistecca di maiale Siciliano* was given me by a friend in Rome as an authentic and typical peasant dish from his native Sicily, although I am sure it has been refined a bit in transit from that island to the United States. Nevertheless, it ranks as probably my favorite (*one of my favorites*, anyhow) methods for preparing pork chops. The ideal utensil for this dish is a ten- or twelve-inch skillet (whichever holds the chops more snugly) with a tight-fitting lid.

1	*tbsp olive oil*
1	*clove garlic, sliced thinly*
4	*pork chops, 1-inch thick*
1/4	*cup dry white wine*
1/2	*cup stock*
2	*tbsp tomato paste*
1/2	*tsp oregano*
	salt
	freshly ground pepper
	mushroom liquid (page 283)
1	*cup fresh mushrooms, sliced*
1/2	*cup green pepper, cut into thin 1-inch slices*

Trim the chops of excess fat. Cut off and reserve the mushroom stems; slice the caps. Sauté the garlic in the oil until browned, then discard. Brown the chops in the same oil on both sides. Combine the stock and wine and warm slightly. When the chops are golden, add the stock and wine and bring to a boil. Remove the chops from the liquid and lower the fire. Add the tomato paste, oregano, salt, pepper, and 2 tablespoons of mushroom liquid. Return the chops to the pan, add the sliced mushroom caps and sliced green pepper and cook slowly for another 10 minutes, adding a bit more stock if necessary to obtain a creamy sauce.

Place the chops on a warm platter and pour the sauce over them. This dish is excellent served with boiled rice or *risotto* (page 261).

BRAISED PORK CHOPS WITH MUSHROOMS

Braised pork chops with mushrooms is another "different" method for preparing pork chops and just as delicious as the others. This dish produces a thin sauce merely because it's intended; no attempt should be made to thicken it. To serve, just spoon the pan juices over the chops and the plain boiled rice that is recommended with this dish.

> 4 *pork chops, at least 1 inch thick*
> 1 *tbsp oil*
> 12 *medium mushroom caps*
> 4 *tbsp shallots or green onions*
> *(white stems only), chopped*
> 2/3 *cup stock*
> 1/3 *cup dry white wine*
> 1/2 *tsp thyme*
> *salt*
> *freshly ground pepper*

Preheat the oven to 325°. Trim the excess fat from the chops. Sauté the chops in barely enough oil to cover the bottom of the skillet. When they are browned, transfer the chops to a flat, lidded, oven-proof baking dish large enough for them to lie flat. Arrange the mushroom caps, carefully wiped but not washed, on top of the chops and sprinkle with a bit of salt and freshly ground pepper. Meanwhile, sauté the shallots or onions in the same pan as the chops for about 3 minutes. Add the stock and wine, combined and heated, and boil moderately while scraping all the bits and pieces from the sides and bottom of the pan. Pour the liquid over the chops and mushrooms, sprinkle with the thyme, a bit of salt, and freshly ground pepper. Place the baking dish, covered, in a 325° oven and bake for 1 hour or until the meat is tender to the fork. If necessary, add a bit more stock in order to have about 1/2 cup of pan juices when ready to serve. Plain boiled rice is the perfect accompaniment to this dish.

CÔTES DE PORC AU MOUTARDE [Pork Chops in Mustard Sauce]

Côtes de porc au moutarde is a method for cooking pork chops that is unlike any other I have ever seen, and that covers a lot of ground! The mustard that gives this dish its delightful piquancy must be the Dijon type—the French call it *moutarde blanche* (white mustard)—which is now available at most specialty food counters and on the regular shelves of many supermarkets, at least in the New York area. It is a hot mustard, but it has flavor and really sets this dish apart. Each pork chop should be large enough for one person—about an inch thick.

4	*pork chops, thick and lean*
1	*tbsp lard or oil*
2	*tbsp shallots or green onions, chopped*
1	*tbsp flour*
1/2	*cup stock*
1/2	*cup dry white wine*
1/4	*tsp salt*
	freshly ground pepper
2	*tbsp Dijon-type mustard*

Brown the chops in the lard or oil on both sides over a brisk fire. Then lower the flame, cover the skillet (it should be large enough for the chops to lie flat), and cook for 15 minutes, turning once. Remove the meat and sauté the chopped onions or shallots until soft. Stir in the flour and cook for 3 minutes, stirring constantly. Heat the combined stock and wine to the boiling point and add to the roux. Stir with a wire whip or wooden spoon until smooth; then add the salt and several grinds of pepper. Return the chops to the skillet, cover, and cook over a low fire until the meat is tender—45 minutes to 1 hour. When they are tender, remove the chops to a serving platter and keep warm. Add the mustard to the sauce and blend well. Reheat the sauce, but do not let it boil. Pour the sauce over the chops and serve with boiled rice or *risotto*.

COSTILLAS DE CERDO CON NARANJA [Pork Chops in Orange Sauce]

This recipe for pork chops in orange sauce, given me by a friend in Madrid, is the only one I can remember that combines oranges and pork. But if the golden fruit is good with ducks, why not a porker? By way of an answer, it is! I much prefer this made with freshly squeezed orange juice (just be careful of the seeds) and, since the recipe is based on one chop per consumer, be sure to choose thick ones.

> 4   *pork chops, 1 inch thick*
> *flour*
> *salt*
> *freshly ground pepper*
> 1   *tbsp olive oil*
> 3/4   *cup orange juice*
> 3/4   *cup stock*
> 1   *tbsp sugar*
> 2   *tbsp white raisins*
> 1/4   *tsp fresh nutmeg*
> 1   *tbsp cornstarch dissolved in water*
> 4   *slices peeled orange*
> *parsley, chopped finely*

Mix the flour with a little salt and freshly ground pepper and coat the chops lightly with the mixture. Heat the oil in a pan large enough to hold the chops side by side. Combine the juice, stock, sugar, raisins, and nutmeg in a saucepan and warm till it starts to bubble. Pour this over the browned chops, cover the pan, and simmer slowly for 45 minutes. When it is tender to the fork, remove the meat to a warm serving platter and decorate each chop with a slice of peeled orange. Thicken the liquid with some cornstarch dissolved in a little water (you probably will not need all of it). Pour the sauce over the chops and serve with boiled rice. A little fresh parsley, finely chopped, will add to the appearance of the platter.

PORK ROAST TEDESCO [German Pork Roast]

Pork roast *Tedesco* is a German recipe that I discovered in Italy (I once got an excellent recipe for French bread in Japan!), hence the name—*Tedesco* is the Italian word for *German*. The recipe deviates somewhat from the usual in that it calls for the pork roast to be precarved almost, but not quite, to the bone. This insures thorough cooking and complete penetration of the various flavors.

1	*pork rib roast, 4-5 lb*
	garlic
	salt
	freshly ground pepper
3/4	*cup stock*
3/4	*cup dry white wine*
3	*tbsp onion, chopped*
1	*tsp sugar*
1/2	*tsp Worcestershire sauce*
	rosemary

Have your butcher cut the roast in 1-inch chops, almost to the bone. (Many supermarkets prepare pork roasts like this as a matter of routine.) Preheat the oven to 400°. Rub the meat well with the garlic, then sprinkle lightly with the salt and freshly ground pepper. Put the roast on a rack and let it brown in the 400° oven for 30 minutes. Meanwhile, mix the remaining ingredients and let simmer for 20 minutes without boiling. When the roast is browned, pour the liquid over it, turn the oven down to 350°, and continue cooking for another hour or until the meat is tender. Baste frequently.

When it is tender, remove the roast to a serving platter and keep hot. Boil the remaining liquid down to the consistency of a gravy, scraping all the crusty bits into the sauce. Correct the seasoning and serve with the roast.

KASSLER RIPCHEN KUMMEL [Smoked Pork Chops with Cumin]

Kassler ripchen kummel is an approximation of a dish once served me in Germany for which I could not obtain a recipe. After some experimentation I came up with the following which, quite without modesty, I believe to be as good, if not better, than the original.

There are two types of smoked pork chops—with the bone or without—in the markets around New York. Personally, I prefer the former for this dish because the chops usually are thicker and, besides, pork chops just don't seem like pork chops to me without the bone.

4	smoked pork chops
1	heaping tbsp flour
1	tsp ground cumin
2	tbsp oil
1/2	cup dry white wine
1	cup stock
	thyme
	salt
	freshly ground pepper
3/4	cup sour cream
	paprika

Mix the flour and ground cumin and dredge the chops well on both sides. Sauté the chops in oil until browned, using a skillet with a tight-fitting lid. Heat the stock and wine together and pour over the chops as soon as both sides are golden. Add a pinch of thyme, fresh pepper, and very little salt. Cover and simmer for 30 minutes.

After 30 minutes test the chops with a fork and, if tender, remove to a plate and keep warm. If too much liquid remains in the skillet, turn up the fire to the fullest and reduce the liquid to about 1/4 cup. Remove the skillet from the fire and blend the sour cream into the liquid, mixing well. Return to the fire and heat, but *do not boil.* Correct the seasoning and pour the sauce over the chops on a serving platter. Sprinkle generously with paprika and serve with boiled rice or mashed potatoes.

RÔTI DE PORC AUX NAVETS [Roast Pork with Turnips]

In the outdoor market in Nice early each morning we used to buy the finest little turnips—not much bigger than a crabapple, tender, and endowed with a quietly soft aroma. These were the turnips for which *rôti de porc aux navets* was created, but your chances for finding a dozen such turnips in an urban market are so small that I am recommending the medium ones, quartered.

> 1   3-lb pork roast, loin or leg
> 3   tbsp lard or oil
>   salt
>   freshly ground pepper
> 3   tsp sugar
> 3/4   cup stock
>
> 3   medium-large turnips, quartered, or 12 small turnips,
>   if available

Preheat the oven to 400°. While 1 tablespoon of the fat is heating in a roasting pan, wipe the meat with a paper towel and rub it with salt and fresh pepper. When the fat has covered the bottom of the pan, place the meat in the center, fat side up. Sprinkle with 2 tablespoons of the sugar and put into a 400° oven for about 15 minutes or until well browned. Add 1/4 cup of the stock, heated, turn down the oven to 300°, and bake for another hour, basting regularly.

Peel the turnips and heat the remaining 2 tablespoons of oil in a skillet. Wipe the turnips dry and brown them in the fat. Add the remaining teaspoon of sugar, about 1/4 teaspoon of salt, and several grinds of fresh pepper. Next add 1/4 cup of stock and cover the pan tightly. Turn the fire down and cook for 15 minutes. Remove the turnips from the stock, arrange them around the roast, and add 1/4 cup of stock to the roasting pan. Cook the roast and turnips for another hour or until the meat is tender to the fork. Remove the pork to a warm platter and arrange the turnips around it. Remove the grease from the pan juices, then pour the juices into a gravy boat, and serve on the side.

PORC AUX OLIVES [Pork and Olives]

Porc aux olives—a recipe that has its roots in the olive belt of the French Midi—is an uncomplicated formula for preparing a pork loin in a somewhat different manner. The non-French angle comes in my suggestion that the finished dish be served with *risotto Milanese*. Experience has shown me that the two blend well and, after all, Milan isn't that far from southern France.

1	*3-lb pork loin*
2	*cloves garlic, sliced*
1-1/2	*cups stock*
1/2	*cup dry vermouth*
1/2	*tsp marjoram*
	salt
	freshly ground pepper
1/2	*cup green olives, pitted and halved*
2	*egg yolks*
2	*tbsp heavy cream or* crème fraîche

Preheat the oven to 325°. Make several incisions in the roast with the point of a knife and insert slivers of the garlic buds. Rub the roast with a little salt and a few grinds of fresh pepper. Put the roast, uncovered, in the 325° oven. Combine the stock, vermouth, and marjoram and heat just to the boiling point. When the roast is browned, pour the hot liquid over it and continue cooking, basting regularly, until the roast is done—at least 2 hours. After 1-1/2 hours add the olives to the sauce.

Remove the roast to a warm serving platter. Pour most of the fat off the pan juices; then adjust until you have about 1 cup of liquid, adding a bit more stock if necessary. Bring to the boil, scraping the sides and bottom of the pan carefully. Mix the egg yolks and cream thoroughly, then stir in 1 tablespoon of the hot juice. Off the fire, stir the combined eggs and cream into the sauce and stir until thick.

This dish goes perfectly with *risotto Milanese (page 264).*

PORC AU RIZ À LA YOUGOSLAVIE [Pork with Rice à la Yugoslavia]

I discovered *porc au riz à la Yougoslavie* in France, and I'll admit I haven't the slightest idea where Yugoslavia comes into the picture. (Personally, I would have voted for Hungary.) All I know for certain is that this is a flavorful colorful method for preparing pork that is neither chops nor roast. I prefer shoulder, boned and cut into one-inch pieces.

1	lb stewing pork, cut up
1-1/2	tbsp oil
3/4	medium onion, chopped
1	clove garlic, crushed
1	tbsp paprika
1	cup dry rice
1/2	tsp salt
	freshly ground pepper
1/2	cup tomato juice
1	tbsp tomato paste
2-1/2	cups stock
2	sweet red peppers or 2 whole pimientos

Sauté the pork in the oil until well browned, cover the pan, and cook another 15 minutes. Remove the meat from the pan and keep warm. Add the onion to the oil and cook until soft, and then add the crushed garlic. Pour in the rice and stir well to make sure every grain is well coated with oil. Mix in the paprika, salt, and several generous grinds of fresh pepper; then return the meat. Pour the stock, tomato juice, and tomato paste, combined and heated, into the rice and add the sweet red peppers, cut or broken into pieces the size of a silver dollar. (If you are using pimientos, hold them until the rice is nearly cooked.) Cover the pan and cook over a very low fire until the rice has absorbed all the liquid and the meat is tender. Fluff the rice with a fork and serve from the casserole.

SPEZZATINO DI MAIALE CON FETTUCINI [Braised Pork with Noodles]

Braised pork with noodles is one recipe in which the end result does not
bring the two starring components into actual contact. The pork and the
noodles are served separately, but they were served as one entrée when I
first tasted them and they obviously belong togther. Besides, the noodles
are served in my favorite manner and can easily be prepared by themselves
whenever a quick, easy, and delicious pasta course is desired.

1-1/2	*lb lean pork, cut into 1-inch pieces*
2	*tbsp oil*
2	*tbsp butter*
2	*onions*
2	*stalks celery*
2	*carrots*
1	*clove garlic, crushed*
1	*tbsp flour*
3/4	*cup stock*
1	*tbsp tomato paste*
	pinch of oregano
	pinch of basil
about 1/2	*tsp salt*
	freshly ground pepper
1/2	*cup dry vermouth*

NOODLES

1/2	*lb egg noodles, 1/4-inch wide*
about 4	*quarts boiling water, salted*
3	*oz Parmesan cheese, grated*
2	*tbsp butter, soft but not melted*

Sauté the pork in the combined oil and butter until browned; then
remove with a slotted spoon and keep warm. While the meat is cooking,
chop the onions, celery, and carrots into small (about 1/4-inch) bits. When

you remove the meat, put the vegetables and garlic into the same oil, sprinkle with the flour, and cook, stirring often, over a moderate fire for 5 minutes. Pour in the combined stock and tomato paste, a pinch each of oregano and basil, salt, and several good grinds of fresh pepper. Return the pork meat to the pan and heat through; then turn the fire low and simmer for 45 minutes or until the meat is tender to the fork. Stir in the vermouth, taste for salt, and simmer another 15 minutes. Serve with the pasta.

While the meat is cooking, drop the noodles into the well-salted water, boiling hard. Cook according to the instructions on the package or until the noodles have the right degree of tenderness (not too much!) when tasted. The butter should be allowed to stand in a warm place for at least 30 minutes until soft, but not melted. As soon as they are done, drain the noodles and pour them into a hot serving bowl. Add the soft butter and the freshly grated Parmesan. Toss until thoroughly mixed and serve immediately—with the *spezzatino* sharing the place of honor.

RÔTI DE PORC AUX PRUNEAUX [Pork Roast with Prunes]

The combination of meat and fruit is rather commonplace in continental cookery, particularly in Switzerland and Germany. *Rôti de porc aux pruneaux* however, is French—and as delicious as any type of pork roast I have ever tasted. The recipe is simple once you get the fruit inside the roast, and even that isn't too difficult if you freeze the pitted prunes first—a *tour de chef* I did *not* learn in France. You should have four people ready to greet this roast when it emerges from the oven.

8	*prunes, pitted*
1	*loin pork roast, about 2-1/2 lb*
	salt
	freshly ground pepper
1	*cup stock*
2	*tbsp Madeira or port*
2	*tsp cornstarch dissolved in water*

Place the pitted prunes in the coldest part of your freezer and let them remain overnight until they are like stones.

Have the butcher cut the bones at the back of the roast, but do not remove them. Preheat the oven to 350°. Trim off almost all the exterior fat. With a thin-bladed knife pierce the roast from end to end through the thick of the meat. Enlarge this hole to about 1/2 inch, using the steel from a carving set or the handle of a wooden spoon. When the hole is ready, force as many of the frozen prunes as possible into the opening, working from both sides if necessary. When you are satisfied that the cavity is filled, sprinkle the roast well with salt and freshly ground pepper and put it in an open roasting pan (a 12-inch glass skillet is ideal). Put it in a 350° oven, bone side down. While the meat is browning, heat the combined stock and Madeira just to the boiling point. If the roast starts to exude prune pulp from the extremes of the cavity, scrape it up with a knife and spread it on top of the roast like a glaze. Don't let it scorch on the bottom of the pan. When the meat is nicely browned, spoon the heated wine and stock over it and let it cook for about 2 hours, basting often with the stock. (You don't have to worry about overcooking a pork roast.) If the liquid starts to cook away, add more wine and stock in the same proportions, so that there will be about a scant cup of liquid remaining when the roast is removed. Thicken this liquid with the cornstarch and water, cooking just enough to effect a perfect blend. Slice the roast (at the table, if desired) and serve the sauce on the side, preferably with creamy mashed potatoes.

COSTILLAS DE CERDO ARAGONESE *[Pork Chops, Aragon Style]*

This recipe for *costillas de cerdo* originated in Zaragoza, capital of ancient Aragon and the only city I ever visited that had two operating cathedrals (the bishop shuttled between them!). If she had introduced Henry VIII to this Aragonese specialty, Katherine of Aragon might have saved her marriage and the whole of England might have escaped excommunication! Incidentally, thin pork chops are *out* for this dish.

> 4   *pork chops, 1 inch thick*
>
>
> *MARINADE*
>
> 1/3   *cup olive oil*
>   2   *cloves garlic, crushed*
> 1/2   *tsp freshly ground pepper*
> 1/4   *tsp powdered cloves*

Marinate the chops in the remaining ingredients for 4 or 5 hours, turning regularly. When ready to cook the chops, strain the marinade and divide the oil into two equal parts.

>   *flour*
>   2 *medium onions, minced*
>   1 *tbsp wine vinegar*
>   1/2 *cup stock*
>   1/2 *cup dry white wine*
>   *salt*
> about 1/4   *tsp freshly ground pepper*
>   *pinch of saffron*

Dry the chops, flour lightly, and then brown in half the oil from the marinade. In a second skillet sauté the onions in the rest of the oil until golden. Add the vinegar and cook until it is evaporated. Add the meat to the onions and with the stock, warmed, rinse the pan in which the chops were cooked. Scrape well, making sure that all the browned bits are included when you add it to the meat and onions. Pour in the wine and grind in the fresh pepper. Taste for salt. Mix the saffron in a bit of the warm liquid and, when it dissolves, stir it into the cooking juices. Cook, uncovered, until the meat is tender and the liquid is reduced and slightly thickened. Serve with rice.

RÔTI DE PORC À L'ORANGE [Roast Pork and Orange]

Oranges have long been used in cooking to complement the savory richness of a duck. *Duckling à l'orange* is familiar to menus all over the United States. But seemingly not as many cooks are as aware that oranges can perform the same magic for fresh pork. I have included a recipe for pork chops cooked with orange in this chapter—one that I found in Spain—but *rôti de porc à l'orange* is for a full roast and comes from the French Côte d'Azur where oranges grow, but seldom ripen. Consequently, we used to prepare this roast with oranges from North Africa, but the ones from Florida, Texas, or California will serve just as well.

1	*3-lb pork roast, leg or loin*
3	*tbsp butter*
2	*tbsp shallots or green onions, chopped*
1/2	*cup stock*
1/2	*cup orange juice*
about 1	*tsp salt*
	freshly ground pepper
1/2	*tsp thyme*
1	*orange*
1	*1-oz jigger Grand Marnier or curaçao*
1	*tbsp cornstarch*

Preheat the oven to 350°. Brown the roast on all sides in the butter, sautéing the shallots or onions at the same time until golden. Pour the combined stock and orange juice, warmed, over the roast and add the salt, thyme, and several grinds of fresh pepper. Roast for a minimum of 2 hours, basting regularly.

Cut the orange in two and peel one half very thinly, so that very little white pulp is included with the outer rind. Cut this rind into narrow 1-inch strips and blanch them for 2 minutes in boiling water. Remove and dry them. Cut the other half of the orange into thin half-slices. When it is done, remove the roast to a warm platter and surround with the orange slices. Remove as much fat as possible from the cooking juices and, if necessary, add enough stock to approximate 1 cup of liquid. Bring this liquid to a boil, scraping the pan carefully; then add the blanched orange rind and a jigger of liqueur. Add 1 tablespoon of liquid to the cornstarch and mix until smooth. Add this to the sauce, a little at a time, stirring constantly; cook until you have achieved the desired consistency. Correct the seasoning. Pour some of the sauce over the meat, orange slices, and serve the remainder on the side. This dish is a natural for wild rice.

BAKED "BARBECUED" RIBS

During our years in the Far East and Europe we always had a yard or a terrace to support a barbecue of some type, but our New York apartments have been different. We developed baked "barbecued" ribs to fill the barbecue void, and it works very nicely with spare ribs. Of course, the ribs aren't actually barbecued, but who's complaining? Not many outdoor cooks are going to top this method of preparing ribs. Incidentally, the sauce is essentially the same as the Forbes Park sauce in chapter six, except that the stock is used to steam the ribs before it is added.

4	*lb meaty spare ribs*
1	*cup stock*
1	*bay leaf*
2	*tbsp oil*
1/2	*medium onion, chopped*
1	*clove garlic, crushed*
1	*cup stock (above)*
1	*tbsp brown sugar*
1	*tbsp vinegar*
2	*tbsp tomato paste*
1	*tbsp Worcestershire sauce*
1	*tsp soy sauce*
	salt
	freshly ground pepper

Put the ribs into a heavy Dutch oven-type pan, pour the stock over them, add the bay leaf, and cover the pan tightly. Steam the ribs over a low fire for 1 hour, then remove, and strain the stock for use in the sauce. If too much fat has accumulated, spoon off as much as possible to leave a nearly pure stock. Discard the bay leaf.

Heat the oil in a saucepan and sauté the onion until it is lightly browned. Add the crushed garlic, and cook another minute or so. Pour in the stock you have reclaimed from the ribs and add all the other ingredients except the salt and pepper. Mix thoroughly; then simmer, covered, for about 30 minutes. Add salt to taste plus several good grinds of fresh pepper. Preheat the oven to 350°. Dip the ribs in this sauce and arrange them flat in the bottom of a large baking pan. Put the pan of ribs, uncovered, into a 350° oven and bake for 1 hour, basting every 10 minutes with more of the sauce. When they are done, remove the ribs to a hot platter. If any sauce is left from basting, pour it into the baking dish, add 1/2 cup of stock, and bring to a boil. Scrape the bottom and sides of the pan carefully to accumulate all the browned bits. Correct the seasoning. Pour some of the sauce over the ribs and serve the remainder on the side.

PORC GOULASCH AU NORMANDE [Braised Pork in Cider]

Normandy is noted in culinary circles for its cheeses and dairy products, its calvados (apple brandy), and its cider, not necessarily sweet. Any dish that bears the Normandy label is certain to include one of these ingredients, and with *porc goulasch au Normande* it is cider. The idea of using cider in cooking is not new to the United States (I was brought up on cider apple butter in the Midwest), but there are few American dishes that also include chestnuts as a basic component. When you master this dish, you will be one of a small minority of Americans who have combined cider and chestnuts in the preparation of a ragout—and you can be sure it is an elite corps! This is a recipe for four chestnut and cider buffs.

16	chestnuts
1-1/2	lb pork (boned shoulder), cut into 1-1/2-inch pieces
2	tbsp oil
2	onions, chopped coarsely
about 1/2	tsp salt
	freshly ground pepper
1/2	tsp paprika
1	tbsp flour
1/2	cup stock
3/4	cup cider
1	bay leaf
	marjoram
	thyme

The biggest problem in any recipe that includes chestnuts is shelling and peeling them — so let's get that off your mind first of all. Take a sharp knife and cut a thin strip off the flat side of each chestnut, exposing the meat. Put the nuts into cold water and, over a hot flame, bring to a full boil. Boil for about 2 minutes, then remove from the fire, and shell with a heavy knife while they are still warm. Once the outer shell is removed, the inner skin must be peeled away; then the nuts are ready for use.

Sauté the pork, together with the coarsely chopped onions, in the oil until both are lightly browned. Sprinkle the salt and several grinds of pepper on top; then stir in the paprika and make sure the meat is completely coated. Use more paprika, if necessary. Next blend in the flour and mix carefully with the oil. Warm the combined stock and cider and, when it reaches the boiling point, pour into the roux and stir until smooth. Add the bay leaf and a pinch each of the marjoram and thyme. Cook, covered, over a very low flame for 45 minutes. Then add the peeled chestnuts, whole, and cook—still covered—another 45 minutes. Keep a close eye on the liquid and add a bit of stock, if needed. When the meat and chestnuts are tender, remove any surplus fat from the sauce and serve immediately. A green salad is the perfect accompaniment.

CHINESE PORK CHOPS

The fact that Chinese pork chops are prepared in a sweet-sour sauce undoubtedly accounts for their name because the pork chop, in that form, simply does not exist in China. We did find this recipe in the Far East, however, but in Manila, where most of the Chinese-Filipinos don't take chopsticks too seriously. We use this version for the two of us, but it can easily be doubled.

2	*tbsp oil*
1	*clove garlic, sliced*
2	*pork chops, 1 inch thick*
2	*tbsp cornstarch*
1	*carrot*
2	*green onions*
1/2	*green pepper*
1/4	*cup white vinegar*
1/4	*cup sugar*
1/2	*cup stock*
5	*water chestnuts, sliced*
2	*tbsp cornstarch mixed with water*
	salt
	freshly ground pepper

Sauté the garlic in the oil until browned, then discard. Dust the chops liberally with the cornstarch and brown in the same oil. After turning once, cover the the pan and cook slowly until tender—about 45 minutes.

Cut the carrot in two, lengthwise, and with a potato peeler slice off about 10 very thin slices from the center; discard the rest. Cut the onions and carrot strips into 1-inch lengths and break the pepper, cleaned, into bite-size bits.

When it is tender, remove the meat to a warm plate. Put the carrot, onions, and pepper in the same fat and sauté for just a moment. Add the stock, water chestnuts, vinegar, sugar, salt, and pepper and cook for about 2 minutes, stirring well to get the browned bits off the pan. Add the constarch and water mixture, a little at a time, until the sauce achieves the proper consistency—rather thick. Return the chops to the sauce, cover the pan, and let simmer slowly for 2 minutes. Serve over boiled rice.

JAMBON À LA CRÈME [Ham in Cream Sauce]

Jambon à la crème is a typical example of how the French love to serve ham in thin slices, even when prepared as an entrée. It is a simple dish to prepare and perfect for a light lunch or supper. The French would definitely serve it as an entrée, which in France is *not* the main course; an entrée on the French menu is a dish served between *(entre)* the introductory and main courses. This *plat* would not be considered substantial enough for a main course along the Rhône, but, regardless of how it is served, it is delicious.

8	*slices boiled ham*
2 to 4	*tbsp fresh butter*
1/2	*cup dry white wine*
1	*tbsp flour*
3/4	*cup stock*
1/2	*cup* crème fraîche *(page 282) or sour cream*

Have your dealer slice 8 slices of ham uniformly about 1/16-inch thick. Melt 2 tablespoons of fresh butter in a heavy skillet and cook each piece of ham individually on both sides, adding more butter as necessary. When it is cooked but not browned, roll each slice and place it on a very warm serving platter.

When all the slices are cooked and arranged on the platter, pour the wine into the cooking juices and, over a very hot fire, reduce by at least one-half. Stir the flour, mixed with a little water, into the liquid and blend with a whisk. When it is smooth, add the stock and continue to cook over a very hot fire until the sauce thickens. Off the fire, stir the cream into the sauce and simmer very slowly for 3 to 5 minutes. Pour the sauce over the ham and serve with boiled rice.

JAMON DE JEREZ [Ham with Sherry]

Jamon de jerez a Spanish recipe for preparing ham steaks, immediately brings up the question of what a ham steak really is. And the answer, of course, is whatever you choose to make it. My definition is "a piece of ham not less than three-eighths of an inch thick and large enough for one person." The steaks in this recipe should be about four by five inches if canned ham is used, or about a half slice if the steak is cut directly from the ham.

The flavor of this ham, incidentally, can be altered considerably by the choice of sherry. In Ibiza, where I first tasted *jamon de jerez, Tio Pepe* (trademark of a low-priced—in Spain—dry sherry) was used, but a very different result can be obtained by using a cream sherry.

4	*ham steaks*
2	*tbsp butter*
1	*tbsp shallots or onion, chopped*
1-1/2	*tbsp flour*
1/2	*cup stock*
1/2	*cup sherry*
1	*tsp tomato paste*
	salt
	freshly ground pepper
1	*cup* crème fraîche *(page 282) or sour cream*

Sauté the steaks in the butter until lightly browned, then retire to a hot plate, and keep warm. Measure the amount of juice remaining in the skillet and discard all but 2 tablespoons. Put the shallots or onion in the pan and sauté until tender; then add the flour and cook slowly, stirring constantly so that the flour will not burn, for about 2 minutes. Add the combined stock and sherry, heated just to the boiling point. Grind in a bit of fresh pepper and, if the ham is not salty, add a bit of salt; be careful not to oversalt. When a creamy sauce is achieved, remove the skillet from the fire and blend in the cream. Return to the fire and heat gently without boiling. Arrange the steaks on a warm serving platter and pour the sauce over them.

HAM AND EGGS GOLDENROD

Ham and eggs goldenrod is our traditional Easter Sunday breakfast—a dish that has evolved over the years from simple creamed eggs on toast to a rather sophisticated offering that can brighten any brunch menu. The ham steaks herein specified are visualized as full-fledged slices, each sufficient for two persons. If canned hams are used, each steak should be of a size sufficient for one person.

2	*ham steaks, halved*
3	*eggs, hard-boiled*
3	*tbsp butter*
3	*tbsp shallots or green onions, chopped*
2	*tbsp flour*
1	*cup stock*
1/2	*cup heavy cream*
	salt
	freshly ground pepper
	pinch of nutmeg
2	*dashes Tabasco*
2	*dashes cayenne pepper*
2	*tbsp Madeira*
	parsley, chopped

While preparing the eggs, broil the ham steaks until browned on both sides.

Shell the eggs, chop the whites coarsely, and force the yolks through a sieve. Sauté the shallots or onion in the butter, being careful not to brown. Add the flour and cook gently, stirring constantly, until done—about 2 minutes. Add the stock, warmed, and stir until a smooth *velouté* sauce is achieved. When the sauce is quite thick, add the cream, salt, pepper, nutmeg, Tabasco, and cayenne pepper. Continue to stir until the sauce begins to thicken again, and then add the egg whites. Turn the fire low and let simmer until the sauce is quite thick; it must not be runny. Spoon the sauce over the ham steaks and top with the egg yolk. A bit of chopped parsley adds color.

SCHINKEN IN MADEIRA [Ham in Madeira]

I have never been able to understand the almost universal preference in the United States for sherry over either Madeira or Marsala for cooking. In my book sherry has a definite place in the kitchen, but Madeira, which is easily available and just as reasonably priced as *good* sherry ("cooking sherry" is for the juvenile delinquents), blends itself into infinitely more kitchen triumphs with greater finesse. The French and the Germans both prefer Madeira (Italians lean to Marsala, and there's nothing wrong with that), and so do good cooks all over the world. *Schinken* in Madeira, from Germany, is a sample of what you can achieve with good ham and good wine from a Portuguese island. The thickness of the ham should provide for four reasonably hungry *Schinken* votaries.

> 1 *ham steak, 1-1/2-inch thick*
> 1 *tsp oil*
> 1 *medium onion, chopped*
>   *salt*
>   *freshly ground pepper*
> 1/2 *cup Madeira*
> 3/4 *cup stock*
> 1 *bay leaf*
> 1 *tbsp cornstarch dissolved in water*

Heat the oil in a skillet large enough to hold the slice of ham. Brown the ham lightly on both sides, then remove, and keep warm. Sauté the onion in the same fat until golden, and add a pinch of salt and several grinds of fresh pepper. Return the steak to the pan and pour over it the combined wine and stock, heated almost to the boiling point. When the stock starts to bubble, turn the fire low, add the bay leaf and simmer, covered, for about 45 minutes or until the steak is tender to a fork. Remove the steak to a warm serving platter and carve. Remove the bay leaf, thicken the sauce with the cornstarch dissolve in very little water. Pour over ham and serve with little boiled potatoes and with pureed chestnuts as a vegetable.

HAM AND CHEESE CASSEROLE

Ham and cheese casserole is a perennial favorite from Indiana (as far as we are concerned)—a recipe we have carried all over the world and found to be equally delicious in any clime. The whole casserole can be put together hours in advance, if desired, and placed in the oven an hour before serving, leaving the cook with most of the evening to devote to guests or the bridge game. This is another excellent one-dish meal, needing only a green salad to make it complete.

2	*tbsp butter*
1-1/2	*tbsp flour*
about 1/4	*tsp salt*
	freshly ground pepper
1-1/2	*cups stock*
	cayenne pepper
2	*tbsp heavy cream*
3	*medium potatoes, sliced thinly*
2	*medium onions, sliced thinly*
1	*lb ham, sliced*
1	*cup cheddar cheese, coarsely shredded*

Heat the butter in a saucepan and cook the flour until you have a golden roux. Add the salt and several grinds of pepper, and then pour in the stock, heated to the boiling point. Stir until the sauce is smooth, then add a pinch of cayenne. Off the fire, stir in the cream, mix thoroughly, and set aside without further cooking.

Preheat the oven to 350°. Butter a large oven-proof casserole. Put a layer of sliced onions on the bottom and cover with a layer of potatoes, then a layer of ham with a sprinkle of cheddar on top. Pour about 1/4 of the sauce over the ham and repeat the layers—onions, potatoes, ham, grated cheese, and sauce—until the casserole is full. The top layer should be of potatoes. Pour the remainder of the sauce over the contents until the liquid shows slightly above the potatoes. Sprinkle the rest of the cheddar over the top and bake in the oven for 1 hour or until the potatoes are done. This casserole will keep itself hot for at least 15 minutes after being removed from the oven.

SCHINKEN IN WEIN [Ham in Wine Sauce]

Schinken in wein is a good way to prepare a piece of precooked ham—a two- or three-pound chunk of canned ham, for instance. This German recipe called for table wine originally, but I have found that the Madeira, while hardly German, does blend better with the flavor of the *schinken*.

> 1   piece precooked ham, 2 - 3 lbs
> 1   medium onion, chopped
> 1   tbsp oil
> 1   tbsp flour
> 3/4   cup stock
> 3/4   cup Madeira
>   thyme
>   freshly ground pepper
>   salt, if necesary

Preheat the oven to 350°. Place the ham in an uncovered baking dish or pan. Sauté the onion in the oil until golden, using a small skillet. When the onion is transparent, add the flour and cook well without browning, stirring constantly. Stir in the combined wine and stock, warmed, together with 2 grinds of fresh pepper and a pinch of thyme; then simmer over a low flame until completely blended. Pour the sauce over the ham and bake in the oven for 45 minutes, basting frequently. If the liquid becomes too low, add more stock, a couple of tablespoons at a time.

Remove the ham from the liquid and slice on a serving platter. Taste the sauce for salt (it may not need any if the ham is salty) and pour over the meat.

JAMBON AU GRUYÈRE [Ham and Swiss Cheese]

Ham and Swiss cheese is a common combination in the United States, but it usually ends up on rye bread with mustard. This ham and Swiss includes the mustard, but from that point it strays way out in the French equivalent of left field. It is an unusual taste sensation, and one I believe you will enjoy. Ham and Swiss cheese, accompanied by only a crisp salad, makes a delightful light lunch. This recipe allots two ham slices to a person:

8	*slices ham*
1	*slice Swiss cheese, 1/2-inch thick*
3	*tbsp butter*
3	*tbsp flour*
2	*cups stock*
	salt
	freshly ground pepper
1	*tsp wine vinegar*
1	*tsp Dijon-type (hot) mustard*
2	*tbsp rum, light or dark*
2	*tbsp bread crumbs*
	butter, melted

The ham slices should be thin enough to roll easily without breaking, but thick enough to have substance. The Swiss cheese (prefer Gruyère to Emmenthaler for this dish because it usually is more solid) should be cut into 8 1/2-inch sticks, about the same length as the width of the ham. Roll each piece of cheese in a slice of ham and place on the bottom of an oiled oven-proof casserole large enough to hold them all, side by side.

Preheat the oven to 450°. Melt the 3 tablespoons of butter in a saucepan and stir in the flour to make a smooth roux. Stir constantly. Heat the stock to the boiling point and pour it into the roux. Stir hard with a wire whip or its equivalent until you have a smooth *velouté*. Add a pinch of salt, several grinds of pepper, the vinegar, mustard, and rum. Simmer slowly for 5 minutes then pour over the ham. Sprinkle the bread crumbs and top with a little melted butter. Bake in the oven, uncovered, for 15 minutes. Serve at once.

JAMBON DE FÊTE AU PORTO [Fiesta Ham with Port Wine]

If you are looking for a really festive method for preparing ham—one your neighbor or delicatessen won't duplicate—try *jambon de fête au Porto,* a recipe I discovered in France several years ago. I have adapted it for a half ham to make it available for smaller families, but a whole ham can be prepared by increasing the quantities by about one-half. This recipe orginally specified a raw ham, but, because precooked hams seem to be the absolute rule in the United States, I have also adjusted to that fact of life.

1/2	*precooked ham, about 7 lbs*
1	*large onion, chopped*
1	*large tomato, peeled, seeded, and chopped*
1	*clove garlic, minced*
1-1/2	*cup port wine (ruby port preferred)*
1/2	*cup stock*
1	*bay leaf*
	thyme
	salt
	freshly ground pepper
1	*egg yolk*
1/2	*cup* crème fraîche *(page 282) or heavy cream*

Preheat the oven to 375°. Trim the skin off the ham very carefully, leaving a generous layer of fat. Score the fat with a knife and put the ham into a roasting pan. Arrange the onion, garlic, and tomato around the ham and pour over it the stock and 1 cup of wine, combined and warmed.

Add the bay leaf, a pinch each of thyme and salt, and several grinds of fresh pepper. Put the ham into a 375° oven and bake, uncovered, for 1-1/2 hours, basting frequently. If the liquid gets low, add more stock; there should always be about 1 cup of liquid in the pan. At the end of 1-1/2 hours, remove the ham to a warm platter and let set at least 30 minutes before carving.

Put the liquid and vegetables remaining in the roasting pan into a blender or through a food mill until smooth. Pour into a saucepan and add the remaining 1/2 cup of port. Heat just to the boiling point; then, off the fire, add the cream and egg yolk, previously mixed, and blend into the sauce thoroughly. Now return the pan to the fire and boil until the sauce starts to thicken. Carve the ham and arrange the slices on a warm serving platter. Pour some of the sauce over it and serve the remainder on the side.

Jambon de fête is excellent served with baked sweet potatoes and with pureed chestnuts (page 245) on the side.

HAM AND BAKED SAUERKRAUT

For most of my life I was not what might be termed an all-out *aficionado* of sauerkraut. I didn't particularly dislike it, but it stirred no adrenalin and I usually continued on down the menu. My wife, on the other hand, has always loved sauerkraut, probably due to her Pennsylvania Dutch ancestry, and for years she quested a method of preparing the dish that would win me over. Ham and baked sauerkraut is it! This recipe, inspired by a meal of *choucroute garnie* she once enjoyed in a Marseilles restaurant with the improbable name of *Tavern Charlie*, is geared to the appetites of four people.

> 1   *ham steak, center cut, 1 inch thick*
> 2   *tbsp oil*
> 2   *cans sauerkraut (about 14 oz each)*
> 3/4 *cup stock*

Cut the ham steak into four equal pieces and brown well in the oil. Drain the sauerkraut thoroughly, discard the juice (or drink it, if that happens to be your cup of tea), and pour the sauerkraut into a saucepan with no other liquid. Set the pan on a sheet of foil, doubled, on as low a flame as possible and steam the sauerkraut for 20 minutes, stirring occasionally. Remove the browned ham from the skillet and pour in the stock, warmed. Scrape the skillet carefully until all the browned bits are absorbed by the stock; then put the sauerkraut into the stock and cook at high heat for 5 minutes. Preheat the oven to 350°. When the sauerkraut is cooked as indicated, pour it and the stock into an oven-proof casserole and arrange the ham on top. Cover the casserole and cook the ham and sauerkraut for 30 minutes. If you are not ready to serve at that time, you can lower the oven to 250°, add 2 tablespoons of stock, and let it cook, still covered, another 15 or 20 minutes. According to my wife, mashed potatoes are a *must* with this dish.

HAM AND NOODLES

Ham and noodles is an ideal dish for using the remains of a baked ham without the impression of leftovers. It is also good enough to justify buying the ham specifically for this purpose. This recipe dates back to our days in Italy when we could buy the noodles freshly cut, but the dry noodles are perfectly acceptable. This casserole should take care of four appetites.

2	*tbsp onion, chopped*
2-1/2	*tbsp butter*
1/2	*small green pepper*
2-1/2	*tbsp flour*
1-1/2	*cup stock*
1/2	*cup milk*
1	*cup cheese, grated*

2 *tbsp Madeira or sherry*
   cayenne pepper
   salt
   freshly ground pepper

8 *oz egg noodles, 1/4-inch width*
3 *quarts water, salted*
2 *cups cooked ham, cut into bite-size pieces*
   milk, if necessary
   paprika

Preheat the oven to 350°. Sauté the onion in the butter until soft, add the pepper, cut into thin 1-inch slivers, and cook another 3 minutes. Add the flour, blend into the butter, and cook over a low flame for at least 2 minutes. Add the stock, warmed, to the flour, stirring constantly; when blended, add the milk and 2/3 cup of the cheese. (We always used Emmenthaler in Europe with some grated Parmesan, but I really prefer the mixture of sharp cheddar and Parmesan, grated together.) When the sauce is creamy, add the Madeira and taste for seasoning.

Meanwhile, cook the noodles in the salted water until done, but still firm to the bite *(al dente)*. Strain and put them into a mixing bowl, add the ham and the cheese sauce, and mix thoroughly. Pour into a buttered oven-proof casserole. If the mixture looks at all dry, add a little milk, pouring it in on the side. Top the noodles with a few dabs of butter and sprinkle with the remaining cheese and a generous helping of paprika. Bake in the oven for 30 minutes.

JAMBON MADÈRE [Ham Steaks with Madeira]

One of the most difficult cuts of meat to obtain in either France or Italy is the ham steak. There seems to be an unwritten law in both countries that requires the ham to be sold and served in paper-thin slices. If he wants the thicker slice, one usually has to buy the whole or half ham and carve it himself.

Nevertheless, we did fall heir to a good ham steak once in a while, and *jambon Madère* was one of our favorite ways to prepare it. Today, with ham steaks as available as the nearest meat counter, this is a regular feature of our menu planning. This recipe assumes that each ham steak will be large enough for two persons.

2   ham steaks, 3/4 inch thick
2   heaping tbsp orange marmalade
1   level tbsp dry mustard

1/4   cup stock
1   jigger (2 oz) Madeira or Marsala
1   tbsp cornstarch dissolved in water

Preheat the oven to 400°. Blend the marmalade and dry mustard thoroughly and spread on top of the steaks. Place the steaks side by side in the bottom of a large baking pan and bake in the oven until slightly browned.

Remove the steaks to a hot serving platter and keep warm. Add the stock to the juices remaining in the bottom of the pan and stir until all the juices and browned bits are absorbed. Add the Madeira and let the sauce cook down by at least one-third, adding a little of the cornstarch dissolved in cold water to thicken slightly. Pour the sauce over the steaks and serve at once, preferably with mashed yams.

If you decide to bake only 1 steak for 2 persons, the amount of the sauce should remain about the same.

GLAZED HAM LOAF

Glazed ham loaf is beyond doubt the best method I've ever found for using the remains of the ham when your appetite demands a change. This recipe produces a ham loaf which not only is a delight to the palate but also has eye appeal, thanks to the basting process. It has the added advantage of being as good when sliced cold as hot. Glazed ham loaf is very good with baked potatoes. For four people, plus a little, use the following.

1 1/2   *lb cooked ham*
1/2   *lb raw veal*
1   *small onion, minced*
1/2   *tsp thyme*
1/2   *tsp marjoram*
1   *tbsp Worcestershire sauce*
1/2   *tsp salt*
2   *eggs, lightly beaten*
3/4   *cup stock*
1/4   *cup milk*
8   *crackers, finely crushed*

1/4   *cup brown sugar*
1   *tsp dry mustard*
1   *cup stock (optional)*
1   *tsp cornstarch dissolved in water (optional)*

Preheat the oven to 350°. Put the ham and veal through a meat grinder or have your butcher do it for you; then blend with the onion, thyme, marjoram, Worcestershire sauce, and salt. Stir the lightly beaten eggs into the meat, then 1/4 cup of the stock and the milk. Add the cracker crumbs, a little at a time, until you achieve a firmness that will allow the meat to hold its shape. You may not need all the crumbs, or you may need a bit more. Form the meat into a loaf and put it into a baking pan. Bake the loaf for 1-1/2 hours, basting frequently with the sauce. To prepare the sauce, combine the brown sugar and mustard, then stir in the remaining cup of stock, warmed. When it is cooked, let the loaf stand for 15 minutes before carving. If you want a sauce to go with it, add 1 cup of stock to the cooking juices and scrape the pan well as the stock comes to a boil; then, off the fire, thicken with 1 teaspoon of cornstarch dissolved in a little water. Correct the seasoning and serve on the side.

JAMBON PERSILÉ [Jellied Ham with Parsley]

In France a good butcher is very often an accomplished cook, particularly in preparing pâtés, sausages, terrines, and all forms of *charcuteries.* During my years in Nice the number-one chopping block at the Boucherie Anglaise was presided over by Jean Petit, a master butcher who would bone a shoulder of lamb with the sure skill of a surgeon, then season the interior carefully before rolling and tying it! Every afternoon he would disappear into the shop's basement kitchen to prepare the specialties for the next day, and one of his best was *jambon persilé*. This is not his recipe, as he always started his stock from scratch, using one or more calves feet to provide the gelatin. Since calves feet are not easy to come by unless you own a calf, I start this formula with good rich white stock.

1-1/2	lb cooked ham, including some fat
1-1/2	quarts (6 cups) jelled white stock
2	cups dry white wine
1	bay leaf
4	shallots or 2 green onions, chopped
	thyme
	chervil
	tarragon
1/2	cup fresh parsley, chopped
1	tbsp wine vinegar
6	peppercorns
	salt

Separate the fat from the lean ham and cut both into 1/2-inch cubes. Set the fat cubes aside, but dump the lean ones into the combined stock and wine. Add the shallots or onions, salt, peppercorns, bay leaf, and a pinch each of the thyme, chervil, and tarragon. (The herbs can be varied.) Bring the liquid to a boil, then turn the flame low, and simmer until the meat is very tender. Remove the meat to a bowl with a slotted spoon, and then strain the liquid. Put the liquid back and reduce over a hot flame to about 1-1/2 cups. Let it cool; then add the wine vinegar and chopped parsley, just as it starts to thicken. Mix the cooked ham with the fat bits and pour the cooled stock over them. Stir as the stock starts to jell, then chill completely. Serve as an hors d'oeuvre or as a luncheon entrée.

CHAPTER VI

Sauces

Sauces enhance good meat but
They <u>never</u> conceal poor quality.

ANON

I am sometimes asked (and not too kindly!) why I—a small-town boy from the Gravy Belt of the Midwest—have suddenly begun to speak of "sauces," apparently relegating my native gravies to that nebulous place called limbo.

Nothing could be further from the truth! All my life I have been a devotee of the gravy boat (as witness my generous waistline), but at the same time I have learned that continental sauces are something else again. About the only thing they have in common with gravy is the fact that they are both founded in cooking juices, and both are invariably more tender than the meat.

In France, for example, a cook almost never uses water or milk in the preparation of a sauce except, perhaps, the simple white (béchamel) sauce, and even then he is likely to prefer cream. The accepted ingredients for a "sauce" include stock, cream, butter, eggs, egg yolks, and wine, among other things (not all at once, thank heaven!) and flour is not the only thickening agent. The end result can differ considerably from our familiar "gravy," and quite often the difference will bring cheers from the consumer.

When I first outlined this book, I envisioned a long list of sauce recipes because there are so countless many that have their base in the stockpot. But as I brought the work to completion, I realized that most of the many sauces included in this book are presented as an integral part of the dish they complement and thus are difficult to divorce. The important thing is to understand that the same techniques can be applied to other dishes, once you have the knack, and the possibilities are endless.

Consequently, I am limiting the recipes in this chapter to a few of the classics that can be used in many ways and are the foundation for many dishes—and other sauces. I have placed the Italian pasta sauces in their own enclave in the midst of chapter eight because they really are a breed apart—essentially meat sauces put together for the glorification of pasta. Those that remain in this section are essentially basic sauces of multiple application.

On the subject of sauces in general, I want to emphasize the importance of two ingredients that must go into each and every one of them. These essentials, without which no sauce can succeed, are constant attention and tireless stirring. I know of no sauce that can be brought to perfection of its own volition; it must be forced. The saucepan should be at the front of the stove where it is always under observation, and the sauce should be stirred as close to constantly as is possible in view of the other chores attendant to the production of a full meal. Only in this way can you effect the perfect amalgamation that sires the perfect sauce.

The most common ingredient for thickening a sauce—as for my beloved Midwestern gravy—is flour. And the secret for using flour so as to avoid lumps, which ruin any production, is to make sure that every fleck remains separate from every other as it goes into the sauce. That sounds like quite a requirement, but it really isn't as difficult as it may seem. If you make a roux, allow it to cool a bit, and then add your boiling liquid all at once—you will achieve this result. If there is any tendency for the flour to lump under this method, a brisk stirring, preferably with a wire whip, will straighten out matters quickly.

On the other hand, when you must add flour to a potential sauce that is already cooking, the matter becomes more complicated. The favorite method of the French cook is to use beurre manié *(page 280), and the way he mixes the flour and butter—using the warmth of his hands to melt the butter and effect a perfect combination—is by all means the best. I know my fellow Americans well enough, however, to understand that few of them will be willing to use their hands in this operation, so I suggest the fork method—and I have never yet found a lump in any sauce I made with* beurre manié *prepared in this fashion.*

Another method is to warm the butter in a pan, stir the flour into it as if making a roux, and then add this hot mixture to the sauce, a little at a time. This is effective because it also insures that each minute grain of flour is coated with butter before it goes into the sauce. If the coating is 100 percent effective, lumps are impossible. In other words, the presence of lumps in a sauce means that the flour was not properly broken up by the butter or by whatever emulsifying agent was used. Flour mixed with plain water is an open invitation to trouble in the construction of any sauce.

Cornstarch and arrowroot are very effective thickening agents, particularly if you desire the semitransparent gloss they give to a sauce. The Chinese, who have through the centuries perfected one of the world's greatest cuisines, use this type of starch almost exclusively for thickening and, as a result, most oriental sauces have that almost jellied appearance that is not as familiar in western kitchens.

There is no question that the use of cornstarch or arrowroot produces a perfect effect in a sauce such as the Chinese sweet-and-sour, but it is doubtful that boeuf bourguignon *would look as appetizing to our critical eye if the sauce had a transparent cast. As a matter of fact, good old fashioned chicken gravy one of the greatest of the native American sauces—would lose a lot of its eye appeal if another starch were substituted for the familiar flour base.*

Egg yolks in heavy cream are another effective thickening agent, particularly for cream sauces (see poulet au champagne). *The usual ratio is two egg yolks beaten into three or four tablespoons of heavy cream for each estimated cup of sauce. If both flour and egg yolks are used in the same sauce (see* Königsberger klops), *one egg is usually sufficient for a cup of sauce. In every case the blending of the egg yolks, either with the cream or a bit of the hot sauce, must be thorough, and they must be added to the liquid* while the sauce is completely off the fire! *If they are added while the sauce is actively cooking, the eggs are likely to separate and spoil, at the least, the appearance of your sauce. Carefully utilized, this is a very effective method for thickening cream sauces.*

Two methods for thickening sauces that are widely used on the Continent are almost unknown in the American kitchen. The first of these is beating plain, unsalted butter into the sauce at the last minute (see bifteck d'Aphrodite). *This is effective when the stock (and wine, if included) has been reduced by hard boiling to a portion of its original volume. The butter will give the sauce a velvety sheen as well as help to thicken it. It is a method well worth experimentation.*

The second method for thickening is using crème fraîche *(page 282), a French phenomenon that is alien to our shores.* Crème fraîche *is a sweet cream matured with the aid of natural ferments until it develops the consistency of ice cream and a warm, nutty flavor all its own. It is* not *a sour cream, and it is widely used in France as a thickening agent because it can be boiled without disintegrating. This is not true of the sour cream sold commercially in the United States, which dissolves in a sauce the second the first bubbles start to break the surface. (That is why I continuously warn against allowing any sauce with sour cream to reach even those very first bubbles. To keep its creamy consistency, the sauce must be warmed carefully and served without delay.)*

The recipe for crème fraîche *given in chapter nine produces a similar cream (it is sometimes called* crème double, *incidentally), but I do not offer it as an exact replica. It is a good cream, however, and has most of the properties of its French cousin. Besides being excellent for sauces, it is a magnificent topping for berries or almost any dessert calling for whipped cream.*

Someday our friends at Borden's, Kraft's, or another of the great dairy organizations are going to market crème fraîche *commercially in this country and, as soon as they give the public just a little education, they'll make a killing!*

Finally, I want to emphasize the quotation that heads this chapter—one of the truest observations ever made concerning sauces of any kind:

> *"Sauces enhance good meat but*
> *They never conceal poor quality."*

WHITE SAUCES

Continental cooks recognize two basic white sauces that can be used in a thousand different dishes—one made with milk, the other with stock. Although primarily interested in products of the stockpot, we must include both sauces in this consideration because they are inseparable in any study of cuisine. The two sauces, of course, are *béchamel* (made with butter, flour, and milk) and *velouté* (made with butter, flour, and stock).

ROUX

The foundation of both *béchamel* and *velouté* sauce is what the French term *roux*—the combination of flour and butter cooked for several minutes before any liquid is added. French cooks often make roux well in advance and store it for use as needed. This is all right for a restaurant chef making innumerable sauces on short schedule, but I can see no need for the average cook working in his kitchen to store a roux.

The amount of flour used in the roux determines the ultimate thickness of the sauce. The ordinary *velouté* or *béchamel* uses flour in the ratio of 1-1/2 tablespoons to each cup of liquid. A sauce to be used as a base for a soufflé will need twice as much flour for the same liquid. For use in a casserole, such as macaroni and cheese, the ratio may be only 1 tablespoon to 1 cup of liquid.

I have found that the most effective method for making either sauce is to prepare the roux and remove it from the fire for several minutes. Then pour in the liquid, boiling hot, all at once and beat it with a wire whip until smooth. Incidentally, most continental cooks frown on aluminum for making sauce. Stainless steel, enamel, tinned copper, or Pyrex are preferred. A wooden spoon and a wire whip are also valuable adjuncts to the operation.

VELOUTÉ or *BÉCHAMEL*

> 2 tbsp butter
> 3 tbsp flour

Melt the butter over low heat, blend in the flour with a wooden spoon, and stir continuously while the roux is cooking—at least 2 minutes—but avoid browning the flour. Remove from the fire.

> 2 cups chicken stock, boiling
>   or
> 2 cups milk, at boiling point
>   salt
>   white pepper

Add the desired liquid to the roux all at once and beat with a wire whip until smooth; then continue to boil for 1 minute, stirring constantly. Stir in salt and white pepper to taste while the sauce is off the fire. If the sauce is not to be used immediately, float a thin film of melted butter or warm milk over the surface to prevent formation of a skin.

SAUCE MORNAY

Sauce Mornay can be made from any of the three preceding white sauces. Merely add 1/4 to 1/2 cup of grated cheese to 2 cups of boiling sauce, then remove from the fire, and stir until the cheese is melted and blended into the sauce. The amount of cheese used is according to taste. The cheese normally used in a Mornay sauce is Swiss Gruyère and Italian Parmesan in about equal proportions. There is no reason why grated cheddar cannot be substituted, if desired.

SAUCE BRUNE [Brown Sauce]

Sauce brune is one of the most basic of all sauces and one that is almost invariably used as a foundation for other foods rather than as a sauce in its own right (see *boeuf en miroton*). This recipe will make slightly less than two full cups of sauce.

      2   *tbsp butter*
      1   *medium onion, chopped*
      3   *slices bacon, chopped*
      2   *tbsp flour*
  1-1/2   *cups stock*
            thyme
            oregano
            salt
            freshly ground pepper

Sauté the onion and the bacon in the butter until the onion is well browned, but not burned. *This can only be accomplished by careful attention,* and the same is true with sautéing the flour! When the onions are browned, remove them and the bacon from the skillet with a slotted spoon and reserve. Cook the flour in about 2 tablespoons of the remaining fat until the flour is browned without scorching. Watch carefully and stir often. Next add the stock, warmed, and stir constantly until the mixture is smooth. Return the bacon and onion to the sauce and add a pinch each of thyme and oregano, 2 twists of freshly ground pepper, and salt to taste. Cover the skillet tightly and let the sauce simmer very slowly for 20 minutes. Taste again for seasoning, then strain, and discard the solids. The sauce can be stored in the refrigerator for several days, if necessary.

VELOUTÉ DE POISSON

Make the *velouté* sauce exactly as shown on page 226, but substitute 2 cups of boiling fish stock (page 56) for the chicken stock. This makes an excellent sauce for fish dishes.

SAUCE BRETONNE

Sauce Bretonne is one of the most famous of the basic sauces dedicated to the glorification of fish, just a step beyond the standard *velouté de poisson.* This sauce can transform an ordinary poached fish into a culinary work of art and the necessary fish stock (chapter three) can be made in a matter of minutes.

> 2 *cups* velouté de poisson
> 2 *tbsp butter*
> 2 *tbsp celery, minced*
> 3 *tbsp onion, minced*
> 4 *medium mushrooms*
> 3 *tbsp* crème fraîche *(page 282) or whipping cream*

Heat the sauce over a very low flame for several minutes while the celery, onion, and mushrooms are cooking in 1 tablespoon of butter until soft, but not browned. Add the *velouté* to the vegetables and slowly bring to a boil; then reduce the flame and simmer slowly for another 5 minutes. *Off the fire* stir in the cream, then the remaining tablespoon of butter, a little at a time. The sauce is now ready for use. A little melted butter poured over the top will prevent a skin from forming, if you plan to keep the sauce for a short time before use.

FORBES PARK BARBECUE SAUCE

When it first opened some 20 years ago, Manila's Forbes Park residential development was the scene of more barbecues and cookouts to the square hectare than any similar area in the history of the Far East! Every type of meat from the traditional spareribs and hamburgers to chickens, turkeys, and whole beef tenderloins went on the charcoals—and most of the sauces tasted as if they had a ketchup base. This sauce was one that was different as well as delicious, and it became a favorite of ours for those joint reasons. Try it on any type of meat the next time you plan a cookout or with spareribs right now in your oven (see baked "barbecued" ribs). This recipe should turn out about two cups of sauce.

```
3    tbsp oil
1    medium onion, minced
2    cloves garlic, crushed
2    cups stock
2    tbsp brown sugar
2    tbsp vinegar
4    tbsp tomato paste
2    tbsp Worcestershire sauce
2    tbsp soy sauce
     salt
     freshly ground pepper
```

Heat the oil in a heavy saucepan and sauté the onion until lightly browned. Add the garlic and cook another 1 or 2 minutes. Pour in the stock, warmed, and add all the other ingredients except the salt and pepper. Bring the liquid to a boil, blending all the components carefully; then turn the fire low and simmer, covered, for 30 minutes. Now taste for salt and add as needed (the strength of the soy sauce can make a difference) together with several good grinds of fresh pepper. Continue to simmer until the sauce achieves the consistency of a heavy tomato sauce.

ITALIAN FISH SAUCE

Italian fish sauce is a typical Mediterranean fish sauce that I discovered in Italy, although it could have originated in Provence—or even Spain for that matter. Its primary reason for being is for use in baking almost any fish that lends itself to oven cooking.

1	*medium fish head*
1/4	*cup onion, chopped*
1	*clove garlic*
1/2	*cup canned bell tomatoes, strained*
1/2	*cup stock*
1/2	*cup water*
	pinch of oregano
	salt
	freshly ground pepper

Mix all the ingredients, season, and cook slowly for 30 minutes. Remove and discard the fishhead. Force the remainder through a food mill or a coarse sieve.

1/2	*green pepper, thinly sliced*
1	*tbsp tomato paste*
1/2	*cup stock*
1	*tbsp cornstarch dissolved in water*

Add the sliced pepper, tomato paste, and stock to the strained stock (above) and simmer another 10 minutes. Off the fire, add the dissolved cornstarch, then reheat to thicken. You should now have a little more than a pint of the sauce ready for use as specified.

SAUCE NORMANDE

Sauce Normande, a somewhat richer cousin of *sauce Bretonne,* is also used to enoble fish, but not as lavishly. When making the fish stock for the *velouté de poisson,* take a cup of the stock and let it boil over a fairly high flame until reduced to one-half its volume.

1	*cup* velouté de poisson
1/2	*cup fish stock, reduced*
1/2	*cup mushroom liquid (page 283)*
3	*egg yolks*
1/4	*cup heavy cream*
3	*tbsp butter*

Combine the *velouté,* the stock, and the mushroom liquid—all warmed—and boil over moderate heat until reduced by approximately one-third. Mix the egg yolks with 1/8 cup of the cream and, when the liquid is sufficiently reduced, remove it from the fire and stir in the combined yolks and cream. Return the sauce to the stove and cook very moderately until thickened, stirring constantly. Remove the sauce from the fire and stir in the remaining 1/8 cup of cream; then beat in the butter, bit by bit. Melted butter over the top will prevent a skin from forming if the sauce is not used at once. This is superb on poached salmon!

SAUCE SUPRÊME

Sauce suprême is the sauce that Raymond Olivier, famous *patron-chef de cuisine* of Paris' *Grand Véfour* restaurant, says should result whenever a *velouté* is prepared with chicken stock. *Sauce suprême* is a *velouté* with *crème fraîche* added, and Olivier believes that the sauce without the cream is only half complete. It is a magnificent sauce for chicken and can be used anytime a *velouté* is specified—particularly in making *lasagne al forno*.

>   2   cups sauce velouté
>   1/2   cup crème fraîche *(page 282)*

Heat both the sauce and the *crème fraîche* and add the cream to the sauce, a spoonful at a time, stirring constantly. Remove the sauce from the fire as soon as the combination is effected. If you are not going to use the sauce immediately, pour a small amount of melted butter on top to prevent a skin from forming.

SAUCE AU RAIFORT [Horseradish Sauce]

Sauce au raifort is a grand sauce for cold meats of almost any type—particularly boiled beef, corned beef, and pastrami—and for lots of hot dishes as well. All you need is a good *velouté* sauce and plenty of horseradish, plus a bit of sour cream to blend the whole. To formalize:

>   1   cup velouté *sauce (page 226)*
>   1/2   cup fresh horseradish
>   2   tbsp sour cream

Mix the *velouté* and the horseradish and let stand for at least 1 hour. It should be understood that the strength of horseradish varies with its age, so the final test must be in the tasting. If the horseradish is at all subdued after the hour, add more to taste. Finally, stir in the sour cream and blend thoroughly. Serve very cool.

CHAPTER VII

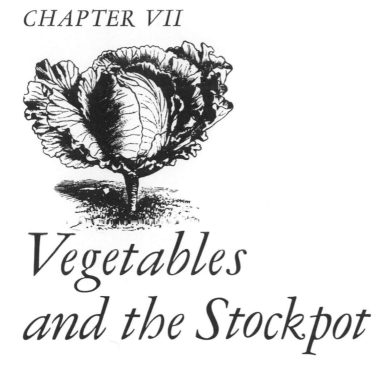

Vegetables
and the Stockpot

Let the first onions flourish there,
Rose among roots, the maiden fair,
Wine scented and poetic soul
Of the capacious salad bowl.

ROBERT LOUIS STEVENSON, 1897

Stevenson's instructions to his gardener really constitute a delightful quatrain, and that's the reason I chose it to head this chapter. From here on, however, we concern ourselves not with vegetables destined for the salad bowl, but rather with hearty, flavor-packed legumes that can stand, unashamed, on any table and demand their rightful ranking with the meat.

Much has been written about cooking vegetables with as little water as possible, and there can be no question that the method is correct. The only constribution water can make to vegetables is to keep them moist during the cooking process, so that the necessary heat doesn't burn them. And in return water demands a toll, often excessive, in food values extracted. With the proper kind of cooking utensil and the right degree of fire, vegetables—some of them, that is—can be cooked with almost no water; thus nutritional qualities—the greater percentage of them—remain in the vegetable and are not discarded with the cooking water that is drained and too often thrown away.

There was a time when the average cook drowned vegetables in water, cooked them to a pulp, and successfully extracted not only their nutrition but their flavor as well. I can remember in my childhood thinking that all cooked cabbage had to be brown in color with an aroma and flavor reminiscent of Monday's steaming laundry. I never could stomach the dish until, as an adult, I learned that it could be thoroughly cooked and still retain its color, its flavor, and a pleasing crispness—not that of raw cabbage, but just enough resistance to the teeth to let you know the food had not died in abject surrender.

And the best cabbage I have ever eaten was that cooked in stock—in the flavorful, aromatic stock that results from cooking a generous piece of corned beef with onions, carrots, turnips, or even potatoes until the water really has something to contribute to the cabbage. We've even made delicious soup from that same stock after the cabbage had been cooked and sent to co-star with the fragrant corned beef.

The point is that water—pure and wholesome as it may be—can never contribute anything to cooking a vegetable except fire insurance. On the other hand, good stock—under the proper circumstances and in combination with the right vegetables—can make a very definite contribution, and that is what this chapter is all about.

Not all vegetables lend themselves to this type of cooking, and those we shall not consider. Rather, I shall present a few thoughtfully selected examples of what good cooks have learned to do with vegetables and stock in combination.

SPARAGIO PARMIGIANO [Asparagus au Gratin]

Sparagio parmigiano is to my mind the finest method for preparing asparagus except, of course, simply steaming it until tender but not limp, then eating it (with your fingers, of course) dipped in melted butter or vinaigrette dressing. As a matter of fact, if you use fresh asparagus for this dish, you prepare them in the same way except that, once they are cooked, you go a step further. If the canned white asparagus is used, it should be heated in its own juice before the sauce is applied.

> 1   lb fresh asparagus
>   or
> 1   1-lb can white asparagus
> 1   cup Mornay sauce (page 226)
> 1/4   cup Parmesan cheese, freshly grated

Preheat the oven to 450°. If you are using fresh asparagus, clean it carefully and peel away with a potato peeler the hard skin from the bottom 3 inches of each stalk. Assort the stalks according to thickness and tie them in bundles of 6 or 8. The time required to cook them will vary with the thickness, so in this way you can remove the thin spears when done, leaving the thick ones for a few minutes longer. The spears should be put into boiling water, salted, until tender, but not limp—between 12 and 16 minutes, according to size. If you are using the canned white asparagus, heat the spears in their juice and then discard the liquid.

Place the cooked asparagus in a flat oven-proof casserole with all the tips at the same end; pour the Mornay sauce over them, but leave the tips free. Sprinkle with the grated Parmesan and put into the oven until the cheese is browned.

FAGIOLINI VERDI CON FUNGI [Green Beans with Mushrooms]

Fagiolini verdi con fungi is a simple method for preparing green beans and mushrooms with more than ordinary flavor. Chicken stock is preferred, but the all-purpose stock will serve very well. And there is no reason why you can't add a good pinch of garlic powder if you choose.

1	*lb fresh green beans*
6	*green onions, chopped*
1/4	*lb fresh mushrooms*
2	*tbsp butter*
2	*tbsp stock*
1/2	*tsp salt*
	freshly ground pepper
	almonds, slivered (optional)

Preheat the oven to 350°. Wash the beans and cut them into 2-inch slices. Chop the onions into 1/2-inch lengths and slice the mushrooms thinly. Place the beans in the center of a sheet of aluminum foil and fold up the edges to form a leak-proof package. Add the remaining ingredients, then fold over the top of the foil and crimp to form a tight package. Put this package on a pie or cake tin and place in the oven. Bake for about 40 minutes, at which time the beans should be tender. Shake the package a time or two during the cooking period. This dish can be garnished with slivered almonds, if desired.

GREEN BEANS AUSTRIAN STYLE

I am including green beans Austrian style because the recipe is entirely typical of the way Austrians prepare vegetables. No cook between Arlberg and Vienna would ever think of cooking vegetables in a minimum of moisture and serving them with only a bit of melted butter. Instead, tradition insists on the use of milk or cream, flour, stock, herbs, and plenty of other vegetables in combination. And some of the results are amazingly good. Try this one on four persons.

1	*lb fresh string beans*
	salted water, boiling
1	*tbsp butter*
1/2	*medium onion, chopped*
1	*tbsp flour*
1	*tsp dillweed*
1	*tbsp parsley, chopped*
1/2	*cup stock*
1	*tsp vinegar*
about 1/2	*tsp salt*
	freshly ground pepper
1/2	*cup sour cream*

Wash the beans and cut into 3/4-inch lengths. Cook in the boiling water, sufficient to cover, until tender—about 20 minutes. Drain and discard the liquid. Melt the butter and sauté the onion until soft. Blend in the flour and cook until it starts to turn golden. Add the dillweed and parsley, then the stock, boiling hot. Stir until the sauce is smooth. Add the vinegar, salt, and several grinds of fresh pepper. Then pour in the beans and cook for about 5 minutes, making sure that the sauce doesn't get too dry; add more stock, if necessary. Remove the pan from the fire and stir in the sour cream, mixing thoroughly. Return to a low fire and warm gently, making sure that the sauce does not boil. Pour into a hot serving dish and serve at once.

AUBERGINES À L'ORIENT [Oriental]

Of all the lexicographers on record, the one who ranks lowest on my list is the chap who looked at an *aubergine*—or perhaps it was a *melanzana*—and decided that its English name should be *eggplant!* There is nothing about the vegetable to suggest an egg, and the word certainly isn't euphonious. I believe one reason why eggplant is not as popular in the United States as in Europe is its name. Certainly no one would voluntarily choose *oriental eggplant* over *aubergines à l'orient* or even *melanzanna orientale*. I really don't know why the term *orient* applies to this dish unless it is the ginger. But I do know it is an excellent way to prepare eggplant, *aubergines*, or *melanzana*.

2	*large onions, thinly sliced*
2	*tomatoes, peeled and seeded*
2	*cloves garlic, peeled*
2	*small or 1 large eggplant*
	oil
1/2	*cup stock*
1/4	*cup dry white wine*
about 1/2	*tsp salt*
	freshly ground pepper
1/4	*tsp ginger*

Prepare the onions and set aside. To seed the tomatoes, cut them in half horizontally; then quarter each half. Peel the garlic, but do not chop it. Wipe the eggplant carefully, but do not peel. Discard a thin slice from each end and cut the eggplant to slices about 3/4-inch thick.

In a large skillet with a lid, heat the oil and sauté the eggplant slices, 2 or 3 at a time, until lightly browned. Put on a warm plate. You will need at least 1/2 cup of oil, adding a little at a time, but the finished dish will not be oily. Place all the browned slices back in the original pan and pour the combined stock and wine, warmed, over them. Put the onions and tomatoes on top of the slices and bury the whole garlic cloves in the liquid. Add the salt and several good grindings of fresh pepper, then sprinkle the ground ginger over the whole. (If you can buy dried ginger root and grate it yourself, the taste is greatly improved.) Cover the pan and simmer very slowly for 45 minutes. Remove the lid for the last 15 minutes if the sauce is too thin. *Aubergines à l'orient* is a superb accompaniment to lamb in almost any form.

CAROTE E CIPOLLE RUSTICO [Carrots and Onions, Country Style]

Carote e cipolle rustico, a combination of vegetables not often seen in the United States, is a delicious accompaniment to roast meat, particularly beef. The onions, of course, are the small white ones—the smaller the better. The carrots should also be as youthful as possible.

3	strips bacon, chopped
1	tbsp butter
16	small white onions
6	small carrots, cut into 3/4-inch chunks
	salt
	freshly ground pepper
1/2	tsp sugar
1/2	cup stock
	parsley, chopped

Sauté the bacon in the butter in a heavy-bottomed saucepan until the fat has been rendered; then remove the cooked meat and discard. Peel the little white onions, cut a thin strip off the root end of each, and then pierce the end with the point of a knife. Put them in the bacon fat with the carrots and cook over a moderate flame until the onions are lightly browned on all sides. Put a pinch of salt and several grinds of fresh pepper into the pan. (Easy on the salt until you taste; the bacon may have been salty.) Add the sugar and stock, heated. Cover the pan and simmer over a low flame until the vegetables are tender and the stock is reduced to a glaze. Sprinkle with chopped fresh parsley and serve.

CAROTE AL BURRO [Carrots in Butter]

Carote al burro demands the use of genuine stock—bouillon cubes in water won't do. The reduced stock and butter combine with the sugar to produce a glaze on the carrots that is pleasing to the eye and doubly so to the palate. Remember that the cooking time of carrots varies with their size and age. The only sure way to know when they are done is to fork one from the saucepan and eat it.

8	*medium carrots*
1-1/2	*cups stock*
1	*tsp sugar*
4	*tbsp butter*
	salt
	freshly ground pepper
	parsley, chopped

Peel the carrots and cut them in 1-inch chunks. Put them in the stock together with the sugar, 2 tablespoons of the butter, a good pinch of salt, and several grinds of fresh pepper. Cook over a moderate fire for about 45 minutes or until the carrots are tender and the stock is reduced to about 3 tablespoons. If more stock is needed before the carrots are tender, add it a little at a time, but don't let the carrots cook dry. When the carrots are tender, add the remaining 2 tablespoons of butter and cook another 5 minutes. Pour into a hot serving dish and sprinkle with the chopped parsley.

CÉLERIS À LA BONNE FEMME   [Celery Home Style]

Celery in the United States is almost always eaten raw or as part of another dish. In most of Europe, however, celery is commonly cooked as a vegetable and with results that make me wonder why Americans in larger numbers don't do the same. *Bonne femme* on a French recipe usually means that the dish is prepared in a simple manner. *Céleris á la bonne femme* is admittedly more complicated than boiling potatoes, but I think you'll agree the results pay off.

1	*large bunch celery*
2	*tbsp butter*
1	*small onion, chopped*
1	*small carrot, shaved*
1	*medium tomato, peeled, seeded, and chopped*
1/2	*cup stock*
1	*bay leaf*
	salt
	freshly ground pepper

Quarter the celery lengthwise, discard the heavy leaves, and cut into 1-1/2-inch lengths. Heat the butter in medium saucepan and sauté the onion and carrot until the onion is golden. Add the chopped tomato, the celery and the stock, then the bay leaf, a good pinch of salt, and freshly ground pepper. Cover the pan and simmer for 45 minutes or until the celery is tender. You now have an excellent vegetable to go with your meat and potatoes!

PURÉE DE MARRONS [Puréed Chestnuts]

Some years ago the Propellor Club of Nice, a group of Americans and their friends dedicated to the promotion of the United States Merchant Marine and good eating—not necessarily in that order—held their annual Thanksgiving dinner at the Hôtel de Paris in Monte Carlo. The French version of a traditional American meal was something to experience, although a bit west of tradition. The food was excellent, however, and I will never forget the pureed chestnuts served with the turkey. Americans have hinted at this combination with chestnut dressing, but the puree is something else again. Here's enough to make a magnificent accompaniment to turkey, duck, guinea hen, or even roast chicken—not to mention ham!

> 1   *lb chestnuts*
>   *cold water*
> 2   *cups chicken stock*
> 3   *stalks celery, cut in to 3-inch pieces*
> 4   *tbsp butter*
> 1/2   *cup milk, hot*
>   *salt*
>   *freshly ground pepper*

Make a small cut in the flat side of each chestnut and put them into a pan with enough cold water to cover. Bring to a boil and boil for 2 minutes. The chestnuts should peel rather easily while still warm; if not, return to the water and boil 1 or 2 minutes more. When they are peeled (the inner skin may give the most trouble), put the nuts into the stock together with the celery, bring to a boil, and then simmer for 45 minutes or until tender. Drain and discard the celery, reserving the stock. Mash the chestnuts with a potato masher (a ricer is even better); then add the butter, softened, and about 1/2 cup of the stock, which should still be hot. (The chestnuts are sure to cool during the pureeing process.) Next, add the hot milk, a little at a time, until you achieve the consistency of mashed potatoes. If you need more liquid, use hot milk. Taste for salt, add a few grinds of fresh pepper, and serve as a delicious vegetable.

CARROTS AND PEAS, FLEMISH STYLE

Carrots and peas Flemish style has its origins in Belgium, where a lot of good food has been produced in the past few centuries. It is simple, tasteful—and rich! But, of course, you aren't going to eat this every day.

8	*small young carrots, sliced*
5	*tbsp butter*
1	*cup stock*
1/4	*tsp sugar*
about 1/2	*tsp salt*
	freshly ground pepper
2	*cups fresh peas, shelled*

Sauté the carrots in 4 tablespoons of the butter for 5 minutes; then pour in the stock, heated, the sugar, salt, and several grinds of fresh pepper. Cook gently until the carrots start to become tender—about 20 minutes; then add the peas. Cover the pan and cook over a medium fire for 10 minutes. Then remove the lid and cook another 5 minutes, reducing the liquid to about 1/4 cup. Stir in the final tablespoon of butter and pour into a hot serving dish.

RAGOUT DE PIMENTS DOUX [Stewed Sweet Peppers]

The idea of cooking sweet peppers to serve as vegetables has never really caught on in the United States. This is really unfortunate, because sweet peppers lend themselves admirably to this treatment and make a welcome break from the traditional green vegetables that grace every American table. In Italy they prepare *ragout de piments doux* with green, red, and yellow sweet peppers with striking effect. I have never been able to locate fresh yellow peppers in the United States, but the red ones blend very well with the green, and the green peppers serve all right by themselves if that becomes necessary.

about 1-1/2   *lb green and red sweet peppers*
     1   *large onion, sliced*
     2   *cloves garlic, crushed*
     2   *tbsp oil*
     2   *tbsp flour*
     1   *cup stock*
        salt
        freshly ground pepper
     2   *large tomatoes, peeled, seeded, and chopped*
        parsley, chopped

Seed the peppers and cut them into large pieces—about the size of a silver dollar. Cook the peppers and the onion in the oil until the onions are golden, but not browned. Add the crushed garlic, then stir in the flour, and mix thoroughly. Heat the stock and add to the pot, stirring to achieve a smooth sauce. Taste for salt and a few grinds of fresh pepper. Add the chopped tomatoes, then cover the pan, and cook very slowly for 30 minutes. Pour into a warm vegetable bowl and sprinkle with the chopped parsley.

CAULIFLOWER AU GRATIN

I have no idea where the idea of serving cauliflower with a cheese sauce originated. I have recipes for cauliflower *au gratin* from France, England, Germany, and even my home state, Indiana, which would seem to indicate that this is a good way to serve the vegetable in any language. The Mornay sauce should be made in advance.

     1   *medium head cauliflower*
about 2   *quarts water, salted*
     2   *cups Mornay sauce (page 226)*
   1/2   *cup cheddar cheese, grated*
        paprika

Preheat the oven to 450°. Separate the cauliflower into flowerets and cook in the water, boiling, for 12 minutes or until tender. Drain them thoroughly, then place in an oven-proof casserole, stem sides down, and pour the sauce, warmed, over them. Sprinkle the grated cheese over them and top with generous sprinkles of paprika. Bake in the oven until the top is browned.

PETIT POIS AUX CHAMPIGNONS [Peas with Mushrooms]

Petit pois aux champignons is a simple and effective method for cooking fresh peas and mushrooms together to produce a vegetable dish that you could serve with pride to your rich uncle. The peas must be fresh, and two pounds will produce close to two cups when shelled. The difference in taste is worth the effort of shelling two cups of peas.

> 2   *lb fresh green peas*
> 1/2 *lb fresh mushrooms*
> 1   *bouquet garni (composed of 2 celery leaves, 1 sprig parsley,*
>   *and 1 small bay leaf*
> 1/4 *cup chicken stock*
>   *salt*
>   *freshly ground pepper*
> 1   *tbsp butter*

Be sure the peas are fresh; shell them. Wipe the mushrooms clean with a damp cloth and slice them thinly. Prepare the *bouquet garni* by tying the celery leaves, parsley, and the bay leaf together with a fine thread. Put the peas, mushrooms, and the *bouquet* into a saucepan with a tight-fitting lid, pour in the stock, and add a pinch of salt, 2 grinds of pepper, and the butter. Cover the pan and cook as slowly as possible for about 40 minutes, stirring occasionally. At this time the peas should be tender and the liquid almost all boiled away. Remove the *bouquet* before serving.

CIPOLLE FARCITE [Stuffed Onions]

Onions, stuffed to serve as a main course, are not too well known in the United States, but the loss is ours. Here is a simple Italian recipe—easy to prepare and more than moderately good. The Tuscans, from whom I obtained this formula, prefer the big, purple onions that dominate Tuscany, but I have found that the large yellow onions (Bermuda or Spanish by preference) will serve just as well.

4	*large onions*
1	*lb ground beef*
2	*tbsp oil (olive oil preferred)*
1	*cup tomato puree*
1	*tbsp tomato paste*
1	*cup cooked rice*
1/2	*tsp oregano*
	salt
	freshly ground pepper
1/2	*cup stock*
1/2	*cup Parmesan cheese, grated*

Peel the onions and cut a *very* thin slice from the root end so that each will stand alone. Place in boiling water for 5 minutes, then drain carefully. Cut a 1/3-inch slice off the top of each onion and, with a sharp tool of the kind used to form melon balls, scoop out the interior of each onion, leaving a shell about 1/4-inch thick.

Chop the pulp thus obtained and combine with the beef. Sauté this mixture in the oil and, when browned, add the rice and mix thoroughly. Next add the oregano, tomato puree, tomato paste, salt, and pepper. Simmer for 30 minutes. Preheat the oven to 350°. Use the tomato mixture to stuff the four onion shells and spread what remains over the bottom of a greased baking dish large enough to hold the onions side by side. Pour the stock over the mixture in the dish, place the onions on top, and sprinkle the grated Parmesan over the whole. Bake in the oven for 45 minutes.

NAVETS AU MATELOT [Turnips, Sailor Style]

Navets au matelot lifts turnips out of the ordinary and makes a special dish of them. I am not sure how the French navy got involved in this recipe, but the turnips are good regardless of origin. This is presumed to be the vegetable course for four people.

8	medium turnips
2	medium onions
1-1/2	tbsp butter
1	tbsp flour
1	cup stock
1/2	cup dry red wine
1/2	tsp salt
	freshly ground pepper
	parsley, chopped

Peel the turnips and cut them in large segments. Chop the onions very finely and sauté both the turnips and onions in the butter until the onions are transparent. Stir in the flour, making sure it is well blended with the oil. Heat the stock and pour it into the pan, then stir until smooth. Add the wine, salt, and several grinds of fresh pepper. Cover the pan and cook slowly for about 30 minutes. Watch the pan carefully and add more stock, if needed. When they are tender, turn them into a warm serving dish and sprinkle with the parsley.

JARDINIÈRE D'ÉTÉ [Summer Vegetables]

Jardinière d'été is an ideal vegetable dish for a festive dinner because it has a festive appearance and a festive flavor. Even the preparation can be festive because it may be prepared well in advance and placed in the oven thirty minutes before serving. This should provide vegetables for six people.

    1   *lb green beans, cut into 1-1/2-inch lengths*
    6   *cauliflower buds*
    2   *carrots, cut into 1-inch chunks*
    1   *lb peas, freshly shelled*
        salt
        freshly ground pepper
  1/2   *cup stock*
    4   *tbsp butter*
        chervil

Put the beans, cauliflower, and carrots into salted hot water and cook over moderate heat for 20 minutes. Melt 1 tablespoon of the butter in a saucepan, put the peas into it, and steam, covered, over a low fire for 10 minutes. Preheat the oven to 325°. Select a large, flat (preferably oval or oblong) oven-proof casserole and arrange the vegetables in separate sections; the green beans divided with one-half at each end, the peas in the center, with a row of alternating carrot, chunks and cauliflower buds dividing each section. Pour the cup of stock warmed, over the vegetables and sprinkle with the remaining 3 tablespoons of butter, melted, and the chervil. Sprinkle with salt and several grinds of fresh pepper, cover tightly (with foil if there is no tight-fitting lid), and cook in the oven for 30 minutes.

CIPOLLE AL FORNO [Baked Onions]

Cipolle al forno is another recipe from Tuscany, although I often had trouble finding the small white onions in a province that produces the finest purple onions in the world. But for this dish, only the small white ones will serve, and they are plentiful in most parts of this country.

Informatively, the reason for piercing the root end of the onions with a knife is to insure their holding their shape while cooking instead of disintegrating.

> 24   *small white onions*
>   *water*
> 1/2   *cup stock*
> 1/2   *cup dry white wine*
>   1   *tbsp parsley, chopped*
> 1/2   *tsp oregano*
>   1   *tsp sugar*
>   2   *tbsp butter*

Preheat the oven to 325°. Put the unpeeled onions into sufficient cold water to cover, bring to a boil, and then cook over a moderate fire for 10 minutes. Drain the onions and, when they are cool, peel them; cut a thin slice off the bottom (root end) and pierce the exposed surface with the point of a knife. In the meantime combine and warm the stock and wine. Add the oregano, parsley, and sugar. Mix well and then pour over the onions in an oven-proof casserole. Cook the onions, tightly covered, in the oven for 1 hour. Remove the lid, dot the onions with butter, and bake uncovered, another 10 minutes or until the onions are tender and the liquid is almost evaporated.

MACARONI AS A VEGETABLE

Americans do not use macaroni as a vegetable as commonly as do the Italians and many of the French, and there is no use pretending that macaroni is a vegetable because it definitely is not. Macaroni can, however, fill in for a vegetable beautifully, if properly prepared, and this is a method I learned in San Remo.

1   *cup elbow macaroni*
2   *cups stock*
    salt
    freshly ground pepper

Heat the stock to the boiling point and add the macaroni slowly. Reduce the fire and cook over moderate heat until the macaroni is tender. This is a matter of your own taste, and the only way to know when it is done is to fish out an elbow now and then and eat it. Taste for seasoning, too, before serving and be sure to grind plenty of fresh pepper into the dish. If the stock gets too low before the macaroni is to your taste, add more; if there is too much liquid, ladle some of it out. The macaroni, when served, should be well moistened, but not soupy.

LEGUMI ALLA CONTADINI [Vegetables, Peasant Style]

Green beans are the dominant component of *legumi alla contadini*, an Italian dish, but it is because they are the firm vegetables and don't cook up. If you set out to make a ragout of vegetables—and why not—this could be the end result. I am quite sure I have had this combination, or something very close to it, in Provence as well.

        1   *lb green beans, cut into 1-1/2-inch lengths*
        3   *slices bacon, chopped into 1/2-inch pieces*
        1   *tsp butter*
        2   *large onions, chopped*
        2   *large tomatoes, peeled and seeded*
    1/4   *tsp oregano*
about 1/4   *tsp salt*
          freshly ground pepper
    1/2   *cup stock*

Soak the beans in cold water for 20 minutes. Sauté the bacon in the butter, but do not let brown. Remove the bacon when done and cook the onion in the same oil until transparent. Reserve the bacon. Cut each tomato into eighths and put in with the onions. Drain the beans carefully and add them to the tomatoes and onions, then return the bacon. Add the oregano, salt, and several grinds of fresh pepper. Add the stock, heated, cover the saucepan, and simmer until the beans are tender—about 40 minutes. By this time the stock should have almost evaporated. Taste the beans for seasoning and pour into a hot serving dish.

Tour de chef: A crushed bud of garlic doesn't hurt this ragout in the least.

PETITS POIS DU MÈNAGE [Peas, Home Style]

Petits pois du mènage is hardly the home style we Americans have been brought up to recognize, but that doesn't alter the fact that this is an exceptionally good way to prepare spring peas. Frozen peas can, of course, be substituted, but the rewards for preparing really fresh peas are well worth the extra effort.

> 4   *strips bacon*
> *boiling water*
> 4   *green onions*
> 3   *tbsp butter*
> 1   *tbsp flour*
> 1   *cup chicken stock*
> 2   *cups fresh peas, shelled*
> *basil*
> *marjoram*
> *salt*
> *freshly ground pepper*

Cut the bacon into 1/4-inch squares, blanch in boiling water for 10 minutes, and then dry on a paper towel. Sauté in their own fat until browned. Remove most of the green part of the onions and cut the whites into 1/2-inch lengths. Melt the butter in a saucepan, stir in the flour, and cook for 2 minutes, stirring constantly. Heat the stock to the boiling point and add it to the roux all at once, stirring with a wire whip until smooth. Lower the fire and pour in the peas together with the onions and the browned bacon. Add a pinch each of basil and marjoram, then salt, and freshly ground pepper to taste. Cover the pan and simmer over a low flame for 15 minutes or until the peas are tender. Taste again for seasoning and serve with pride.

CHAPTER VIII

The Italians Call It Brodo

Open my heart and you will see
Graved inside it, "Italy."

ROBERT BROWNING, 1855

The first time I ever tried to buy bones for stock from an Italian butcher (later I got them free), I learned something elemental about Italy and Italian butchers. They may not understand exactly what an American means when he pulls fondo di cucina *out of his dictionary, but any* macellaro *will understand* brodo *instantly.*

The closest English equivalent to brodo *is broth or bouillon and, like them,* brodo *is often used as a soup. Basically, however,* brodo *is a good stock for cooking and* brodo ristretto *(reduced) is a good, rich stock. The method for producing* brodo *is identical to that for stock, and concentrated* brodo *can be bought, to mix with boiling water, just like bouillon cubes. And just like stock or bouillon, homemade* brodo *is much to be preferred to the concentrated product dissolved in water.*

The idea of including an Italian chapter in this book—even though excellent Italian recipes are scattered all through it—was born of the thought that I had no logical place for such favorites as lasagna al forno, *my favorite pasta sauces, and the* risottos, *which are as Italian as the Tiber.*

*If I stray a bit from the stockpot in the midst of the pasta, don't be alarmed. The sauces that give them meaning are rich in stock or—more appropriately—*brodo!

I am sure that Browning fell so deeply in love with Italy—an emotion easy to understand—at least partly because of the brodo.

BASIC PASTA

There is only one fundamental difference between the basic Italian egg pasta and grandmother's noodles; the pasta is kneaded and rolled to absorb as much flour as possible and is relatively dry when finished. Grandmother's noodles were more moist and were often left in the open air to dry before using. Both are delicious, but here we are concerned with the Italian version, which can be cooked in boiling water—just like macaroni or spaghetti—and served with the same sauces and, of course, Parmesan cheese. I am recording here the one-egg-plus recipe, which is usually enough for four persons. To prepare for twice as many people, merely double the quantities.

> 1   *cup all-purpose flour*
> 1   *whole egg*
> 1   *egg yolk*
> 3/4   *tsp salt*
> 1   *cup flour (in reserve)*

Put the first cup of flour, the egg, the yolk, and the salt into a mixing bowl and mix thoroughly until a smooth dough is achieved. If necessary, add more flour from the second cup in reserve. Put the dough onto a well-floured bread board and knead it with both hands, adding flour as necessary, until it is firmly elastic and no longer sticky. Divide the dough into 2 parts and roll each section on the floured board until you have a sheet of pasta as thin as you can roll it without breaking the dough. It can now be cut into any shape or width. If you want long ribbons, the easiest way is to roll up the pasta and cut to the desired widths with a very sharp knife and unroll. If you are making a lasagne, cut the rectangles (see *lasagne verdi al forno,* page 265) to the required size without rolling and proceed as with the green noodles. Lasagne can be made with either type of pasta. Incidentally, the green noodles used for *lasagne verdi* can also be cut into strips and cooked exactly the same as the basic pasta.

SMALL NOODLES

Small noodles are merely the basic pasta dough rolled thinly and cut into any desired shape, cooked in boiling salted water, and served with such dishes as *Königsberger klops* or any type of ragout. They are also very good in soup.

Roll the pasta into a thin sheet and cut it into 1/2-inch strips. Cut each strip into 2-inch lengths. Twist each length in the center to form a "bow" and press the center twist so it will hold its shape. This simple shape helps the cooked pasta to maintain its individuality without massing together. Other shapes can be invented as you proceed.

Cook the shaped pasta in plenty of boiling water for about 15 minutes or until as tender as you like it. It must be tasted to determine when this point is reached.

RISOTTO

The world has long known and sung the praises of Italian pastas, and rightly so, but much less is known of the Italian *risottos*, which are just as distinctive and certainly rank with the world's finest methods for preparing rice. The Italians rarely cook rice in plain salted water, preferring to use *brodo* (stock in our book) and almost anything that strikes their fancy. There are meat *risottos*, fish *risottos*, and *risottos* spiced with herbs and enriched with cheese. Some of the more elaborate are main courses in themselves, but most are served to accompany a main dish. Basically, the method for preparing any *risotto* starts by cooking the rice briefly in hot oil, then adding stock in two or three operations until the rice is cooked and has absorbed most of the liquid. I am presenting a few of the basic recipes for *risotto* and, when you master them, you will be in a position to ad-lib your way through a hundred variations. One thing to remember is that no *risotto* is supposed to be dry or mushy. The ideal *risotto* retains some moisture, but the rice is fluffy and the grains don't cling together. A bit of experimentation will show you how. The Italian likes his rice *al dente,* which means he wants it with a bite in it—almost underdone by our standards. This is strictly a matter of taste and, when you make *risotto,* you are the judge of how well the rice is to be cooked.

This is a basic recipe for plain (a matter of opinion!) *risotto.* The formula changes from place to place in Italy.

> 3   *tbsp butter*
> 2   *tbsp olive oil*
> 1   *onion, chopped*
> 1   *clove garlic, crushed*
> 1   *cup raw long grain rice*
> 3   *cups stock (chicken preferred), well seasoned*
>   *Parmesan cheese, grated*

Sauté the onion in 2 tablespoons of the butter and the oil, combined, until it is soft; then add the garlic and immediately pour in the entire cup of rice. Stir the rice until it is completely coated with the butter and oil, then allow to cook another 5 minutes. Pour in 1 cup of boiling hot stock, cover the pan, and turn the fire low. Simmer until the liquid is all absorbed, then add a second cup of stock, and repeat. When the third cup is absorbed, the *risotto* should be ready. Taste for seasoning and consistency. Stir in the remaining 1 tablespoon of butter and about 2 generous tablespoons of Parmesan, fluff with a fork, and serve with more Parmesan on the side.

RISOTTO CON POMIDORO   *[Rice and Tomatoes]*

Risotto con pomidoro is made exactly like plain *risotto* except that after the second cup of stock is absorbed by the rice, the following vegetable mixture is added with the final cup of stock.

      2   tbsp butter
    1/2   onion, sliced
      1   small stalk celery, minced
      6   medium mushrooms, sliced
      2   large tomatoes, peeled, seeded, and chopped
    1/4   tsp salt
          freshly ground pepper
          basil

Heat the butter and cook the onion and celery together until soft. Add the mushrooms and cook another 5 minutes. Then add the chopped tomatoes (they should be very ripe), salt, several grinds of fresh pepper, and a good pinch of basil. Cover the pan and cook over a low fire for 10 minutes. Taste for seasoning, then drain off all the liquid. Add the solids to the *risotto* with the third cup of hot stock and stir before the final simmering.

When the *risotto* is done, add the butter and grated Parmesan as in the original recipe and serve with more Parmesan on the side.

RISOTTO CON FUNGI [Rice and Mushrooms]

Risotto con fungi is another standard *risotto* that is very popular all over Italy. Like most of the variations, this one starts with the regular *risotto* recipe and the mushrooms are added during the cooking of the rice. This is an excellent accompaniment to almost any veal dish.

    1/2   lb mushrooms, sliced
      2   tbsp butter

Sauté the mushrooms in the butter until lightly browned, being careful not to let them steam.

Proceed with the recipe for plain *risotto*, holding the mushrooms in reserve. When you are ready to add the third cup of stock to the rice, put the mushrooms into the rice at the same time. Stir carefully before the final simmering begins. When the rice is done, add the butter and Parmesan as specified, fluff with a fork, and serve with extra Parmesan on the side.

RISOTTO MILANESE   [Rice Milan Style]

There are no limits to the variations that can be made to a basic *risotto*. I am detailing some of the better known ones and once you master the fundamental idea, you can produce a score of *risottos*—all different—out of your imagination. *Risotto Milanese* is a traditional partner to *osso buco* and goes well with almost any kind of ragout.

        2-1/2   *cups stock (chicken preferred), well seasoned*
          1/4   *tsp saffron*
            1   *tbsp beef marrow*
            2   *tbsp butter*
            2   *tbsp olive oil*
            1   *onion, chopped*
            1   *clove garlic, crushed*
            1   *cup long grain rice*
          1/2   *cup dry white wine*
                salt
                freshly ground pepper
                Parmesan cheese, grated

Have your butcher split a 2-inch marrow bone, extract the marrow, and dice it finely. Heat the stock to the boiling point, then keep it simmering until needed. Dissolve the saffron in about 1 tablespoon of hot stock and reserve.

Sauté the onion in the combined oil and butter in a large saucepan (about 3 quarts) until the onion is golden. Add the crushed garlic and the diced marrow, then pour the rice into the pan. Cook for about 5 minutes over a moderate fire until the rice is completely coated with the oil and starting to take on color. Pour in the wine and cook over a hot fire until nearly evaporated. Add the saffron and mix well; then add 1 cup of hot stock, lower the fire, and simmer until the liquid is absorbed. Now add half the remaining stock and repeat the procedure. Finally, use the last of the stock and, when it is about absorbed, taste the rice for seasoning. When the rice is done, stir in 2 tablespoons of grated Parmesan and serve with more Parmesan on the side.

LASAGNE VERDI AL FORNO *[Baked Green Noodles]*

The twin snacks of Italy, particularly that part north of Naples, are pizza and *lasagne al forno*. The pizzas in most instances are a rather pale product compared to the American pizzas, which are—hard to believe! —a product of the past quarter-century. But the lasagne is invariably good—sometimes better than other times, but always good. Obviously lasagne is a dish that can be prepared, kept warm, and served in individual portions over a period of time without serious deterioration. This recipe, which features the green *(verdi)* lasagne, can produce an end result superior to most restaurant pastas, either here or abroad. And you won't have to worry about deterioration; it will probably be finished at the first serving. *(Lasagne al forno* is also excellent made with basic pasta.)

1-1/2	*cups fresh spinach, chopped finely*
1/2	*cup water*
2	*cups flour*
2	*cups flour (in reserve)*
2	*whole eggs*
1	*egg yolk*
1-1/2	*tsp salt*
3	*cups pasta sauce* (Bolognese *recommended)*
3	*cups* velouté *or* suprême *sauce*
1	*cup mozzarella cheese, diced finely*
	Parmesan cheese, grated

(An equal amount of frozen spinach can be substituted for the fresh, but experience has shown that the fresh has better coloring and imparts a flavorful nuance to the pasta.) Cook the chopped spinach (be sure all the stems are removed) in 1/2 cup of water for 10 minutes, then puree in a blender until smooth. With a spatula scrape the puree off the sides of the blender into a fine mesh sieve (a tea strainer, for instance) and drain off as much liquid as possible.

Put the first 2 cups of flour into a large mixing bowl. (In Italy most cooks do not use bowls because great marble-topped work tables are standard kitchen equipment, but you are better off with a good mixing bowl in the average American mènage.) Add the eggs, the egg yolk, and the drained spinach puree. Add the salt and mix thoroughly until the dough takes on a uniformly green color. Using the second 2 cups of reserve flour as needed, flour a large bread board and put the dough in the center of it. Knead with both hands, adding flour as necessary, until the dough is firm and elastic. Return to the bowl, which has been cleaned and floured, and let it rest for at least 15 minutes. Divide the dough into 4 parts for easier handling (unless you have a mammoth board). Put the first quarter on the floured board and roll it out, turning and adding flour, until you have a sheet as nearly rectangular as possible and as thin as you can roll it without breaking. Cut this dough into rectangles about 2 by 5 inches and lay them on floured waxed paper. Add the scraps of dough to the second batch of pasta and handle exactly the same—then the third and fourth portions. When it all is cut, put the pasta into a large kettle filled with boiling salted water and cook for 8 minutes. Remove the pasta and dip immediately into cold water for just an instant. Spread them on paper towels.

Preheat the oven to 375°. Butter a large rectangular baking dish—about 9 by 12 inches and 2 inches deep. Porcelain or glassware is preferred. Spread a thin layer of pasta (meat) sauce on the bottom of the dish and cover with a light layer of the *velouté* (if you want a super-duper sauce, use the *suprême*). Then place a layer of the pasta rectangles over the sauces, covering the entire bottom and allowing the pastas to overlap a bit. Cover the pasta with layers of the meat and *velouté* sauces and sprinkle with the diced mozzarella cheese. Now add another layer of pasta, more sauces, and mozzarella, repeating until the dish is filled. Conclude with the sauces on top of the final layer of pasta. Sprinkle generously with grated

Parmesan and bake in the oven for 40 minutes, reducing the heat to 300° when the top is well browned. Let the lasagne stand for at least 15 minutes after removing from the oven, then cut in 3- or 4-inch squares, and serve with more Parmesan on the side.

SALSA LIVORNESE [Spaghetti Sauce, Livorno Style]

I encountered *salsa Livornese* while living in Tuscany's port, Livorno— hence its name. It can be used on all types of pasta and is excellent on *lasagne verdi al forno* (page 265). The beef must be ground at least three times, once with the sausage. It is impossible to cook this sauce too much, as long as you cook it very slowly and don't let it stick to the bottom of the pot.

1	lb beef chuck, ground three times
2	links (1/4 lb) hot Italian sausage
1	cup purple onion, finely chopped
2	tbsp olive oil
2	cloves garlic, minced
1	1-lb can peeled Italian tomatoes, chopped
1	heaping tbsp tomato paste
1	cup stock
1/2	cup dry red wine
1/4	tsp oregano
1/2	tsp basil
1	large bay leaf
	salt
	freshly ground pepper
16	medium mushrooms
2	medium carrots, finely grated

Skin the sausages and mix well with the beef. Put the mixture through the grinder at least once. Sauté the onion in the oil until soft, then add the meat to the same oil and brown. Add the minced garlic just before the meat is browned, then follow with the tomatoes, tomato paste, wine, and stock. Add the oregano, basil, bay leaf, salt, and pepper. Bring to a boil, then lower the flame, and simmer very slowly for 3 hours.

Trim the stems from the mushrooms and dice finely. Add these stems, together with the grated carrots, to the sauce as soon as it starts to boil.

Slice the heads of the mushrooms and add to the sauce during the last 30 minutes of simmering. When it is done, let the sauce stand for 1 hour; then skim as much oil as possible off the top before serving. The sauce improves if left overnight or longer.

MINESTRA DI PASTA E FAGIOLI *[Bean Soup with Pasta]*

Only the Italians would dream of taking a starchy food like pasta and cooking it with the pure starch that distinguishes beans. But the result is amazingly good. There were shops in Livorno's *Gran Marcato* that featured huge sacks of beans *(fagioli)* in a dozen sizes and forms. We tried most of them at one time or another and came up with the firm conviction that the red kidney beans or the large white ones are the best for this *minestra*. The dried beans are infinitely better than the canned varieties for this purpose, too.

1/2	*lb dried beans (kidney or navy)*
1	*large onion, sliced*
1	*tbsp oil*
8	*cups stock*
1/4	*cup Chianti or dry red wine*
1	*rounded tbsp tomato paste*
1/2	*cup celery, chopped*
1	*carrot, sliced*
	salt
	freshly ground pepper
1/2	*lb pasta "bows"*
	Parmesan cheese, grated

Wash the beans carefully and discard any bad ones. Put them in a kettle with sufficient water to cover, bring to a boil, then turn the flame down, and simmer for 20 minutes. Remove them completely from the fire and let stand for about 1 hour. Return then to the fire and simmer slowly, adding more water if needed, for another hour or until they begin to get tender. Now cook the sliced onion in the oil until golden, add the stock and wine, and stir in the tomato paste. Add the celery, carrots, and beans, carefully drained. Add about 1 teaspoon of salt and twists of fresh pepper. Cook gently for about 30 minutes or until the beans are completely tender, then add the pasta, and cook another 15 minutes. Taste again for salt. Serve in soup plates with plenty of grated Parmesan cheese.

MACARONI AND CHEESE MEZZO ITALIANO

To a Midwesterner brought up on "rattrap" cheese, a minor hardship of living in Italy was the total absence from the markets of cheddar cheese, even the plastic processed form. What little we had we imported from Fortnum and Mason in London, and that ran into money. Macaroni and cheese *mezzo Italiano* was developed in Italy (that's why it is "half" Italian) in an effort to get the best possible results from the precious cheddar we did have. It is not really Italian, but any Italian would love it and it did have its roots in our Tuscany kitchen.

1-1/2	*cups elbow macaroni*
2	*quarts water, salted*
1/2	*medium onion, chopped finely*
3	*tbsp butter*
2	*tbsp flour*
1	*cup stock*
3/4	*cup canned tomatoes, strained*
1	*cup mild cheddar, coarsely grated*
	salt
	freshly ground pepper
	dash of cayenne
	paprika

Put the macaroni in the boiling salted water and cook for 10 minutes. Drain and keep warm. While the macaroni is cooking, sauté the onion in the butter in a heavy-bottomed pan. When the onions are soft, add the flour and cook for 2 minutes, stirring constantly. Cut the tomatoes into small pieces, mix with the stock, and heat almost to the boiling point. Add this to the flour and stir until smooth. When the sauce starts to thicken, add about 2/3 cup of the cheese, a pinch of salt, several grinds of fresh pepper, and the cayenne. Cook until the cheddar is melted, stirring constantly. Preheat the oven to 350°. Butter a 1-1/2-quart baking dish and put about half the drained macaroni in it and top with half the sauce. Stir lightly. Add the rest of the macaroni, then the sauce, and stir again. Spread the remaining 1/3 cup of the cheddar over the top and sprinkle generously with paprika. Bake in the oven for 30 minutes and serve with a fresh green salad on the side. This is an excellent one-dish meal.

SALSA BOLOGNESE   [*Spaghetti Sauce, Bologna Style*]

Of all the thousands of sauces produced in Italy for the purpose of exalting the thousands of different types of pasta, *Salsa Bolognese* is easily the best known—and the hardest to define. I have eaten pasta with *Salsa Bolognese* all over Italy, including three or four restaurants in Bologna, and never were any two alike. Each Italian cook has his own version—all similar, but far from identical. I make no claims for this recipe except that it came from Italy, it is my personal favorite of a half-dozen in my possession, and it will improve the flavor of the finest pasta in the world.

    1/2   lb bacon, chopped
    1   tbsp olive oil
    1/4   lb raw ham, diced finely
    1   medium onion
    1   carrot
    2   stalks celery
    1/2   lb veal
    1/2   lb beef

1/2	lb pork
1	cup stock
1/2	cup white wine
1	tsp salt
	freshly ground pepper
	ground cloves
	nutmeg
3	large ripe tomatoes, peeled, seeded, and chopped
1/4	lb fresh mushrooms, sliced
2	chicken livers, diced
3/4	cup heavy cream

Cook the bacon in the oil until lightly browned, then add the ham. (Raw ham or, better yet, genuine Italian *Prosciutto crudo* is preferred, but ordinary ham will serve.) Dice the onion, carrot, and celery very finely, add to the ham, and cook until soft, stirring often. You can put the veal, beef, and pork through the meat grinder, but the Italians seem to prefer it chopped very finely; take your choice. Add the meat to the pot and cook until it changes color; then pour in the stock and wine, combined and warmed. Stir in the salt, plenty of fresh pepper, and a pinch each of ground cloves and nutmeg. Simmer, uncovered, until the liquid is low and the sauce thickened. Now blend in the tomatoes and simmer, covered, for another hour, stirring regularly and adding a bit of stock, if needed, to maintain the proper consistency. Taste for seasoning and hold the sauce until ready to serve. About 15 minutes before serving, add the sliced mushrooms and diced chicken livers to the sauce and simmer until ready to eat. Stir in the heavy cream just before serving.

SALSA ALLA SALSICCIA [Sausage Sauce]

Salsa alla salsiccia is a pasta sauce for which we were never able to find a recipe, so we worked this formula out in our own kitchen. I can say without any pretense at modesty that it is as good, if not better, than any of the originals we tasted in Italy. To prevent it from crumbling, the sausage is left in its long casing until just before serving. Moreover, this sauce was created for the large pasta shells which hold the sauce better than spaghetti or fettucine.

1-1/2 *lb sweet Italian sausage (in one piece, if possible)*
1 *cup stock*
1 *medium onion, chopped*
1 *cup Italian bell tomatoes, drained*
1 *clove garlic, crushed*
1/4 *tsp oregano*
1/4 *tsp basil*
1/4 *tsp thyme*
1/4 *tsp sage*
   salt
   freshly ground pepper
3 *tbsp tomato paste*
1/2 *lb fresh mushrooms, sliced*
1 *tbsp butter*

(Buy the sausage in the long, thin, single piece, if possible; if not, buy pieces as long as possible.) Put the sausage, whole, into a 10-inch skillet and, over a moderate fire, brown on both sides, keeping the skillet well covered. When the sausage is browned, add about 1/4 cup stock and, still covered, let simmer until nearly evaporated. Now add the onion and cook until transparent. Drain the tomatoes well (2 medium tomatoes, peeled, seeded, and chopped, may be substituted) and add to the onion, together with the garlic, oregano, basil, thyme, and sage. Pour in the remaining 3/4 cup of stock and blend in the tomato paste. Taste for salt and add several good grinds of fresh pepper. Cover the pan again and let the mixture simmer for about 45 minutes. Meanwhile sauté the mushrooms in the butter and add to the sauce after about 45 minutes. Again cover the pan and simmer once more for about 15 minutes. If the sauce is too thin, remove the lid and simmer until thickened. With kitchen shears or a very sharp knife, cut the sausage into bite-size bits. Simmer another 5 minutes, then serve with pasta. To repeat, this sauce is particularly recommended for the large pasta shells, which can handle its consistency better than the linear pastas.

SALSA DI POMODORO [Tomato Sauce]

Salsa di pomodoro is one of the simplest Italian sauces for pasta—easily and quickly prepared and delicious on a variety of dishes, such as ravioli and *cannelloni*, and on some meats, particularly veal. Its one requirement is that the tomatoes be fully ripe, because you won't get the desired taste or color otherwise. I have seen this sauce made with canned tomatoes, but the result too often is a super-abundance of tomato seeds and I detest tomato seeds. Italian bell tomatoes are ideal, but the chances of finding two pounds of ripe bell tomatoes in the average American grocery are not too great.

1/4	lb bacon, diced
1	large onion, diced
2	lb very ripe tomatoes
1	clove garlic, crushed
1/3	cup dry white wine
1/3	cup stock
1/2	tsp sugar (optional)
1/2	tsp oregano
	salt
	freshly ground pepper

Fry the bacon until very crisp in a heavy, lidded skillet. Pour off all but about 1 tablespoon of the bacon fat and sauté the onion in the fat until lightly browned. Meanwhile, dump the tomatoes into boiling water for about 30 seconds. If they are really ripe, the skins will come off easily. Cut them in two crosswise and remove all the seeds plus any white pulp you may find. Chop them finely and add to the skillet, together with the crushed garlic, stock, wine, oregano, salt, and pepper. Some people prefer a soupçon of sugar to cut the acid taste of the tomatoes, so add sugar, if desired. Bring the mixture to a boil; then lower the heat, cover the pan, and simmer for 30 minutes. If the sauce is still too thin, continue simmering with the lid removed until the proper consistency is achieved. Some cooks strain the sauce at this point; I prefer the bits and pieces it contains.

MINESTRONE TOSCANO

During our residence in Livorno, the port city of Tuscany, our apartment was situated directly across the *piazza* from the *stadio communale* (the community stadium) where thousands of sports fans gathered on Saturdays and Sundays (don't forget the holidays!) to watch and cheer football, European style. A lady who lived on the floor directly below us used to augment her income by boarding some of the football players, and the food she served them was strictly dictated by their training regime. She once sent us a tureen of her own *minestrone,* just as she made it for the athletes. Amazingly, perhaps, it was made without meat. We enjoyed it so much that we asked for the recipe, which she graciously gave us—handwritten in Italian. For this reason my translation may not be entirely accurate, but it will produce some very good *minestrone!* Comparable ingredients may be substituted when necessary or desirable.

1	tbsp oil
1	medium onion, chopped
1	tsp parsley, chopped
2	large tomatoes, peeled, seeded, and chopped
1	tbsp tomato paste
6	cups stock
1/2	cup Chianti or other dry red wine
2	stalks celery with leaves, chopped
2	carrots, sliced
1	large potato, diced into 1/2-inch cubes
1	cup fresh peas
1	zucchini squash, sliced
1	cup cabbage, shredded
1	tsp salt
	freshly ground pepper
1/2	tsp oregano
1	cup pasta shells

Parmesan cheese, grated

Sauté the onion in the oil until soft; then add the parsley, the tomatoes, and the tomato paste. Mix well, then pour in the combined wine and stock, and stir until blended. Now add the vegetables, salt, oregano, and freshly ground pepper. Turn the fire low and simmer the soup, uncovered, for 45 minutes. Add the pasta and cook another 15 minutes. Serve with plenty of grated Parmesan.

CHAPTER IX

Salmagundi

Our learned friend, Noah Webster, defines salmagundi as "a mixed dish, as of chopped meat and pickled herring with oil, vinegar, pepper and onions."

That is not what this chapter is all about!

Webster does, however, continue: "Hence, a heterogeneous mixture, medley, potpourri."

And that's where we come in.

This chapter makes no rhyme or reason as a unit; it is a "mixture, medley, potpourri" of varied information which I felt should be included, but which doesn't categorize itself in other parts of the book. I believe it is worth studying, and much of its material is referred to in other parts of the book.

Included are information about ingredients and methods and a couple of recipes that don't fit elsewhere. All the information complements that which has preceded it.

BOUQUET GARNI

Traditionally the *bouquet garni* is the combination of a branch of parsley, a branch of thyme, and a bay leaf, used for imparting a herb nuance to foods while being cooked. The herbs (sometimes celery or fennel is substituted or added) are tied together for easy removal. Today, however, fresh thyme is difficult for most Americans to find and the bay leaf poses no removal problem, so the *bouquet* is coming into less use in the United States.

Actually, there is little reason to worry about the appearance of herbs in cooked food. Of all the dried herbs presently available, rosemary is one of the few that can't be easily powdered in the palm of the hand or with a mortar and pestle. (Herbs can be placed in a bit of cheesecloth and tied to form a bag, if desired.) In this book I have favored dried herbs over the traditional *bouquet,* and I know that many modern continental housewives and cooks are doing the same because of the prevalence of dried herbs in the markets, particularly in the Mediterranean areas.

Incidentally, a *pinch* of any herb is simply the amount you can pick up between the thumb and finger. When the thumb is touching the finger before you pick up the herbs, you have a normal pinch. A generous pinch is the amount you can pick up between the two digits when they are not touching each other before you pinch.

BEURRE MANIÉ

Beurre manié (bur-man-yea), a favorite thickening medium of French cooks, has the distinct advantage of being almost infallible insurance against lumps. I've been using it for a dozen years, and I've never yet found a lump, even after minimal cooking.

Beurre manié literally means "handled butter" and that is exactly how a French cook prepares it. Butter and flour are actually mixed together with the hand, letting the warmth of the hand soften the butter to aid the business of working as much flour into the butter as it will absorb. When stirred into a sauce, the butter melts and the released flour permeates the liquid freely. I enjoy watching a skilled cook prepare *beurre manié* because there is no doubt that his hands are swift and effective. I have found, however, that I can make equally good *beurre manié* by forcing the flour into the butter with the tines of a strong table fork. It isn't as fast as the simple hand method, but, if anyone is watching, he won't be worrying about whether you washed your hands—which, of course, you did.

When covered tightly as with a plastic wrap, *beurre manié* can be kept in the refrigerator as long as ordinary butter—and it can be made with margarine if you prefer. The one thing to remember is to add it, in small bits, to a hot liquid only.

CLARIFIED BUTTER

It really is surprising that more American cooks do not make use of clarified butter. The preparation of clarified butter is really simple and its advantages are more than worth the little effort involved. Clarified butter is merely butter with the milk solids removed and, when you realized that milk solids are the first things to burn when you overheat butter, it is easy to see the advantages of clarified butter for frying or sautéing. Pastry chefs prefer clarified butter for fine cakes, and some of them insist that clarified butter, when used to grease cake-tins, will not stick as ordinary butter is apt to do. Clarified butter, alone or with lemon juice, salt, and freshly ground pepper, makes an excellent sauce for asparagus, artichokes, or similar vegetables.

To clarify butter, merely take any amount of butter and melt it very slowly over a low fire until a white froth comes to the top. Skim off this froth and continue skimming until no more forms. At this time the other particles will have settled to the bottom of the pan. Pour the clear melted butter off the sediment very carefully or use a bulb baster to remove it. What you have is the true clarified butter, and it can be stored in the refrigerator for as long as a week. The residue can be used to flavor or enrich stews, soups, or sauces.

GARLIC BUTTER

Garlic bread may be an American innovation (of which we should be proud) or it may have its roots somewhere in the Iberian peninsula. I never encountered garlic bread during my years in Eruope, but I did have a Spanish friend in the Philippines who delighted us all by spreading toast with a very similar concoction. The Spanish are the greatest consumers of garlic on the Continent. The *raison d'être* of garlic bread, of course, is garlic butter, easily prepared.

1   *stick butter*
3   *cloves garlic*
    salt
    freshly ground pepper

Mash the butter in a small bowl and crush the garlic cloves into it. Add a pinch of salt and 2 grinds of freshly ground pepper.

Tour de chef: Try spreading garlic butter on the next steak you grill in your broiler or even over charcoal!

CRÈME FRAÎCHE [Matured Cream]

One of the things that intrigued me about shopping in France during my early days in Provence was to walk into *Le Bon Lait*—a chain of dairy stores throughout the area—order *"un hecto de la crème,"* and watch the lady dish it out with a spoon onto a bit of grease-proof paper and literally wrap it up. Try that with a hundred grams of whipping cream sometime!

The difference, I finally learned, was that I was buying *crème fraîche,* a processed cream that has been matured with natural ferments until it becomes quite thick and develops a distinctly sweet flavor. It is not *sour* cream, and it can be boiled without disintegrating as sour cream always will. The French use it to bind sauces and soups, and fresh berries with *crème fraîche* are a treat never to be forgotten. *Crème fraîche* can be used in almost any situation in which the American cook would use whipped cream—and without whipping.

Someday a smart dairy products firm will introduce *crème fraîche* into the United States, but until they do you can easily make the best substitute.

Stir slightly more than 1 teaspoon of commercial buttermilk into 1 cup of whipping cream. Heat the mixture to barely lukewarm (about 85°)—don't leave it for an instant—and pour it into a glass jar with a loose-fitting lid. Place the jar in a spot where the temperature will stay between 60° and 85° and let it stand until it thickens. This can vary from 6 to 36 hours, depending on the weather; more time is required when the outside temperature is low. When it thickens, stir the cream and put it in the refrigerator, where it should stay fresh for up to 10 days.

MUSHROOM LIQUID

Mushroom liquid is a homemade condiment that can add flavor to various dishes, such as soups, stews, and ragouts. Reduced to simple terms, it really is a mushroom stock—mushroom stems and scraps simmered in water until the flavor is extracted. It is simple to prepare and can be kept in the refrigerator for several days, tightly capped.

Cut the stems off 1/2 pound of mushrooms and place them in 2 cups of water. Bring to a boil, then reduce the flame, and cook slowly until the liquid is reduced by one-half. Strain, discard the solids, and use the liquor for flavoring meats, stews, soups, sauces, or any dish in which a hint of mushroom flavor is an asset.

Needless to say, you still have nearly 1/2 pound of mushroom caps to use in the preparation of any number of different dishes.

THOUGHTS ON COOKING RICE

During my years in the Philippines I never met a man, woman, or child with any knowledge of the kitchen who couldn't take a tin can, if necessary (and it often was, right after the war); toss in a handful of rice, a bit of salt, and some water (no apparent measurements); and turn out beautiful snowy boiled rice—each grain separate from all others and each grain soft, but never mushy.

And it wasn't the type of rice that was responsible. I've seen the Filipinos turn the trick with packaged Louisiana rice from the United States commissary, as well as with their own superb *Wag Wag*—the rice (of many Philippines rices) that fueled our household for many years. Cooking rice came as naturally to them as boiling water does to us occidentals, and the same is true of the Chinese and the Japanese, although the latter usually produce a less dry rice.

But even with the illustrative instruction always available, we were never able, in more than a dozen years, to capture or duplicate that facility. We still have to measure meticulously and watch carefully to avoid burning. But, finally, after all these years we now feel we can undertake the preparation of boiled rice with a good chance of success, even though we don't do it by instinct. This is our method.

Always prefer the long grain rice (examine the package) and cook it without prewashing. Packaged rice in the United States needs no cleaning before preparation and washing only sluices away part of the food values. For every measure of rice (1/4, 1/2 or 1 cup) use 2-1/4 measures of water. Salt should be added at the rate of 1/2 teaspoon to 1 cup of water.

Put the rice into cold salted water and bring to a boil. Then lower the flame, cover the pan tightly, and cook very slowly until the water is all absorbed—about 20 to 25 minutes. We have found that it protects the rice to place a doubled sheet of aluminum foil between the pan and the flame.

When the water is absorbed, the rice should be done unless you prefer it mushy (in which case you start out with more water). The Italian uses less water to come out with his personal preference in texture—*al dente*, which most Americans would translate as "undercooked." A little experimentation will show you the formula that bests suits your personal taste.

Again, when the water is absorbed, the rice should be done, so fluff it with a fork and serve before it cools. If the rice should start to scorch, don't panic. All of it will be okay except the grains at the bottom of the pan that have actually turned color—and they probably won't taste too bad themselves.

I have never been able to develop a taste for cold boiled rice—a favorite food of the Philippines. "You don't insist on all your bread being served hot, do you?" one Fillipino friend asked me when I remarked on the custom. In the Orient rice is truly the staff of life, whereas on this side of the world it is an excellent but not vital food.

Too many Americans don't realize how many different kinds of meat dishes can be better complemented with rice than with potatoes. It is something wonderful to discover.

ON THE CARE AND PEELING OF TOMATOES

There are some among my circle of friends who believe I am just a bit daft on the subject of preparing tomatoes, but I steadfastly maintain that I have never tasted any dish or any beverage that was better for having included tomato seeds, tomato peelings, or both! Canners of tomato juice buy expensive ads to brag about their soft-press processes, designed to extract the juice without breaking the seeds, because they know that a tomato seed can be bitter. Personally, I can think of nothing less enjoyable than trying to pick tomato skins out of the dental recesses after eating tomatoes that were cooked in their overalls.

The business of peeling a tomato is simple and quick, and it makes anything you cook with tomatoes infinitely better in taste and texture. To peel a tomato, I place the tomato in a Pyrex measure in the 2-cup size and cover with boiling water for 30 seconds—less if the tomato is very ripe, more if it is a bit green. A yellow tomato may take more than 1 minute. If I have several tomatoes to prepare, I put them under boiling water one at a time, let them cool a bit, and then peel them. Once the tomato has served its time under boiling water, the skin will surrender easily, even if the tomato has been cooled completely.

To seed—and I never use a tomato in a salad without removing the seeds, just as for cooking—I cut the peeled tomato in half horizontally and remove the seeds with the point of a knife. (You can also cut out any bits of white, hard pulp at the same time.) If I am going to use the tomato in cooking for which its shape is not important, I often squeeze out the seeds and then rinse the tomato pulp with cold water.

Once you have the knack, you should be able to peel and seed a tomato in from 1 to 2 minutes, and the results more than justify that insignificant investment in time.

English Index

Foreign Index